MEMOIRS of
BERNARDO VEGA

MEMOIRS of BERNARDO VEGA

A contribution to the history
of the Puerto Rican community
in New York

edited by César Andreu Iglesias
translated by Juan Flores

Monthly Review Press
New York and London

Originally published by Ediciones Hurácan as *Memorias de Bernardo Vega*,
copyright © 1977 by Ediciones Hurácan.

Library of Congress Cataloging in Publication Data
Vega, Bernardo, 1885–
  Memoirs of Bernardo Vega.

  Translation of: Memorias de Bernardo Vega.
  Includes index.
    1. Vega, Bernardo, 1885–   2. Puerto Ricans—
New York (N.Y.)—Biography. 3. Puerto Ricans—New York
(N.Y.)—History. 4. New York (N.Y.)—Biography.
I. Andréu Iglesias, César. II. Title.
F128.9.P85V4313   1984   974.7'104   84-9128
ISBN 0-85345-655-0
ISBN 0-85345-656-9 (pbk.)

Monthly Review Press
155 West 23rd Street
New York, N.Y. 10011

Manufactured in the United States of America

10 9 8 7 6 5 4 3 2 1

Contents

v

PART 6. MID-CENTURY

Acknowledgments

I would like to give public recognition to the Centro de Estudios Puertorriqueños of the City University of New York, without whose support the preparation of this volume for publication would scarcely have been possible. I am particularly grateful to Professor Frank Bonilla, director of the Centro, and Professor Ricardo Campos, for the interest they showed, from the very outset, in Bernardo Vega's manuscript.

Other persons lent encouragement. Even though I do not list their names my gratitude to them remains. But there is one person whom I cannot overlook: Mrs. Evi Viro de Pietri, who knew Bernardo personally and who, with love and devotion, typed the manuscript.

For all, my Puerto Rican gratitude.

—*César Andreu Iglesias*

1975

The Centro de Estudios Puertorriqueños, now part of Hunter College (CUNY), is also responsible for the preparation of the English edition. Thanks are due to the Centro staff, and specially to Noemí Cabrera, Zunny López, Félix Ojeda, Alicia Pousada, Migdalia Rodríguez, Carlos Sanabria, Amílcar Tirado, and Blanca Vázquez, as well as to Angel Flores and Nicholasa Mohr. We all wish to thank Diana Cuevas, the widow of César Andreu Iglesias, for permission to publish the book in English, and Susan Lowes, Bobbye Ortiz, Lybess Sweezy, and Linda Briggs of Monthly Review Press.

—*Juan Flores*

1984

Translator's preface

When Bernardo Vega was writing his memoirs in the late 1940s, he could only have been dimly aware of the importance they would assume for readers in the United States. For how was he to anticipate, from that vantage point, the immense growth of the emigrant Puerto Rican community in the immediately ensuing years—such that within a decade there would be more of his fellow Puerto Ricans living in New York than in San Juan? How could he have foreseen the historical magnitude of the Civil Rights' movement and its direct repercussions among all oppressed minorities and in U.S. society as a whole? How could he have known that the Vietnam War would unleash such momentous opposition and draw world attention to the system of colonialism and imperialism that has ruled his native Puerto Rico throughout its history? All of the intervening events, and the attendant public interest in the Caribbean, labor migration, racial and ethnic relations, international political economy, third world liberation movements, and working-class history, make the *Memoirs of Bernardo Vega* an invaluable source of insight and understanding.

The collective experience of Puerto Ricans migrating to and re-settling in the urban United States exemplifies these issues as they converge and intersect, and the *Memoirs* is indisputably a classic and authoritative history of that experience. Though it tapers off at the onset of the mass migration, Bernardo Vega's text contains the most detailed and politically coherent account of Puerto Rican life in New York for the three formative decades, from 1916 to the aftermath of World War II. Since its publication in 1977 the Spanish version of the *Memoirs* has served Puerto Rican students and scholars as the major resource for factual knowledge and interpretive analysis about that neglected period, making it possible to demonstrate that

Puerto Ricans are by no means "newcomers" among immigrants and that the unrelenting disadvantage they now endure has been a constant feature of their presence here. Readers of the Spanish have also found in the autobiographical thread of the narrative an engaging personal access to those stretches of history as they are rescued from oblivion: What would Puerto Rican working-class experience be without the humor and picaresque irony, the humility and determination, the singular tribulations and triumphs of everyday life?

To the historian the book is a hidden treasure of rare glimpses going back to the late nineteenth-century Caribbean, the times of José Martí and Eugenio María de Hostos, when Cuban and Puerto Rican revolutionary leaders converged on New York to plot their next steps against Spanish colonial rule. To the general reader it is a testimonial novel, a life story recounting the adventures of a unique yet representative pioneer among Puerto Rican migrants.

Beyond its historical and literary qualities, Bernardo Vega's memoirs have also been of key value to the Puerto Rican political movement, both in the United States and in Puerto Rico. They demonstrate the vibrancy and high degree of organization of Puerto Rican social and political life in New York from the earliest days. And Bernardo Vega is particularly well qualified to tell this story. Born in 1885, he participated in the early years of the Federación Libre de Trabajadores, formed in 1899 as the Island's first large-scale working-class organization. He was a charter member of the Partido Socialista, which was founded in 1915 in his hometown of Cayey. As a cigar worker *(tabaquero)*, he belonged to the most educated and politically advanced sector of the Puerto Rican working class. From early on he recognized that the workers' struggle needed to be directed not only at the local bosses and colonial elite on the Island, but at the whole system of imperialist exploitation based in the United States.

And, as the *Memoirs* narrate, he carried this revolutionary perspective with him when he came to New York. In the "iron Tower of Babel," as he referred to the metropolis, his internationalism could only intensify, as he witnessed workers of all nationalities subject to the same pattern of exploitation, fighting side by side for justice. His patriotic love for Puerto Rico grew stronger as he realized that his compatriots were no better off in the land of opportunity than they had been back home, and that the forced migration of colonial peoples was just another way of holding them in bondage.

It is on the basis of this experience, reinforced and made concrete by decades of activism and self-education, that Bernardo Vega offers a remarkably balanced, clear-headed political understanding whose pertinence to the Puerto Rican problematic has endured, intact, down to the present day. The dialectics of nationalism and socialism, that complex relation so frequently polarized in colonial liberation movements, finds confident and practical elucidation in the pages of the *Memoirs*. The Puerto Rican independence movement in particular can continue to gain guiding perspectives on the vexing problem of the strategic and tactical relation between Puerto Ricans on the Island and in the United States.

Bernardo Vega spent the last years of this life in Puerto Rico, where he carried on his untiring political activities. In the late 1950s, at the age of 75, he came under renewed surveillance, and was among the leaders of protests against House Un-American Activities Committee investigations of Puerto Rican Communists. Then, inspired by the triumphant Cuban Revolution, Bernardo helped to consolidate the Movimiento Pro Independencia (MPI), the most important independence organization to emerge after the war and the forerunner of the Partido Socialista Puertorriqueño. He was a constant source of political guidance and inspiration until the last days of his life in 1965.

The *Memoirs* were evidently a rich but unwieldy manuscript when Bernardo entrusted them to his long-time friend and comrade César Andreu Iglesias. A prominent leader of the Puerto Rican labor, independence, and socialist movements since the 1930s, César Andreu Iglesias was also an excellent writer of political and literary works, and was therefore an ideal person to undertake the necessary editing. His introduction recounts some of that painstaking process and suggests many of the personal and political dimensions to the book. The longer introduction to the Puerto Rican edition by José Luis González (not included here) carries that political analysis still further: González, a well-known Puerto Rican writer who also knew Bernardo Vega and was a close friend of César Andreu Iglesias for over twenty years, focusses on the importance of the *Memoirs* within the ongoing political and ideological debate in Puerto Rico.

Yet as integral as the book is to the overall national problematic and to the perspectives within Puerto Rico that have emerged over the past decades, there is no doubt that it is the Puerto Rican community in the United States that stands to gain the most, and most directly, from Bernardo Vega's many lessons. For Puerto Ricans living here, many with limited access to Spanish, the English-language edition of the *Memoirs* is an event to celebrate, marking a new stage in the people's historical self-awareness. No book offers the millions of Puerto Rican readers in the United States so many continuities and connections, so many recognizable and identifiable life experiences, so many incentives to recapture the buried past and to strike out against an unsatisfactory present. Bernardo himself was fully aware of the deeper programmatic value of his memoirs when he wrote, in words that deserve special emphasis: "Without a doubt, in order to stand on our own two feet Puerto Ricans of all generations must begin by affirming our own history. It is as if we are saying—we have roots, therefore we are!"

—Juan Flores

Introduction
César Andreu Iglesias

In a preface written in 1955, Bernardo Vega explained the reason for his book, claiming that "an honest recollection was needed, a memoir, telling of how Puerto Ricans have lived and what they have accomplished in New York." Not that he considered himself "the best person to do this"; he simply felt that someone should do it, and, impressively enough, he didn't sit around waiting for others. If there was a job to be done, he'd take it on. Men like him are rare in Puerto Rico, or anywhere in the world.

As we read Bernardo Vega's book, we are immediately struck by his reverence for history. Not just the history of the so-called great men, of which there are but a handful, but history as it is forged by men in their everyday lives. With this in mind he wrote, "We Puerto Ricans must affirm our own history."

Bernardo Vega was out to awaken our knowledge and understanding of ourselves. He was not one for uncritical exaltation. No one, in fact, could be further from blind patriotism than Bernardo Vega, an internationalist in the full sense of the word. At the same time, no one has been more attached to his homeland. This sense of balance, without which there can be no fair opinion or accurate assessment, guided Bernardo Vega throughout his life.

Some people are inclined to view the Puerto Rican experience as a historical repetition of earlier migrations to the United States, such as those of the Irish or the Italians. There are similarities, Bernardo Vega says, but the Puerto Rican case is more complex. And he goes on to point out some of the differences: "We came from a colony and had no citizenship of our own." On the other hand, he continues, "Our racial tolerance introduced an element which was foreign to the prevailing mode of interaction." This "racial open-mindedness on the part of the Puerto Ricans was not viewed kindly, even by other immigrants who were themselves being stepped on by the blue-blooded Americans."

There were also important differences, according to Bernardo, in the various stages of the migration. Puerto Ricans who arrived later found the ground already broken, since they at least had family and friends who had settled here. Speaking of those who made up the vanguard from earlier times, he said, "If the cigarworkers [*tabaqueros*] hadn't had that spirit of struggle and had been intimidated and become fatalistic, would those who followed have had the advantages they are enjoying today?"

This does not mean, of course, that the present generations are without their problems. Problems there are, and severe ones. But there have been advances, thanks to the persistence of the Puerto Ricans—which is precisely what, in Bernardo Vega's opinion, has been their most important contribution to the culture of the United States. "Our efforts," he wrote, "might be considered inconsequential, but they have been positive. The demands of black Americans for greater economic opportunity and political rights were given a major boost by the example of tolerance shown by the Puerto Rican workers. We live with them and they have lived with us in spite of those who hated us both."

Second in order of importance in this contribution to a "better understanding of racial matters" has been the "diffusion of our music." That's right, Bernardo claims, our music in its full Caribbean and Latin American dimension, and our language—Spanish—have served to enrich the culture of the United States. Not that we are so presumptuous as to believe, he explains, that Hispanic culture was previously unknown in this country. That there have been Spaniards here, and Mexicans in the Southwest, long before us is well known. The role of the Puerto Ricans, though, has been a very special one—that of taking Hispanic culture out of the academies and universities, where it was traditionally studied, and bringing it to the level of everyday life in the big cities. Here is how Bernardo himself put it:

> When I came to this city in 1916 there was very little interest in Hispanic culture. For the average citizen, Spain was a country of bullfighters and flamenco dancers. As for Latin America, no one could care less. And Cuba and Puerto Rico were just two islands inhabited by savages whom the Americans had beneficently saved from the clutches of the Iberian lion. Once in a while a Spanish

theater company would make an appearance in New York. Their audiences never amounted to more than the small cluster of Spaniards and Latin Americans, along with some university professor who had been crazy enough to learn Spanish. That was it!

The constant growth of the Puerto Rican community gave rise to riots, controversy, hatred. But there is one fact that stands out: at a time when there were no more than half a million of us, our impact on cultural life in the United States was far stronger than that of the 4 million Mexican-Americans. And the reason is clear: though they shared with us the same cultural origins, people of Mexican extraction, involved as they were in agricultural labor, found themselves scattered throughout the American Southwest. The Puerto Ricans, on the other hand, settled in the large urban centers, especially New York, where in spite of everything the circumstances were more conducive to cultural interaction and enrichment, whether we wanted it that way or not.

Bernardo gives special weight to the fact that it was the cigar-workers who exerted the greatest impetus to the migratory movement from Puerto Rico, and from Cuba as well. This is an emphasis that may seem subjective—a kind of partiality in favor of cigarwork-ers—but one which, I believe, constitutes still further evidence of his singular greatness. For it would have been easy for him—given his formal education, his remarkable autodidactic knowledge, and his business successes (as limited and short-lived as they may have been)—to leave cigarmaking behind. . . . But he never did! His pride and joy was to be a cigarworker, which he would always display as a sign of his unflinching identification with the working class.

For Bernardo Vega, then, the preponderance of cigarworkers in the migrant population was of paramount importance. In his own words:

We were not submissive men who came here to serve as mere tools of the ruling class by depressing the living conditions of the workers and helping in the destruction of the unions. On the contrary, if the Puerto Rican workers failed to contribute more effectively to the struggles of the labor movement, it was because the American trade union leaders never showed the least interest in winning them over. As is clear in these *Memoirs,* our compatriots had to force their way into the labor unions. I remember very well the many times that we Puerto Rican cigarworkers had to defend our strikes and picketlines against scabs of various European nationalities. That's how firmly

socialist ideas were rooted among us. And the cigarworkers who came
before us, let it be noted, held in highest esteem the republican ideas
and the ideal of human brotherhood put forth by Betances, Hostos,
Molina León, and Pachín Marín. . . . Our emigration was not like a
herd of cattle obeying the lash of the whip, but one of men who
identified with the common good.

This wish to help clarify what happened in the past inspired
Bernardo to think of writing a "memoir" that would take stock of
"how Puerto Ricans have lived and what they have accomplished in
New York." But realizing that "there are many people who don't
care for dry historical prose," he wanted his narrative to read something like a novel. He was not interested in writing a work of
"fiction," but in putting in print a book of history with wide popular appeal.

With this in mind, he wrote an account of his life in the third
person, creating a character whom he called Bernardo Farallón. I
think he chose to do it that way because of his sense of modesty. He
also may have considered it a way of lending his story the highest
possible measure of objectivity. But he doesn't get very far at concealing his identity—half way through the book he seems to forget
about his fictional characters altogether, and to concentrate on his
chronicle of historical facts. It should also be noted that he baptizes
his character with his own name and chooses as a surname
Farallón—the name of the rural area where he was born.

One day Bernardo Vega came to me with this manuscript and
asked me to edit it for publication. I read it with tremendous
interest, but the next time we got together I expressed my displea-
sure with the form in which he had chosen to write it. In my
opinion, we were talking about a work of inestimable value, and I
saw no reason to conceal or disguise his testimony. The sincere and
straightforward narrative was its greatest source of interest, and its
novelistic aspects added little. For that reason, I argued, we should
undertake to rewrite it in the first person. He did not accept my
suggestion!

Unable to agree, we postponed the discussion to a more opportune time, especially since we were both engulfed in all kinds of
activity. Unfortunately, however, that day of peace and quiet never
came to pass.

Ten years have passed since Bernardo Vega's death, and only now
have I come to fulfill my obligation to edit the manuscript. I have

relied exclusively on my own judgment, though I am confident that Bernardo Vega would have agreed with what I have done. I have left those characters which he himself, in his preface, described as "imaginary." He began his remarks with the subhead, "How to separate the literary and the historical parts of these chronicles." And that is what I have done.

But at the same time another confession is in order: I did not completely eliminate the literary aspect. As the reader will see, Bernardo did a remarkable job of historical research concerning Hispanic and Puerto Rican people in New York during the nineteenth century. He wanted to incorporate those findings into his narrative, and to do so made use of a literary convention—he meets up with his Uncle Antonio. In accordance with that intention, which I believe enriches the work, I have included the historical antecedents, which include the Vega ancestry and a good deal of undocumented material, as though it were based on the account of Uncle Antonio. This addition is justified not only because of my respect for the author, but also—and above all—because it makes a good point of departure and an indispensable link to the events concerning the struggle for the independence of the Antilles and the Cuban and Puerto Rican communities in New York. Bernardo Vega gives a full history of those events and of the important people who make their appearance in the pages of the book. He states specifically that "they are historical figures and their actions are subject to the judgment of history."

For my own part, I have done my utmost to transcribe the manuscript as rigorously as possible and to preserve the style of the original. Beyond that, I shall finish this introduction by referring to the article I published on June 15, 1965, in *El Imparcial* on the occasion of Bernardo Vega's death.

I entitled the article "The Last *Tabaquero*" for several reasons, one being that on the afternoon when he died in his home in the Santiago Iglesias housing development in San Juan, Bernardo Vega was rolling his last cigars. A few minutes later I found a piece of paper on his workbench on which he had written the following words: "It is up to the young people to carry on the struggle and to complete our work." It seems that death overcame him just as he was preparing a short course on political education for the younger members of the Movimiento Pro Independencia.

That was Bernardo Vega. Throughout his life, until he was well into his eighties, he succeeded in bringing mental and manual labor into harmony with each other. A magnificient example of humanity, to the very end of his life he continued serving his fellow human beings. From beginning to end, he was able to translate theory into practice and to unite his actions with his words.

Bernardo was born in Farallón, a neighborhood outside of Cayey. As a young boy he took up the trade of cigar-roller. At several points in his life he came into possession of a sizable fortune. Never, though, was he anything other than a *tabaquero* in body and soul. He was, no doubt, the last standby of a tradition of native-born *tabaqueros,* born into the midst of those shops of yesteryear which constituted genuine working-class universities. Those were the shops of Caguas, Cayey, Bayamón, and Puerto de Tierra which forged a veritable legion of men with a high level of social conscience, skilled artisans who were proud of their trade and revolutionary in thought and action. And when I say that Bernardo Vega was the last of that tradition, it is because he remained faithful to it until the very hour of his death.

He attended the founding convention of the Partido Socialista, held in 1915 in Cayey, as the delegate from that town. A militant in the trade union and political movements, he fought at the side of Santiago Iglesias, with the difference that, unlike Iglesias, he was always against colonialism and struggled for the independence of his country. He emigrated to the United States in 1916 and was for several decades an outstanding leader in El Barrio. In 1926, along with other compatriots, he founded the Liga Puertorriqueña e Hispaña, in which was foreshadowed the civic, economic, and cultural battles waged by the growing Puerto Rican community. In the following year he founded the popular weekly magazine *Gráfico,* and was its editor for some years. A humorous and forceful writer, he contributed regularly to the important newspapers *Nuevo Mundo* and *Liberación*. He was a member of Henry Wallace's Progressive Party when Wallace left his position as vice-president and ran for the presidency of the United States, working as national director of the party's Hispanic section. He later returned to Puerto Rico and became involved again in the struggle within the ranks of the Partido Socialista. He did all he could to salvage that party from opportunism and to lead it back to the path of liberation struggles. When he became convinced that this was impossible, he turned his efforts to the Partido Independentista Puertorriqueño. Then he joined the

Movimiento Pro Independencia (MPI). From 1961 on he served as organizational secretary of the national office, and there wasn't a town he didn't visit in the course of his untiring work. His own labors thus stand as his most prominent monument.

What is most remarkable about Bernardo Vega is that he never seemed to grow old. Within a few minutes of meeting him, any young man would feel on an equal footing. His love of life and the sheer pleasure that he derived from the struggle were contagious—everyone around him was affected by it. He was an extraordinary self-taught man, with a solid educational and cultural background. It was my privilege that he considered me a friend for many years, and I believe that he deserves the highest praise: he was a teacher of life.

His legacy to posterity is contained in these *Memoirs*. As the reader will see, they are not simply Bernardo Vega's life story. They are much more than that, and for that reason they represent a contribution to the history of the Puerto Rican community in New York.

December 1975

Part 1
THE EMIGRANT LIFE

1. From my hometown Cayey to San Juan, and how I arrived in New York without a watch

Early in the morning of August 2, 1916, I took leave of Cayey. I got on the bus at the Plaza and sat down, squeezed in between passengers and suitcases. Of my traveling companions I remember nothing. I don't think I opened my mouth the whole way. I just stared at the landscape, sunk in deep sorrow. I was leaving a girlfriend in town . . .

But my readers are very much mistaken if they expect a sentimental love story from me. I don't write to pour my heart out—confessions of love bore me to death, especially my own. So, to make a long story short, the girl's parents, brothers, relatives, and well-wishers declared war on me. That's not exactly why I decided to leave, but that small-town drama of Montagues and Capulets did have an influence. Anyway, I left Cayey that hot summer, heavy of heart, but ready to face a new life.

From an early age I had worked as a cigar-roller in a tobacco factory. I had just turned thirty, and although it was not the first time I had left my hometown, never before had I put the shores of Puerto Rico behind me. I had been to the capital a few times. But now it meant going farther, to a strange and distant world. I hadn't the slightest idea what fate awaited me.

In those days I was taller than most Puerto Ricans. I was white, a peasant from the highlands (*a jíbaro*), and there was that waxen pallor to my face so typical of country folk. I had a round face with high cheekbones, a wide, flat nose, and small blue eyes. As for my lips, well, I'd say they were rather sensual, and I had strong, straight teeth. I had a full head of light chestnut hair, and, in contrast to the roundness of my face, I had square jaws. All in all, I suppose I was rather ugly, though there were women around who thought otherwise.

3

I did not inspire much sympathy at first sight, I'm sure of that. I have never made friends easily. No doubt my physical appearance has a lot to do with it. I hadn't been living in New York for long before I realized how difficult it was for people to guess where I came from. Time and again I was taken for a Polish Jew, or a Tartar, or even a Japanese . . . God forgive my dear parents for my human countenance, which was after all the only thing they had bequeathed me!

I arrived in San Juan at around ten o'clock in the morning. I ordered the driver to take me to El Comercio, a cheap hotel I knew of on Calle Tetuán. I left my suitcase and went out for a walk in the city.

The sun warmed the pavements of the narrow streets. I longed for the morning chill of my native Toa valley. I decided to go for a ride in a trolley car and say goodbye to an old schoolteacher of mine. To her I owed my first stop. Her name was Elisa Rubio and I have fond memories of her to this day. In her little house in Santurce she told me glowing things about the United States and praised my decision to emigrate. I would have a chance to study there. To this day, after all these years, her exaggerated praise echoes in my mind: "You have talent and ambition. You will get ahead, I am sure. And you'll become famous " Heaven forgive my well-meaning teacher.

On my return to the old section of San Juan, I spent the afternoon taking leave of my comrades. There was Manuel F. Rojas, who had been elected secretary general of the Partido Socialista at the constituent assembly recently held in Cayey, my hometown, which I had attended as a delegate. With him were Santiago Iglesias, Prudencio Rivera Martínez, and Rafael Alonso Torres . . . They all were unhappy about my decision to leave because of the loss it would be for our newly organized workers' movement. But they did not try hard to dissuade me. As socialists, we dig our trenches everywhere in the world.

I returned to the little hotel tired and sweaty. Before going up to my room I bought the daily newspapers—*La Correspondencia, El Tiempo, La Democracia*. In shirtsleeves, I threw myself onto my bed and plunged into the latest events of the day.

In those days our newspapers were not as big as they are today—none were over twelve pages. The news, especially about foreign affairs, did not take up much space. But our native writers waxed eloquent in endless polemics—original commentaries, sharp criticism, and plenty of our local humor. They reflected the life of the whole society—or rather, of its ruling class—with uneven success, but in any case they were more truthful than they are today, for sure.

Night fell, and I washed up, dressed, and went back out in the street. I had a long conversation with Benigno Fernández García, the son of a prestigious Cayey family. We talked about the European war, in which the United States was soon to be involved. Then I returned to my hotel, went to bed, and tried to sleep, but it was impossible. My mind was full of memories and my heart ached. Until then I had been acting like a robot, or a man under the influence of drugs. Now, alone in the darkness of my room, I recalled my mother's tears, the sad faces of my little brothers . . . I just couldn't get to sleep.

Once again I went back into the streets. It had rained. A pleasant breeze blew through the city. The bright moon lit up the streets. The damp pavements glistened. And I took to walking, up one street and down another, in an intimate chat with the cobblestones of that city which means so much to Puerto Ricans.

Dawn caught me by surprise, seated on one of the benches in the Plaza de Armas now and then looking up at the big clock. The cheerful rattle of the first trolley car brought me back to sad reality. Within a few minutes the bold tropical sun had taken possession of San Juan, and the streets were crowded with people. Gentlemen in jackets and hats left home to go to work. But the largest crowds were made up of people flocking in from the countryside, dealers in agricultural produce. Cornflakes had not yet replaced corn on the cob, though things were already headed in that direction.

The hours passed quickly. At around two in the afternoon I boarded the boat, the famous *Coamo* which made so many trips from San Juan to New York and back. I took a quick look at my cabin, and went right back up on deck. I did not want to lose a single breath of those final minutes in my country, perhaps the last ones I would ever have.

Soon the boat pushed off from the dock, turned, and began to move slowly toward El Morro castle at the mouth of the harbor. A nun who worked at the women's home was waving *adiós* from high up on the ramparts; I assumed she meant it for me. As soon as we were on the open sea and the boat started to pitch, the passengers went off to their cabins, most of them already half seasick. Not I. I stayed up on deck, lingering there until the island was lost from sight in the first shadows of nightfall.

The days passed peacefully. Sunrise of the first day and the passengers were already acting as though they belonged to one family. It was not long before we came to know each other's life stories. The topic of conversation, of course, was what lay ahead: life in New York. First savings would be for sending for close relatives. Years later the time would come to return home with pots of money. Everyone's mind was on that farm they'd be buying or the business they'd set up in town . . . All of us were building our own little castles in the sky.

When the fourth day dawned even those who had spent the whole trip cooped up in their cabins showed up on deck. We saw the lights of New York even before the morning mist rose. As the boat entered the harbor the sky was clear and clean. The excitement grew the closer we got to the docks. We recognized the Statue of Liberty in the distance. Countless smaller boats were sailing about in the harbor. In front of us rose the imposing sight of skyscrapers—the same skyline we had admired so often on postcards. Many of the passengers had only heard talk of New York, and stood with their mouths open, spellbound . . . Finally the *Coamo* docked at Hamilton Pier on Staten Island.

First to disembark were the passengers traveling first class—businessmen, well-to-do families, students. In second class, where I was, there were the emigrants, most of us *tabaqueros,* or cigar workers. We all boarded the ferry that crossed from Staten Island to lower Manhattan. We sighed as we set foot on solid ground. There, gaping before us, were the jaws of the iron dragon: the immense New York metropolis.

All of us new arrivals were well dressed. I mean, we had on our Sunday best. I myself was wearing a navy blue woolen suit (or *flus,* as they would say back home), a borsalino hat made of Italian straw, black shoes with pointy toes, a white vest, and a red tie. I would have been sporting a shiny wristwatch too, if a traveling companion hadn't warned me that in New York it was considered effeminate to wear things like that. So as soon as the city was in sight, and the boat was entering the harbor, I tossed my watch into the sea . . . And to think that it wasn't long before those wristwatches came into fashion and ended up being the rage!

And so I arrived in New York, without a watch.

2. The trials and tribulations of an emigrant in the iron Tower of Babel on the eve of World War I

The Battery, which as I found out later is what they call the tip of lower Manhattan where our ferry from Staten Island docked, was also a port of call for all the elevated trains. The Second, Third, Sixth, and Ninth Avenue lines all met there. I entered the huge station with Ambrosio Fernández, who had come down to meet me at the dock. The noise of the trains was deafening, and I felt as if I was drowning in the crowd. Funny, but now that I was on land I started to feel seasick. People were rushing about every which way, not seeming to know exactly where they were headed. Now and then one of them would cast a mocking glance at the funny-looking travelers with their suitcases and other baggage. Finally there I was in a subway car, crushed by the mobs of passengers, kept afloat only by the confidence I felt in the presence of my friend.

The train snaked along at breakneck speed. I pretended to take note of everything, my eyes like the golden deuce in a deck of Spanish cards. The further along we moved, and as the dingy buildings filed past my view, all the visions I had of the gorgeous splendor of New York vanished. The skyscrapers seemed like tall gravestones. I wondered why, if the United States was so rich, as surely it was, did its biggest city look so grotesque? At that moment I sensed for the first time that people in New York could not possibly be as happy as we used to think they were back home in Cayey.

Ambrosio rescued me from my brooding. We were at the 23rd Street station. We got off and walked down to 22nd Street. We were on the West Side. At number 228 I took up my first lodgings. It was a boarding house run by Mrs. Arnao, the place where Ambrosio was living.

On my first day in New York I didn't go out at all. There was a lot to talk about, and Ambrosio and I had lengthy conversations. I told him the latest from Puerto Rico, about our families and friends. He talked about the city, what life was like, what the chances were of finding a job . . . To put it mildy, an utterly dismal picture.

Ambrosio himself was out of work, which led me to ask myself, "Now, if Ambrosio is out of a job, and he's been here a while and isn't just a cigarworker but a silversmith and watchmaker to boot, then how am I ever going to find anything?" My mind began to cloud over with doubts; frightening shadows fell over my immediate future. I dreaded the thought of finding myself out in the streets of such a big, inhospitable city. I paid the landlady a few weeks' rent in advance. Then, while continuing my conversation with Ambrosio, I took the further precautionary measure of sewing the money for my return to Puerto Rico into the lining of my jacket. I knew I only had a few months to find work before winter descended on us. If I didn't, I figured I'd send New York to the devil and haul anchor.

Word was that Mrs. Arnao was married to a Puerto Rican dentist, though I never saw hide nor hair of the alleged tooth-puller around the house. She was an industrious woman and her rooming house was furnished in elegant taste. She had a flair for cooking and could prepare a delectable dinner, down to the peapods. At the time I arrived her only other boarder was Ambrosio, which led me to suspect that she wasn't doing too well financially.

But in those days you didn't need much to get by in New York. Potatoes were selling for a fraction of a cent a pound; eggs were fifteen cents a dozen; a pound of salt pork was going for twelve cents, and a prime steak for twenty cents. A nickel would buy a lot of vegetables. You could pick up a good suit for $10.00. With a nickel fare you could get anywhere in the city, and change from one line to another without having to pay more.

The next day I went out with Ambrosio to get to know New York. We headed for Fifth Avenue, where we got on a double-decker bus. It was the first time I had ever been on one of those strange contraptions! The tour was terrific. The bus went uptown, crossed over on 110th Street and made its way up Riverside Drive. At 135th Street we took Broadway up to 168th Street, and then St. Nicholas Avenue to 191st. From our comfortable seats on the upper deck we could soak in all the sights—the shiny store windows, then the mansions, and later on the gray panorama of the Hudson River.

In later years I took the same trip many times. But I was never as impressed as I was then, even though on other occasions I was often in better company. Not to say that Ambrosio wasn't good company, don't get me wrong!

At the end of our tour, where we got off the bus, was a little park. We strolled through it, reading the inscriptions commemorating the War of Independence. We couldn't help noticing the young couples kissing right there in public. At first it upset me to witness such an embarrassing scene. But I quickly realized that our presence didn't matter to them, and Ambrosio confirmed my impression. What a difference between our customs back home and the behavior of Puerto Rican men and women in New York!

We returned by the same route, but got off the bus at 110th Street. We walked up Manhattan Avenue to 116th, which is where the León brothers—Antonio, Pepín, and Abelardo—were living. They owned a small cigar factory. They were part of a family from Cayey that had emigrated to New York back in 1904. The members of that family were some of the first Puerto Ricans to settle in the Latin *barrio* of Harlem. In those days the Nadals, Matienzos, Pietris, Escalonas, and Umpierres lived there too; I also knew of a certain Julio Ortíz. In all, I'd say there were some one hundred and fifty Puerto Ricans living in that part of the city around the turn of the century.

Before our countrymen, there were other Hispanics here. There was a sizable Cuban colony in the last quarter of the nineteenth century, members of the Quesada, Arango, and Mantilla families, as well as Emilia Casanova de Villaverde. They must have been people of some means, since they lived in apartments belonging to Sephardic Jews on 110th Street facing Central Park.

As I was saying, when I took up residence in New York in 1916 the apartment buildings and stores in what came to be known as El Barrio, "our" barrio, or the Barrio Latino, all belonged to Jews. Seventh, St. Nicholas, and Manhattan avenues, and the streets in between, were all inhabited by Jewish people of means, if not great wealth. 110th Street was the professional center of the district. The classy, expensive stores were on Lenox Avenue, while the more modest ones were located east of Fifth Avenue. The ghetto of poor Jews extended along Park Avenue between 110th and 117th and on the streets east of Madison. It was in this lower class Jewish neighborhood that some Puerto Rican and Cuban families, up to about fifty of them, were living at that time. Here, too, was where a good many Puerto Rican cigarworkers, bachelors for the most part, occupied the many furnished rooms in the blocks between Madison and Park.

On Park Avenue was an open-air market where you could buy things at low prices. Early in the morning the vendors would set up their stands on the sidewalk under the elevated train, and in the afternoon they would pack up their goods for the night. The marketplace was dirty and stank to high heaven, and remained that way until the years of Mayor Fiorello La Guardia, who put the market in the condition it is in today.

Many of the Jews who lived there in those days were recent immigrants, which made the whole area seem like a Tower of Babel. There were Sephardic Jews who spoke ancient Spanish or Portuguese; there were those from the Near East and from the Mediterranean, who spoke Italian, French, Provençal, Roumanian, Turkish, Arabic, or Greek. Many of them, in fact, could get along in five or even six languages. On makeshift shelves and display cases, hanging from walls and wire hangers, all kinds of goods were on display. You could buy everything from the simplest darning needle to a complete trousseau. For a quarter you could get a used pair of shoes and for two or three cents a bag of fruit or vegetables.

At the end of our visit to this neighborhood, Ambrosio and I stopped off for dinner at a restaurant called La Luz. We were attracted by the Spanish name, though the owner was actually a Sephardic Jew. The food was not prepared in the style that was familiar to us, but we did notice that the sauces were of Spanish origin. The customers who frequented the place spoke Castilian Spanish. Their heated discussions centered on the war raging in Europe. From what I could gather, most of them thought that the United States would soon be involved in the conflict, and that the Germans would be defeated in the end.

I was impressed by the restaurant because it was so hard to believe that it was located in the United States. There was something exotic about the atmosphere. The furniture and decor gave it the appearance of a café in Spain or Portugal. Even the people who gathered there, their gestures and speech mannerisms, identified them as from Galicia, Andalusia, Aragon, or some other Iberian region. I began to recognize that New York City was really a modern Babylon, the meeting point for peoples from all over the world.

At this time Harlem was a socialist stronghold. The Socialist Party had set up a large number of clubs in the neighborhood.

Young working people would get together not only for political purposes but for cultural and sports activities and all kinds of parties. There were two major community centers organized by the party: the Harlem Terrace on 104th Street (a branch of the Rand School), and the Harlem Educational Center on 106th between Madison and Park. Other cultural societies and a large number of workers' cooperatives also worked out of these centers. Meetings and large indoor activities were held at the Park Palace, an auditorium with a large seating capacity. Outdoor public events were held at the corner of 110th Street and Fifth Avenue. All kinds of political, economic, social, and philosophical issues were discussed there; every night speakers aired their views, with the active participation of the public.

Housing in that growing neighborhood was for the most part owned by people who lived there. In many buildings the owners lived in one apartment and rented out the rest. There was still little or no exploitation of tenants by absentee landlords who had nothing to do with the community. The apartments were spacious and quite comfortable. They were well maintained precisely because the owners themselves lived in the buildings. Clearly, the Jewish people who lived in Harlem back then considered it their neighborhood and felt a sentimental attachment to it. Several generations had grown up there; they had their own schools, synagogues, and theaters . . . But all of this changed rapidly during the war and in the years to follow.

It was late, almost closing time, when we reached the León brothers' little cigar factory. Antonio, the eldest, harbored vivid memories of his little hometown of Cayey, which he had left so many years ago. His younger brothers, Pepín and Abelardo, had emigrated later but felt the same kind of nostalgia. There we were, pining for our distant homeland, when Ambrosio finally brought up the problem at hand: my pressing need for work. "Work, here?" the elder brother exclaimed. "This dump hardly provides for us!" Thus, my dream of rolling cigars in the León brothers' little factory was shattered. My tribulations in the iron Tower of Babel had begun.

3. Proletarians extend a hand, but hunger pinches and there is no remedy but to work in a weapons factory

The following day Ambrosio and I began the challenging task of looking for work. We set out for the neighborhood where the bulk of the cigarworkers then lived: the blocks along Third Avenue, between 64th and 106th streets. Spread out over this large area were a lot of Puerto Ricans. There were also a lot in Chelsea, and up on the West Side of Manhattan, which is where the ones with money lived.

After Manhattan, the borough with the largest concentration of Puerto Ricans was Brooklyn, in the Boro Hall area, especially on Sand, Adams, and Pearl streets, and over near the Navy Yard. Puerto Rican neighborhoods in the Bronx and the outlying parts of Manhattan were still unknown.

Between 15th and 20th streets on the East Side there were the boarding houses that served as residences primarily for Puerto Rican *tabaqueros*. I especially remember the houses owned by Isidro Capdevila and Juan Crusellas. They were where Francisco Ramos, Félix Rodríguez Infanzón, Juan Cruz, Lorenzo Verdeguez, Pedro Juan Alfaro, and Alfonso Baerga were staying.

In 1916 the Puerto Rican colony in New York amounted to about six thousand people, mostly *tabaqueros* and their families. The broader Spanish-speaking population was estimated at 16,000.

There were no notable color differences between the various pockets of Puerto Ricans. Especially in the section between 99th and 106th, there were quite a few black *paisanos*. Some of them, like Arturo Alfonso Schomburg, Agustín Vázquez, and Isidro Manzano, later moved up to the black North American neighborhood. As a rule, people lived in harmony in the Puerto Rican neighborhoods, and racial differences were of no concern.

That day we visited a good many cigar factories. The men on the job were friendly. Many of them even said they would help us out if we needed it. That's how cigarworkers were, the same in Puerto Rico as in Cuba, the same in Tampa as in New York. They had a strong sense of *compañerismo*—we were all brothers. But they couldn't make a place for us at the worktable of any factory.

I spent the days that followed going around the city and visiting places of interest. A "card-carrying" socialist, I made my way down to the editors of the *New York Call,* the Socialist Party paper which back then had a circulation in the hundreds of thousands. I showed a letter of introduction given to me by Santiago Iglesias before I left San Juan, and they welcomed me like a brother. Some of the editorial staff spoke our language and showed great interest in the situation in Puerto Rico. We talked about the conditions of the workers, strikes, and the personality of Iglesias . . . They insisted that I come back that afternoon to talk to Morris Hillquit, the leader of the party.

My conversation with Comrade Hillquit centered around the question of the political sovereignty of Puerto Rico. In his opinion, our country should be constituted as a republic, while maintaining friendly relations with the United States. He told me that was what he advised Santiago Iglesias. "I do not understand," he added, "how that political position could not appear in the program of the Partido Socialista of Puerto Rico."

I left very impressed by my meetings with the North American comrades. A few days later I introduced myself to the Socialist Section of Chelsea. The secretary was an Irishman by the name of Carmichael. He attended to me in a friendly fashion and signed me up as a member, after which he introduced me to a comrade by the name of Henry Gotay. A sailor by trade, Henry was a descendant of Felipe Gotay, that celebrated Puerto Rican who commanded one of the regiments of Narciso López' army in its final and unsuccessful invasion on Cuba. Henry in turn introduced me to Ventura Mijón and Emiliano Ramos, two Puerto Rican *tabaquero* militants. They belonged to an anarchist group led by Pedro Esteves and associated with the newspaper *Cultura Proletaria,* the organ of the Spanish anarchists in New York.

In Henry's judgment, Mijón, Ramos, and Esteves were simply degrading their own intelligence and wasting their time preaching such a utopian cause. Henry was a man of deep socialist convictions. I had lunch that day with him and Carmichael at a Greek place on

27th Street and Eighth Avenue. It was an interesting experience—it was the first time I ever drank whisky. As I was not used to alcoholic beverages, I got very drunk and my two new friends had to carry me home. That was the first time I was dead drunk in New York!

Liquor in those years was dirt cheap. A hearty shot of the best brand went for a dime. All the bars had what was called "free lunch," with an endless assortment of tidbits free for the taking: cheese, ham, smoked fish, eggs, potatoes, onions, olives . . . I must admit I was a frequent client of those taverns in my needier days. I would nurse my ten-cent shot and stuff my face with free goodies. What a shame when a few years later prohibition put an end to those paradises of the poor!

My drunk cost me several days in bed. All I had to do was take a drink of water and the whisky would roll around in my stomach and I'd be drunk all over again. But once I was back on my feet I headed straight for the Socialist Club. I was there often, and Carmichael, Henry, and I became close friends. They helped me straighten out some personal problems and went to great lengths to find me a job. But times were very bad. There simply was no work, and with every passing day I saw my situation grow bleaker and bleaker . . . "As a last resort," my friend said, "when your money runs out and you can't pay your rent, bring your belongings here and sleep in the club. And as for food, don't worry about that either. There'll be some here for you. The party has an emergency fund for cases like this." Those words gave me such a lift!

In the following days I visited Local 90 of the Cigarmakers' Union, which was a local led by the "progressives" in the union. Jacob Ryan held the post of secretary. I showed him my "travel card," establishing me as a member of the Puerto Rico chapter of the International Cigarmakers' Union/A.F.L. I wasn't given much of a welcome; my meeting with the secretary was cold and formal.

I immediately started attending union meetings at the hall up on 84th Street off Second Avenue. There I met many countrymen who had been living in New York since the end of the century. The militancy of those Puerto Rican cigarmakers had been a decisive factor in the election of progressive candidates to leading positions in the local.

Despite all my efforts, after more than a month in New York I was still unemployed. If I didn't find something soon I knew I'd be in serious straits. How much longer could I stretch the little money

I had? The bills I had sewn int[...]
course sacred, so I decided to res[...]
"buy" a job. Yes, sure, I had alrea[...]
to catch the innocent. I knew ho[...]
foreigners by "selling" them im[...]
somewhere, and even the slightes[...]
showed up, along with my friend[...]
of work, at one of those infamous a[...]
set our hopes on the employment [...]

Day in, day out, we would go [...]
some remote "workplace." More [...] [...] out that
the street number, and even the street, was completely unknown to
anyone. Other times we would track down the address, only to find
an abandoned building. We would of course go back to the agency
and explain what had happened, but they would only treat us like
idiots who couldn't even find our way around town. Finally it began
to dawn on us that we were being made fools of.

One day I woke up with that *jíbaro* spirit boiling in my blood.
When we got there, the agency was full of innocent new victims. I
went straight up to the man in charge and raised holy hell. I yelled
at him—partly in English but mostly in Spanish—and demanded
my money back immediately. A few Spaniards heard the noise and
joined me in a loud chorus, demanding the return of their money
too. Two employees of the agency grabbed me by the arms and tried
to throw me down the stairs. But the Spaniards jumped to my
defense. Finally the boss of the place, afraid of a serious scandal and
police involvement, gave all of us our money back.

At the next meeting of the Socialist Club I recounted my experience at the employment agency, and it was decided to make a
complaint to the authorities. I later found out that they did in fact
conduct an investigation, and that the agency had its license suspended. The fact is, though, that the injustices of those infamous
agencies continued, and that Puerto Ricans became their most
favored prey.

In those years, and for a long time to come, the Socialist Party,
the Cigarmakers' Union, and the Seamen's Union were the only
groups that were concerned about defending foreign workers. The
other labor unions either showed no interest, or were too weak to do
anything, as in the case of the Dressmakers' Union, which later
became the powerful International Ladies' Garment Workers'

...d also be mentioned that the Fur and Leather
...n showed its solidarity with the struggles of foreign

...st influence was strong among the Jews. Many of their
...zations worked with the Socialist Party and the labor unions.
...st outstanding of all were the Jewish Workmen's Circle and the
...iberal-minded newspaper *Forward*.

I began to move in these circles and go to a lot of their activities.
Truth is, though, that as far as finding work is concerned none of it
did me any good. On top of that, the landlady at our rooming
house, Mrs. Arnao, began to ask us every single day whether or not
we had found work. Even though we would pay her religiously every
week, she started to have an unpleasant look on her face.

At the same time, the warm hospitality we had enjoyed at the
boarding house was cooling down. There was not such a variety of
food as in our first days there. The rooms weren't cared for as
carefully as they had been at the beginning. The hatchet finally fell
on a Friday, after dinner. Suddenly Mrs. Arnao informed us that she
was thinking of going away on a trip and that we would have to
move out.

Figuring that misery makes poor company, Ambrosio and I decided to part ways. We headed off in different directions. Before
long word had it that my friend had found work in a gunpowder
factory. As for me, I took up lodgings at the house of a certain
Rodríguez, a cigarmaker from Bayamón who had a boarding house
on East 86th Street. It was actually the first floor of a modern
building. The apartment was spacious and comfortable. The room-
ers in the house were mostly Hungarians and Czechs. The style of
life in the neighborhood was strictly European, filled with traces of
old Vienna, Berlin, and Prague.

Mr. Rodríguez' wife was an excellent Puerto Rican woman. To
her misfortune, however, her husband drank whisky the way a camel
drinks water. When he was sober he was mild-mannered and good
natured, but when he took to drinking, which was usually the case,
he liked to pick fights.

Several Puerto Ricans were also staying in the house, very good
people to be sure. Many others of the same caliber came by to visit.
Among them I got to know Paco Candelas, J. Amy Sanjurjo,
J. Correa, Pablo Ortíz, and Pepe Lleras. It was a pleasant neighborhood: the atmosphere was neat and clean, the people friendly and

open-minded. Everyone would express themselves in their own tongue. Most people spoke English, but poorly, and always with a foreign accent.

There were excellent restaurants in the neighborhood. You had your choice—Hungarian, German, Czech, Italian, Montenegran . . . Quite a few of them would imitate the style of cafés in Vienna and Bohemia. The area was full of good-looking women, especially Hungarian. A lot were blonde, though you'd also see dark-haired ones with that distinctive gypsy beauty. I must admit that it was those women, who looked so much like the ones from my home country, that most appealed to the romantic side of me. But what could a man do who was out of work and down to his last pennies?

But I enjoyed the neighborhood anyway. On 86th Street there were five theaters where they not only showed films but put on live shows. I loved the diversity of people. Nearby was the German colony, where the socialists were active in all community affairs. There were many meeting places there, most notably the Labor Temple. Down a little ways was the Czech area, with its center of activity being the Bohemian National Hall *(Narodni Budova),* between First and Second avenues. The followers of Beneš and Masaryk used to meet there before Czechoslovakia became an independent state.

Around the time that I went to live in that part of town a good many Puerto Ricans were beginning to move in too. Many Hispanics, especially Cubans from the time of José Martí, lived on those streets. Right in the heart of that area, in fact, at 235 East 75th Street, is where our illustrious countryman Sotero Figueroa lived for many years.

It certainly was a good thing that I liked the neighborhood, because the truth is that my situation was desperate. Winter was near and I didn't even have adequate clothing. As fall set in I spent my days feeling the lining of my jacket and that precious return fare to Puerto Rico. But I wasn't about to give up until the eleventh hour . . .

One morning my fellow townsman Pepe Lleras invited me to go with him to Kingsland over in New Jersey. My good friend Lleras, who was also unemployed, convinced me that the only place we would be able to find work was in the munitions industry. So off we went to one of those immense plants. When asked in the personnel office if we had any experience, we said yes. I was so set on landing something that I almost went so far as to say I had grown up playing with gunpowder!

That was my first job in the United States. The war in Europe was at its height. The Germans had just suffered a setback at Verdun. In the United States, war material was being produced in enormous quantities. The work in the munitions plant was very hard. Only those hardened by rigorous labor could stand it. It really was too much for the soft hands of *tabaqueros* like ourselves. They would work us for eight hours without a break. Even to do your private business you had to get permission from the lead man of the work crew, and he would only relieve you for a few short minutes. Never before had I experienced, or even witnessed, such brutal working conditions.

Pepe and I would be out of the house at five in the morning. It took us almost two hours to get there. The work day started at seven and we would spend the whole day surrounded by all kinds of grenades and explosives. Most of the workers were Italians of peasant stock, tough as the marble of their country. There were also a lot of Norwegian, Swedish, and Polish workers, most of them as strong as oxen . . . Pepe Lleras and I, though better built than the average Puerto Rican, were beaten to a pulp after two weeks.

On the way home we would collapse onto the seat of the train like two drunks, and when we got home we hardly even felt like eating. Our hands were all beaten and bloody and felt like they were burning. After massaging each other's backs, we would throw ourselves into bed like tired beasts of burden. At the crack of dawn, feeling as though we had hardly slept more than a few minutes, we'd be up and off to another day's labor.

One day—we hadn't been there long—we met up with a stroke of hard luck. We used to get there a few minutes before work began to change into our work clothes. It so happened that one afternoon at the end of the day we couldn't find our street clothes. We complained to the man in charge, but he only responded sneeringly, "What do you think this is, a bank or something? If your clothes are stolen, that's your tough luck."

It sure was our tough luck. The clothes that were stolen were the only good clothes we had, and for me the loss was greater still—for along with my suit jacket went my passage money back to Puerto Rico. It was as though my return ship had gone up in flames.

4. The customs and traditions of the *tabaqueros* and what it was like to work in a cigar factory in New York City

Since the day we had our street clothes stolen and had to come home from work in rags, Pepe and I started thinking of quitting work at the munitions plant. But we had no other job in mind, or time to look for one. One day I found Pepe gloomier than a rooster after a cockfight. I tried to console him, but he just broke down, crying his heart out. The job was even more unbearable for him than it was for me. He got sick and gave up.

I kept up that fierce daily battle for another few weeks. But one morning I caught sight of a bunch of rags on fire alongside a powder keg and, had I not grabbed an extinguisher and put out the fire just in time, right there and then I might have taken leave of the world of the living.

For fear of losing my skin, time had come to give notice. Payday was every two weeks, and I had worked only half that. I decided to leave that day no matter what, though I wanted to be sure of collecting what was due me. The only way I could see was to pick a fight with someone and force them to fire me. I chose as my victim the first co-worker who showed up. The foreman pulled us apart and took us to the office to fire us both. Once I got my pay, I assured the foreman that it was I who had started the trouble and that the other guy was innocent. The foreman shouted, "You son of a bitch!" That was the first time, though certainly not the last, that I was called by that name in the United States.

One day a few weeks later I picked up the morning newspaper and felt my heart skip a beat—that same plant had been blown to bits in an explosion!

With what savings I had I bought myself some clothes for winter. Having no notion yet what that season would demand, I made the sinful mistake of buying two loud colored suits and an equally flashy overcoat. Friends who had already spent a few winters in New York made fun of my new purchases. So there I was, after all that hardship, in the same old straits—flat broke and without the clothes I needed for winter.

It took "El Salvaje," as Ramón Quiñones—another fellow townsman from Cayey and a first-rate *tabaquero*—was called, to get me out of my predicament. Though gentle and good-hearted, he would resort to his fists at the slightest provocation, and was always quick to seize the limelight. He never carried firearms, but tried to solve all his problems with his bare hands. That's how he got the nickname "Wild Man."

One day my friend "El Salvaje" took me down to Fuentes & Co., a cigar factory located on Pearl Street, near Fulton Street, in lower Manhattan. I started work immediately, but within a week they had marked down the price of my make of cigar, and I quit.* When "El Salvaje" found out, he went down to the shop in person and, as was his custom, had it out with the foreman with his bare fists. He had to pay a fine to stop them from locking him up.

As for me, I was actually lucky to leave that job. A few days later I found work at another cigar factory, "El Morito" ("The Little Moor"), on 86th Street off Third Avenue, a few steps from where I was living. At that wonderful place I struck up friendships with a lot of Cubans, Spaniards, and some fellow countrymen, all of whom awakened in me an eagerness to study. Among them, two Cubans who remain prominently in my mind. One of them, Juan Bonilla, had been a close friend of José Martí. He was a noted orator and one of the editors of *Patria,* the newspaper founded in New York by the Apostle of the Cuban Revolution himself. The other was T. de Castro Palomino, a man of vast erudition, who had also gained renown for his role in the liberation struggles of the Antilles.

Of the Spaniards I remember fondly Maximiliano Olay, still hardly more than a boy in those years, who had had to flee Spain to escape charges of complicity in an anarchist assassination of a leading political figure. He was a loyal friend of many Puerto Rican mi-

---

*Cigar prices varied according to the "make" or *vitola*—the quality of the tobacco and the cigarmakers' reputation. The *vitola* was indicated by the cigar ring.

Cigar factories ranged in size from the *chinchal* (workshop), which might include no more than the master cigarmaker and two or three apprentices, to *fábricas* (factories), which employed from fifty to four hundred workers. Some *fábricas* engaged in all phases of cigar production; in others, called *despalillados,* most of the workers were women, who separated the tobacco leaves from the stems.

grants; more than once I heard him claim that destiny had made him a brother of the Puerto Ricans, for one of them had once saved his life.

Maximiliano was born in Collota, a village in the Asturian mountains of Spain. Two of the Guardia Civil on duty in his town were from Puerto Rico. They were friends of his family, who had watched him grow up from early childhood. As a young man he got himself into serious trouble for political activities. He was arrested and the charges against him would have cost him his head. But one of the Guardia Civil hid him and arranged for his escape. He crossed the border into France and managed to get away to New York. "Now you see why all Puerto Ricans are my brothers," Maximiliano would say.

Another good Spaniard and dear friend of Puerto Ricans was Rufino Alonso, whom they used to call "Primo Bruto" ("Dumb Cousin"). Another of the Puerto Ricans I got to know there and still remember was Juan Hernández, the director of the workers' paper *El Internacional*. There was also the fine writer Enrique Rosario Ortiz, and J. Navas, Tomás Flores, Francisco Guevara, Ramón Rodríguez, Matías Nieves—known as "El Cojo Ravelo" ("Limping Ravelo")—all of whom were active in the cigarworkers' struggle and in the Hispanic community in general.

With workers of this caliber, "El Morito" seemed like a university. At the time the official "reader" was Fernando García. He would read to us for one hour in the morning and one in the afternoon. He dedicated the morning session to current news and events of the day, which he received from the latest wireless information bulletins. The afternoon sessions were devoted to more substantial readings of a political and literary nature. A Committee on Reading suggested the books to be read, and their recommendations were voted on by all the workers in the shop. The readings alternated between works of philosophical, political, or scientific interest, and novels, chosen from the writings of Zola, Dumas, Victor Hugo, Flaubert, Jules Verne, Pierre Loti, Vargas Vila, Pérez Galdós, Palacio Valdés, Dostoyevsky, Gogol, Gorky, or Tolstoy. All these authors were well known to the cigarworkers at the time.

It used to be that a factory reader would choose the texts himself, and they were mostly light reading, like the novels of Pérez Escrich, Luis Val, and the like. But as they developed politically, the workers had more and more to say in the selection. Their preference for works of social theory won out. From then on the readings were most often from books by Gustave LeBon, Ludwig Buchner, Darwin, Marx, Engels, Bakunin . . . And let me tell you, I never knew a single *tabaquero* who fell asleep.

The institution of factory readings made the *tabaqueros* into the most enlightened sector of the working class. The practice began in the factories of Viñas & Co., in Bejucal, Cuba, around 1864. Of course there were readings before then, but they weren't daily. Emigrants to Key West and Tampa introduced the practice into the United States around 1869—at least, I was told that in that year the shop owned by Martínez Ibor in Key West had an official reader.

In Puerto Rico the practice spread with the development of cigar production, and it was Cubans and Puerto Ricans who brought it to New York. It is safe to say that there were no factories with Hispanic cigarworkers without a reader. Things were different in English-speaking shops where, as far as I know, no such readings took place.

During the readings at "El Morito" and other factories, silence reigned supreme—it was almost like being in church. Whenever we got excited about a certain passage we showed our appreciation by tapping our tobacco cutters on the work tables. Our applause resounded from one end of the shop to the other. Especially when it came to polemical matters no one wanted to miss a word. Whenever someone on the other side of the room had trouble hearing, he would let it be known and the reader would raise his voice and repeat the whole passage in question.

At the end of each session there would be a discussion of what had been read. Conversation went from one table to another without our interrupting our work. Though nobody was formally leading the discussion, everyone took turns speaking. When some controversy remained unresolved and each side would stick to a point of view, one of the more educated workers would act as arbiter. And should dates or questions of fact provoke discussion, there was always someone who insisted on going to the *mataburros* or "donkey-slayers"—that's what we called reference books.

It was not uncommon for one of the workers to have an encyclopedia right there on his worktable. That's how it was at "El Morito," where Juan Hernández, Palomino, Bonilla, Rosario, and young Olay stood out as the arbiters of discussion. And when a point of contention escaped even their knowledge, the dogfight, as we used to call it, was laid to rest by appealing to the authority of the *mataburro*.

I remember times when a *tabaquero* would get so worked up defending his position that he didn't mind losing an hour's work— it was piecework—trying to prove his point. He would quote from the books at hand, and if there weren't any in the shop he'd come back the next day with books from home, or from the public library. The main issues in these discussions centered around different trends in the socialist and anarchist movements.

In those years of World War I, a central topic was imperialism and its relation to pacifism. In "El Morito" we had just been reading Henri Barbusse's *Le feu (Under Fire)*. The hair-raising depiction of life in the trenches gave rise to an endless discussion among the socialists, anarchists, and the handful of Germanophiles in the factory. Earlier we had read *La Hyene enragée (The Trial of the Barbarians)* by Pierre Loti, one of the writers often read to pass the time. But this particular book did a great deal to disarm the pacifists. The forceful description of the ruins of Rheims and Arras, the destructive avalanche of the Kaiser's soldiers, so graphically depicted, stirred us to thoughts of revenge and gained our deepest sympathy for the Allies. Just like so many of our comrades in both France and Germany, we fell prey to the call to "defend the fatherland," losing sight of the proletarian internationalism on which socialism is founded. Needless to say, Lenin and Bolshevism were still totally unknown in New York at the time.

When the Catholic newspapers in France took up their campaign against Marx and Marxism, we read the rigorous defense made by the socialist Jean Longuet. His articles kindled lively debates among the *tabaqueros*. For a while the sentiment in defense of France, inspired by Barbusse and Loti, began to lose support. The most militant pacifists among us struck back by arguing: "The French and the Germans both represent imperialist capitalism. We workers should not favor either one of them!" But this revolutionary position was again undermined by the reading of the Manifesto of March 1916, signed by the leaders of pacifist internationalism—Jean Grave, Carlo Malato, Paul Reclus, and Peter Kropotkin. This declaration struck a mortal blow to the worldwide anti-imperialist movement. "To talk of peace," it read, "is to play into the hands of the German government . . . Teutonic aggression is a threat not only to our hopes for social emancipation but to human progress in general. For that reason we, who are antimilitarists, archenemies of war, and ardent partisans of peace and brotherhood among all nations, stand alongside of those who resist."

"Those who resist," of course, were the French. As a result, a growing current of Francophilia spread among socialists. A great majority of *tabaqueros* saw France as the standardbearer of democracy and progress, if not of socialism.

The dominant trend among North American socialists, however, and perhaps among the people of the United States in general, was neutrality. The leading pacifist and anarchist among the Spanish-speaking workers in New York was Pedro Esteves, who put out the paper *Cultura Proletaria*. As I mentioned before, most of the *tabaqueros* believed that the Germans had to be defeated. Many of them enlisted in the French army. Outstanding among them were Juan Sanz and Mario César Miranda, two leaders of the workers' movement who left Puerto Rico and were killed in combat in the first battle of Verdun. Florencio Lumbano, a Puerto Rican cigarworker in New York, also fell on the battlefields of France. Another *tabaquero* to take up arms was Justo Baerga. Years later I was told that he had been seen, old and sickly, in Marseilles.

Many, in fact, are the Puerto Ricans who have fought in defense of other countries. Perhaps for that reason, they have found themselves so alone in their own land. It was right there in "El Morito" that I first heard of the role of the *tabaqueros* in the Cuban wars of independence. There, too, I began to learn of the distinguished contribution our countrymen made to the Cuban revolution. I heard many true stories from the lips of Juan Bonilla and Castro Palomino, who had experienced them first hand. From then on, I was determined to write an account of the participation of Puerto Ricans in the Cuban independence struggle, which after all was a struggle for the independence of Puerto Rico as well.

But life among the *tabaqueros* was not all serious and sober. There was a lot of fun too, especially on the part of the Cuban comrades. Many were the times that, after a stormy discussion, someone would take his turn by telling a hilarious joke. Right away tempers would cool down and the whole shop would burst out laughing.

None of the factories was without its happy-go-lucky fellow who would spend the whole time cracking jokes. In "El Morito" our man of good cheer was a Cuban named Angelito, who was known for how little work he did. He would get to the shop in the morning, take his place at his worktable, roll a cigar, light it, and then go change his clothes. When he returned to his table he would take the cigar from his mouth and tell his first joke. The co-workers nearest him would laugh, and after every cigar he'd tell another joke. He would announce when he had made enough cigars to cover that day's rent. Then he'd set out to roll enough to take care of his expenses. Once this goal was reached, he wouldn't make one more cigar, but would leave his workplace, wash up, get dressed, and head for the Broadway theaters.

A good-looking man, Angelito was tall and slender. He had a charming face and was an elegant dresser. He had arrived in the United States with a single, fixed idea in mind, which he admitted openly to anyone who would listen: he wanted to hook up with a rich woman. Pursuing his prey, he would walk up and down the streets, looking, as he himself would say, for his lottery prize. And the truth is that it didn't take him long to find it. A few months after I started at "El Morito" he landed a rich girl, who was beautiful and a violinist to boot. He married her and lived—in his own words—like a prince. But he never forgot us: time and again he would show up at the shop to tell us of his exploits and bless us with the latest addition to his vast repertoire of jokes.

Around that time news reached us at "El Morito" of a major strike in the sugar industry in Puerto Rico. A call went out for a rally in solidarity with the strikers. It took place on 85th Street near Lexington Avenue, and was attended by over a hundred *tabaqueros*, mostly Puerto Ricans. Santiago Rodríguez presided, and Juan Fonseca served as secretary. Many of those attending stood up to speak, including Ventura Mijón, Herminio Colón, Angel María Dieppa, Enrique Plaza, Pedro San Miguel, Miguel Rivera, Alfonso Dieppa, Rafael Correa, and Antonio Vega. The last mentioned immediately attracted my attention because of the way he spoke, and even more because of his appearance.

While I was listening to Antonio Vega I recalled how my father used to talk all the time about his lost brother, who had never been seen or heard from since he was very young. I'm not sure if it was the memory that did it, but I know I felt deeply moved by the man who bore my last name. He was a tall fellow, with a broad forehead, a full head of gray hair, a big handle-bar mustache, green eyes, and an oval-shaped face . . . When I went up to him he jumped to his feet with the ease of an ex-soldier and responded very courteously when I congratulated him for his speech. We then struck up a conversation, at the end of which we hugged each other emotionally. He was none other than my father's long lost brother.

5. An amorous experience and other incidents that lend substance to this truthful tale

As soon as I had assured myself of a job at the cigar factory, I enrolled in a public school on 86th Street off First Avenue. The other students were mostly Hungarians and Germans. The class was taught by a little teacher of Irish descent. One night she talked of the advantages of being a United States citizen and how to go about becoming one. "How can I become an American citizen?" I asked. She replied that you just have to follow the steps she had outlined. I responded by pointing out that, unlike our Hungarian and German classmates, Puerto Ricans do not really have any citizenship. Outside of Puerto Rico our natural citizenship is not recognized. Without any citizenship to give up, it would seem pretty hard for us to become Americans.

A bit flustered, the teacher could only restate what she had said before: that you just have to give up your own citizenship, follow the steps, and there you have it. And it was the same for everyone who was a resident of the United States!

"Yes, for everyone," I said, "except Puerto Ricans."

The teacher did not like my attitude. She must have thought that I was trying to make her look stupid in front of the whole class. She called the principal who, informed of the situation, felt it his duty to save the teacher from ridicule. After hemming and hawing, he concluded by saying that the problem was that so little is known about Puerto Rico here in the United States.

This incident wouldn't be worth mentioning if it weren't for what happened as a result: they transferred me to a school so far from where I was living that I had to give up my studies. I would have been better off if I hadn't said anything. Which is how I learned that keeping your mouth shut is the key to "success" in the United States.

In those days some fellow Puerto Ricans started a campaign of telegrams to Congress, applying for United States citizenship. I refused to join that campaign because I felt that what we should demand was a resolution to the problem of our sovereignty. Anything else, in my opinion, would only prolong colonial rule over our country. But my position didn't stand a chance in those days.

Luck turned against me again, too. Work in the factory slowed down, and the last hired were of course the first fired. Once again I was unemployed. Again I was to see the changing attitude of my landlady. Even though I still paid her in advance, as soon as she found out that I was out of work she began to treat me like a poor relation. No doubt she was afraid of my becoming a burden, and being of the same blood . . . Well, out of sight, out of mind, as the saying goes, so, with chin up, I was back in the streets. I convinced myself that I ought to be moving to a smaller place anyway, and off I went!

I remembered my Uncle Antonio, whom I had met so recently, and thought I might turn to him for help. He gave me a warm welcome at his house. Not having enough room himself, he took me to a boarding house nearby, on 79th Street between Second and Third. I took a room there. It was very clean, and cost me $2.00 a week. The house, which belonged to a Hungarian family, had a cultured and refined air about it.

Within a few days I got a "table" at a small cigar factory on 103rd Street off Broadway. The owner, a Spaniard from Asturias by the name of Leonardo Viñas, was a kind and cheerful bachelor. He treated his employees in a warm and comradely manner, and paid a good price for quality cigars. This shop had the distinction of being the meeting place of the Latinos. I made friends with Cristóbal Cañas, Alfonso Torres, Lorenzo Semidey, Concepción Gómez García, and Basilio Fernández, all Puerto Ricans. Of the Spaniards I met there I still remember Victor Simón, Anastasio Fueyo, and Juan Cuadrado.

While I enjoyed the friendly atmosphere at work, my boarding house was also very pleasant. The owners, Mr. and Mrs. Bude, came from Hungary and were lovers of music and dance. Jan and Malvina, as they were called, played the accordion and performed some exquisite duets. Their daughter Rina was a renowned pianist. Their older son, Clodoveo, was an excellent baritone. The house, therefore, was full of artists, and what made the place even more pleasant still, they all were socialists.

The Budes loved good literature. The whole length of the foyer was lined with books. On the first floor, a cozy little curtained-off area with windows on the yard served as a reading room. On the middle floor was the parlor, used for parties and receptions. That house, then, was like a regular little hotel with all the refinements of good taste.

At least once a month there would be a social evening attended by the boarders, members of the family, and some friends. The artists of the house made a big hit with their repertoire of Hungarian, Russian, and Spanish music . . .

At my first such evening I made the acquaintance of Lauri Brodi, who delighted us with operatic selections. We quickly became friends. Before long Lauri and I were inseparable, and from friendship we moved on to relations of a more intimate—and more complicated—nature. It was my first love affair in the United States. Lauri, I was told, was a widow. She had a son, Lucio, who was ten years old. Friday nights he would go to the theater with us, but Saturdays and Sundays we went out by ourselves. Not a weekend went by that we didn't attend a concert. Afterward we would go out to eat, always choosing a restaurant with an exotic foreign cuisine. Going out was like taking long journeys through far-off lands. It was a way of fleeing from humdrum everyday life.

We would have continued our excursions indefinitely if it weren't for a sobering incident that brought us back to reality. One Saturday, just as we were about to step out for the evening, a drunken man burst into the house. He asked for a certain woman and gave her name. They told him that nobody by that name lived there. But the man insisted, warning them not to try to fool him because he had seen her going in and out and would find her one way or the other. Then he crossed the threshold and headed resolutely into the hallway. At that moment Lauri and I were coming down the stairs. The intruder threw himself at Lauri like a wild beast. He was carrying a knife. I jumped in and managed to hold him off. The man fell to his knees and the knife dropped to the floor. Just when I thought he was going to pounce on the weapon to renew his attack, he collapsed on the stairs, and began crying like a child, begging forgiveness for what he had done. Then, a second later, his face contorted, he began to rebuke Lauri, accusing her over and over again of infidelity. After having ruined and disgraced him, he said, Lauri had taken his son away and did not let him see him, even though he was paying regularly for his support.

Jan, the landlord, was a tolerant man and knew the meaning of human tragedy. He intervened in the drama, speaking calmly, almost sympathetically, to the intruder. Without condemning his improper conduct, he asked him to leave. But the man fell into a new fit of rage and shouted that he would not. Jan's wife Malvina ran to the telephone and dialed the police. Lauri rushed down the stairs and beseeched her not to call them. Malvina hung up. Meanwhile Clodoveo, the eldest son, grabbed the intruder, bent his arm behind his back and with great skill threw him out into the street. Thus ended the incident, though it took a good deal longer to get over the unhappy consequences.

When questioned by Jan, Lauri admitted that the man had been her husband but that she had divorced him. All of his accusations, she said, were false. She claimed that her former husband was not only an incurable drunk but a sexual degenerate as well. After hearing her out, Mr. and Mrs. Bude rendered judgment—she should be on her way immediately.

Needless to say, our plans for the evening collapsed. Lauri returned to her room and I went out and didn't get back until very late. I got up and left for work early so as not to cross paths with Lauri, who moved out that day. When I came back in the afternoon, Malvina showed me what she had found while cleaning up her room: marihuana cigarettes hidden in a dresser drawer and a few hypodermic needles. According to Jan, they might have been left behind by Lauri in her rush to clear out, but they could also have belonged to an earlier roomer. Whatever the case may be, those discoveries definitely filled me with serious doubts.

Several days later Lucio brought me a letter from his mother. Lauri apologized for having tried to pass for a widow, and declared her ardent love for me. She enclosed her new address and begged me to come and see her. The note upset me even more, how can I deny it? But I had made up my mind to break off with that woman once and for all.

The letters from Lauri continued. They were messages full of promises. She recalled the times we had spent together. She invited me to live and enjoy life, and to put my worries aside. She spoke of the "winter of life" and how by then all that would be left would be memories. I must confess that I was never so tempted in all my life. But the *jíbaro* in me, hearing such siren songs, could only say, "Watch out!"

One afternoon, though, all my uncertainty vanished, and all my temptations along with it. The police broke into Lauri's place and seized a shipment of drugs. They handcuffed the woman and a male friend and took them away. Even from jail Lauri continued to send me letters.

I felt for the lovely woman, but I also felt obliged not to answer her letters. I decided to move out, a painful step indeed since I had been so pleasantly at home in the Bude household. When a woman is insistent and you can't put an ocean between you, make sure you at least strike out in a different direction.

Having moved, though, did not mean that I stopped visiting Jan and Malvina's home. Not for the life of me would I miss out on those delicious evenings. I had made so many good friends there. Associating with people of different nationalities awakened my interest in languages. Aside from perfecting my command of English, I took up Italian and Czech. My classes in Czech were at the Bohemian Center, where I became friendly with a girl from Prague. It was Amalie Lotiska who helped to ease my painful memories of Lauri.

My relations with Amalie were purely platonic. She was a fervently patriotic woman, dedicated to the struggle for the reconstruction of Czechoslovakia. She traveled often around the United States on political missions. She wrote a column in a Czech newspaper. I lost her when the final plans for the establishment of Czechoslovakia were worked out. The girl was off for London. We said goodbye at the pier, and that was the last time I saw her . . . Here's to you, Amalie Lotiska, wherever in Czechoslovakia you may be, or wherever your bones may rest!

Meanwhile, I was living in the house of a great *tabaquero* and even greater Puerto Rican, Flor Baerga. He had amassed a collection of old documents about the emigration of Cubans and Puerto Ricans to New York City. One of his prize possessions was a magnificent photo of Pachín Marín, the Puerto Rican hero who died fighting in the jungles of Cuba. According to writing in the border, the picture was developed at Moreno and López Photographers, 4 East 14th Street. It had the following dedication: "To my dearly beloved friend Flor Baerga—March, 1892."

I used to spend afternoons with Flor Baerga in Central Park listening to all the stories he had to tell about the times when Martí was in New York, the armed expeditions to Cuba, the struggle to carry the revolution over to Puerto Rico. One day as we were walking along 89th Street we read a sign that said, "Apartment to let. No Cubans, Puerto Ricans, or dogs allowed." We looked at it again, translating it into Spanish. The next day I mentioned it at the cigar factory where I was working. It so happened that "El Salvaje," of all people, was around that day and, as we already know, he was a man who would start up with half a crank, as they used to say about the Fords that began coming out at the time. He got a few *tabaqueros* together, marched them right down to the house in question, and in the twinkling of an eye they tore down the offensive sign. And as if that weren't enough, they proceeded to smash a few windows in the building.

Orders were becoming scarcer and scarcer at the factory run by Viñas, the Asturian, and I had to change my place of work. This time I found work at a factory owned by a Galician named Fares on Pearl Street and Hanover Square. It had a large number of educated cigarmakers, among them the Puerto Ricans Santiago Rodríguez, Juan Fonseca, Rafael Acosta, Lalí Jiménez, and Pepe Alicea. There was no official reader, but the owner himself used to read us the daily papers. He was a very progressive man. In his youth he had belonged to an anarchist group. He had vast knowledge, and loved to debate. When the discussion got heated, his language would be as sharp as a razor. At that shop, just like "El Morito," there was constant discussion about the latest topics of the day.

The area around Pearl Street in lower Manhattan was filled with cigar factories. There were even some large firms among them, like Calero, Suárez and Crespo; Cosío and Texeiro; Mancebo and Muiña; Escobar and Díaz; Gangemi, Fuentes, Starlight . . . They were paying their workers around $25.00 a week. Some earned even more, depending on how much was produced on average. In nearly all of those shops work was done by hand. Production "on the mold" was still limited. The tobacco leaves were from Cuba. They didn't use much Puerto Rican tobacco.

Down there I ran into quite a few Puerto Rican businessmen and office employees who were working in the financial district. Many of them had lunch at Borrel's or at a restaurant called La Chorrera, two excellent Spanish places back then. The first was on Water Street near Wall, the second on Front off John Street. There, at least at lunch hour, office workers, *tabaqueros,* and businessmen would eat together and fraternize.

In the evening we cigarmakers would return to our neighborhood, which even then was beginning to be known as Barrio Latino. Many of us used to frequent the theaters on 86th Street. Once they were showing a film with a tropical setting. From what the billboards said the action took place in Puerto Rico. You can imagine the great attraction it had for the Puerto Ricans.

But without fail, Hollywood movies those days always followed the same basic pattern. If the scene was supposed to be Spain, there would be a flurry of flamenco dancers and bullfights; if it was Mexico, the screen was filled with sombreros and lazy men who were always asleep and would wake up only to shoot it out; Frenchmen were effeminate; Italians ate spaghetti; and so on. All foreigners were bandits; the South American countries were inhabited by savages . . . Only the hero—a Yankee, of course—was cleancut, generous, brave, always ready to fight in defense of the innocent girl who in the end collapsed swooning into his arms.

The film that supposedly took place in Puerto Rico was in the same mold. It was filled with half-savage little boys climbing coconut trees like a bunch of monkeys. Barefoot, half-naked women walked along mountain trails carrying huge baskets of tropical fruit, while the men slept flat on their backs in the shade. There were alligators fighting in a lagoon and snakes basking in the warm sun. And the shining Yankee goodguy overcame all dangers to save the naive girl longing to be enlightened by American civilization. The audience, composed mostly of Germans, just laughed. But the Puerto Ricans who were there began to protest, and midway through the film we got together in the lobby of the theater. Panchito Carballo, a *tabaquero* from Caguas, took the lead. With us behind him, he went to the manager's office and delivered our denunciation of the film, demanding permission to speak to the audience from the stage. The manager agreed, and during the intermission Panchito spoke for several minutes in very correct English. He made it clear that he was not blaming the owner of the theater but the film company for producing what he called such "crass stupidity." He condemned that kind of trashy film which only stirs up hatred and prejudice among people. He explained briefly the cultural situation in Puerto Rico, and when he was through he received a long round of applause.

Panchito Carballo was a journalist and magnificent orator. He spoke several languages in addition to his native Spanish. Nor was that the only time he addressed a movie audience. In those war years he also played an active part in the campaign of "three-minute talks" in support of the Allies.*

I didn't give up my plan to continue my studies. Around that time I finished a course in bookkeeping and I was already good at shorthand. I was trying to get out of cigarmaking and find a job in an office. But salaries in that line of work were so low—$10.00 a week at most—that I decided to stay on in my old trade. Besides, the *tabaqueros* were involved in so many exciting cultural activities. I was not going to cut myself off from that environment.

Two of the most important *tabaquero* institutions were the Círculo de Tabaqueros in Brooklyn and the Francisco Ferrer y Guardia school, located at 107th Street and Park Avenue. The Círculo functioned very much in the manner of an old-style European casino, part cultural center and part social club. People would come to play chess, checkers, and dominos. The canteen, where they sold coffee and cigars, was open every night and on holidays. No gambling was allowed, and they did not hold dances. There were frequent lectures and cultural events.

At the Ferrer school the prevailing political tendency was anarchism. For an idea of what it was like, one Sunday afternoon there was a forum conducted by internationally renowned anarchist intellectuals. On the day I am thinking of, Carlos Tresca, who was chief editor of the newspaper *Il Martelo,* spoke in Italian about anarchism and the theories of Darwin; Elizabeth Gurley Flynn spoke in English about free communities and liberated relations among human beings; Pedro Esteves held forth in Spanish about war, peace, and the situation of the proletariat; and, finally, the Catholic anarchist Frank Kelly gave another talk in Spanish about Jesus Christ, the "first Communist." Following the presentations, there was always a

---

*The reference is probably to the so-called four-minute men, members of a national volunteer organization who spoke to movie (and other) audiences to promote the sale of Liberty Loan bonds during World War I. The speakers, who numbered about 75,000 in 1917–1918, limited their addresses to four minutes each.

question-and-answer period. On that occasion Maximiliano Olay served as moderator.

Attendance at these events was never under two hundred. There were women, too, but fewer in number than the men. The most striking thing about the audience was its patience; it would stay alert through programs that sometimes lasted five long hours or more. There was always great interest in the discussion, which was usually carried over to the restaurant on the corner, where many would go for refreshments afterward.

Cigarworkers bought and circulated a wide assortment of books, especially works expressing the most advanced ideas published in America and Europe. There were also many newspapers and magazines advocating all kinds of social and political doctrines. In New York City there were several newspapers published in Spanish: the anarchist *Cultura Proletaria;* the more general-interest *El Heraldo; Las Novedades,* an old-time Spanish paper founded in 1887; and *La Prensa,* a daily that began publishing in 1913. There were a few monthly magazines, too, such as *El Comercio.*

This variety reflected the cultural, political, and civic environment of the Hispanic community in New York in 1917. Cigarmakers and their families made up more than 60 percent of the Puerto Rican population.

Around that time I completed my first year in the iron tower of Babel. One day I found out that my Uncle Antonio was sick. As I mentioned, my father's brother had disappeared from Puerto Rico when he was still a child. For years he had dreamed of returning to his native soil, but, dazzled by the relative prosperity of New York, he postponed the trip time and again. And now, old and ailing, his heart ached, like so many other Puerto Ricans, at the thought of dying on foreign soil.

But for me, my uncle's illness had a positive side, for it brought us much closer together. I spent a lot of my free time with him, listening to him talk for hours on end. That was how I learned the story of his life, and of the struggles and activities of the Puerto Ricans who lived in New York before my time.

What follows is a summary of my Uncle Antonio's story, which covers the sixty-odd years that he lived in the United States. Everything he told me I have been able to verify through historical documents and the accounts of other people. This is the Vega ancestry—and the ancestry of Puerto Rican emigrants as well.

Part 2
HISTORICAL
BACKGROUND

6. The Vega ancestry in America, a wealth of history with a touch of myth

In tracing our family's origins in America, Uncle Antonio could go as far back as his grandfather. During the Spanish war against the Napoleonic invasion, he had served under the command of General José Palafox, the famed defender of Zaragoza. When that battle was over he took part in a Republican conspiracy in Catalonia, for which he was arrested and sentenced to prison in Ceuta. He managed to escape and fled to Panteleria, a little island off Sicily, not far from the Tunisian coast of Africa. There, like many others, he became involved in smuggling.

Uncle Antonio's father—my grandfather—grew up in this environment. As might be expected, he too became a seaman and smuggler. In a frigate sailing under the British flag he traveled to all the ports of the Mediterranean, and to his commercial voyages he added the business of freeing political prisoners from Ceuta.

By 1820 the Latin American wars of independence were in full swing. The Spanish government had unleashed a reign of brutal repression in the colonies. Ceuta was filled with political prisoners from Caracas, Bogotá, Havana, and even from San Juan, Puerto Rico. By bribing the prison guards, ways could always be found to organize an escape.

Their contact with the political prisoners awakened, in both father and son, a keen interest in America. On one occasion a plan was drawn up to rescue eight prisoners, some of whom had been officers in Simón Bolívar's army. They decided to go ahead with the plan and, at an agreed-upon point on the coast, the fleeing fugitives were brought on board. Ill fortune overtook them a few hours later, however, when they realized that a Spanish warship was in hot pursuit. Unable to enter the British port of Gibraltar, they were forced to head out into the Atlantic. In no time, the speedier government ship threatened to overtake them. At that point the old man decided to meet danger head on: he fired several cannon volleys which evidently caught the pursuing vessel off guard, and they managed to get away.

They escaped, but in doing so closed off any chance of reentering Spain. There was no choice but to set sail for America. Thus it was that the first Vegas arrived in the Caribbean. They docked in Curaçao, where they sold their frigate, which had sailed under the British flag, and purchased a ship with a Dutch name. They sailed on to Venezuela, where they unloaded the eight patriots, and from that day on father and son began transporting war supplies for Simón Bolívar's army. The Venezuelans, grateful for all Antonio's grandfather had done, were willing to give him whatever help he needed. And with their years of experience in smuggling, they had little trouble outwitting the Spanish navy.

One day toward the end of 1823, their ship came upon a Yankee schooner off the coast of La Guaira. Exercising his rights as a privateer for the revolution, Antonio's grandfather decided to inspect the vessel. He found himself aboard the *Midas,* which was carrying Cuban emissaries to consult with Bolívar. Their hope was that he would agree to extend the war of independence to Cuba and Puerto Rico. Among their ranks were José Agustín Arango, Juan Antonio Miranda, José Aniceto Iznaga, Fructuoso del Castillo, and Gaspar Betancourt Cisneros.

Since it was already late in the afternoon, the schooner was not allowed to enter the port at La Guaira. But Antonio's grandfather, knowing the purpose of their voyage, stepped in as an intermediary and made arrangements for the emissaries to disembark. It was at this point that the old man and his son first came in contact with the Antillean revolution.

The Cuban delegates were received by Francisco Javier Yáñez, a Cuban living in La Guaira. Through his mediation they were granted an interview with General Antonio Valero, a Puerto Rican who was on his way from Mexico to put himself at the service of Simón Bolívar. He had renounced his commission in the Mexican army when Agustín de Itúrbide, his commanding officer, had announced his intention of abandoning republican principles and declaring himself emperor.*

---

*Spain approved Mexico's proclamation of independence in 1821. A year later Agustín de Itúrbide declared himself emperor, supported by the upper ranks of the clergy and other conservative elements in the society. The Puerto Rican Antonio Valero (1790–1863), who had served the cause of Mexican independence as a

General Valero was enthusiastic about the idea of carrying the war to the Antilles. In Mexico City the Unión Patriótica had already been set up to do just this. It was planning to coordinate its efforts with those in Caracas and Bogotá, and there was already talk of landing five thousand men under the command of General José Antonio Páez, to be transported in a fleet commanded by Juan Padilla. Valero expressed his desire to join the expedition.

The government in Caracas placed at the emissaries' disposal a ship that took them from La Guaira to Maracaibo. From there they traveled on to Bogotá. General Valero became the newest addition to the Cuban mission, his Puerto Rican origins lending an Antillean dimension to the delegation. Their goals went unfulfilled, though, because the Liberator was heavily involved in his campaign in Peru. José Agustín Arango was assigned to continue the mission through the Andes and gain a hearing from Bolívar, while the rest of the emissaries remained in Bogotá to discuss their project with General Francisco de Paula Santander.

General Santander, who ran the government, agreed with the plan to extend the war to the Antilles. It was obvious that once the Spanish troops on the continent had been vanquished, Cuba and Puerto Rico would be Madrid's last stronghold in America. It would no doubt be to the Spaniards' advantage to make the enemy's retreat even more difficult. But with all the military forces committed to the Andean expedition, it would not be possible to open up a new front, especially when there was a sea of water in between. It would all depend on the meeting with Bolívar and the outcome of the Peruvian campaign.

The Cuban delegates returned to New York, which was their base of operations. Meanwhile, Arango went back to La Guaira without having managed to meet with the Liberator. As 1825 drew to a close, General Valero was embroiled in the task of organizing reinforcements for the war in the Peruvian highlands. Arango kept him informed about the activities of the exile community in New York. The Puerto Rican general reiterated his promise to remain at the service of the Antillean revolution, and to speed a hearing with Bolívar he brought Arango into his high command as his private secretary. Months later, in 1826 in Lima, they were able to arrange a

---

leading officer in its army, repudiated the tyranny and rejected the idea of monarchy. Valero left Mexico for South America, joining the struggle for the independence of that continent, led by Simón Bolívar.

formal meeting with the Liberator about the plan to carry the war over to Cuba and Puerto Rico.

By that time the United States government had made clear, directly and indirectly, its opposition to extending the revolution to the Caribbean. Washington preferred that Spain hold on to Cuba and Puerto Rico. When he was talking about those early initiatives on behalf of Antillean independence, I remember how Uncle Antonio used to say: "Our people have yet to give due recognition to General Antonio Valero y Bernabé, that illustrious son of Fajardo. Never did he forget his Antillean homeland, and he was always ready to pledge his sword to the cause of revolution in Cuba and Puerto Rico."

Uncle Antonio, in fact, would often wax eloquent in his exaltation of the past. One of his major concerns was to rescue from oblivion those outstanding personalities, men who, as he put it, "had been disregarded simply for having been born on our little island." New generations, he felt, always ignore our achievements. As a result, "Today's youth are the victims of those who have renounced their country and denied their origins, while seeking to justify their treachery by claiming that Puerto Rico has no history." He would call people like that "rotten bastards" and, as though to overwhelm them with thunderbolts of erudition, he would list the countless Puerto Ricans who had distinguished themselves. On one such occasion I made note of the following names:

Juan Avila, captain of the Spanish army in Flanders, who died a glorious death in Maestrilict; Antonio Pimentel, who excelled in the Italian wars; Andrés Rodríguez Villegas, governor of Margarita Island and Florida; Juan de Amézquita y Quijano, hero in the defense of San Juan during the Dutch invasion and governor of Cuba; Matías Otazo, sergeant major and captain in the Philippines; Felipe Lascano, military governor of Havana; Andrés Franco, general in the kingdom of New Granada; Antonio de Ayala, doctor of theology at the University of Valladolid; Diego de Cárdenas, dean of the cathedral of Caracas; Fernando de Altamirano, distinguished prelate at Tlaxcala; Juan Salinas, treasurer of the city of Caracas; Gregorio Pérez de León, professor at the University of Seville; Francisco M. Rivera, a canon in Yucatán; Demetrio O'Daly, who aided General Riego in the struggle to restore the Constitution of 1812 in Spain; General Juan de Saint Just, hero in the Carlist wars; Felipe Gotay, commander of General Narciso López' second invasion of Cuba . . .

Uncle Antonio made no distinction between the beliefs or convictions of these figures of Puerto Rican origin. To his mind the mere fact of having been born on our Island was ground for praise. This rather naive belief needs to be qualified, of course, by more careful criteria. But his was still a valid response to the foolish idea that Puerto Rico exists in a historical vacuum. Without a doubt, in order to stand on our own two feet Puerto Ricans of all generations must begin by affirming our own history. It is as if we are saying—we have roots, therefore we are!

In continuing his account of the Vega history in the Caribbean, Uncle Antonio told me that following the death of Bolívar in 1830 his grandfather settled on the island of Margarita, off the coast of Venezuela. His son took over a modern ship, one with an auxiliary motor, and continued on his raids. His specialty was contraband perfume, soap, and similar items. Aside from his smuggling, though, he also served as a conduit for revolutionary propaganda to Cuba and Puerto Rico. In those days the port city of New Orleans was a center of activity for the exiles, and it was a port-of-call for Uncle Antonio's father—who was also my grandfather.

One of his smuggling expeditions took my grandfather—as I shall henceforth call him—to Boquerón, on the Cabo Rojo coast. There he met the Puerto Rican woman who became my grandmother. All indications are that she was a woman from the coast who loved the sea. As her family was opposed to her choice of suitor, she agreed to leave home on my grandfather's boat. And they were married, though it is not known in which port in the Caribbean.

Grandfather wanted his wife to stay in his father's house on Margarita, but she refused. She insisted on sharing his seafaring ways and before long it turned out that, being a woman, she was an excellent carrier of revolutionary propaganda to Puerto Rico. She became involved in that sensitive work at the request of some Puerto Rican exiles living in Caracas, who entrusted her with a message to their relatives in San Germán. In carrying out this mission she met Guida Besares, a childhood friend, who had become a *laborante,* as the Spaniards called the separatists in Puerto Rico and Cuba. From that time on the friendship between the two women grew.

My grandmother took her work very seriously. Disguised as a peddler of saints, medallions, and other religious articles and carrying forged papers, she would disembark at some point along the Cabo Rojo, Lajas, or Guánica coasts and move from town to town throughout the western part of Puerto Rico. Her first visits were to the wives of government officials and the novitiates in the families of military officers. Camouflaging in this way the real purpose of the trip, she would deliver the messages entrusted to her in Caracas or New Orleans. Her open display of Catholic symbols helped her outwit the vigilant colonial oppressors.

"But a grave event put a sudden end to these activities," Uncle Antonio said. And in answer to my questioning look, he smiled and explained: "I came into the world."

Even after the birth of Uncle Antonio, my grandmother took on further missions to Puerto Rico. But hardly a year went by before the man who was to become my father arrived on the scene, and with two babies life on board became very difficult. My grandmother wished them to grow up in her home country, and so she entrusted the two infants to her dear friend Guida Besares. "She was the mother who raised us," Uncle Antonio declared.

At first their wandering mother visited her sons in San Germán several times a year. But as time went by her visits became fewer. Life was getting harder and harder for anyone trying to carry on illegal activities in the Caribbean and elude the Spanish authorities. Great Britain joined in the United States' effort to maintain a strategic balance in that part of the world. Both powers allied with Spain in its struggle against any revolutionary undertakings in the Antilles.

Under these conditions, smuggling became a very risky business, as did my grandfather's work as a revolutionary privateer. Longer and longer intervals separated my grandmother's visits to Puerto Rico, until they finally ceased altogether.

Grandmother Guida, as I should rightly call her, moved from San Germán to Caguas in 1855. Uncle Antonio was nineteen years old by then and his brother—my father—was one year younger. My father studied in Caguas, under a tutor named Nicolás Aguayo y Aldea. My uncle was sent to San Juan to take up more advanced studies. And at this time, Puerto Rico was devastated by a cholera epidemic.

Caguas was one of the towns that was hardest hit by that terrible plague. People were falling in the streets and there wasn't even time to bury the corpses. One victim was Grandmother Guida. My father, suddenly an orphan, found shelter in the home of his godfather in Cayey, while Uncle Antonio, over in San Juan, disappeared shortly thereafter, never to be heard from again . . . that is, until we met, many years later, in New York.

Only then was the mystery surrounding Antonio's disappearance finally cleared up. Instead of registering at school in San Juan, he had become an apprentice at Fermín Baerga's cigar factory. In his younger days Baerga had been a wandering cigarmaker: after some time in New York he landed in New Orleans, where he participated in revolutionary expeditions against Spanish rule in Cuba. As the years passed, Baerga withdrew from subversive activities and returned to Puerto Rico, where he set up a little cigar factory in the capital. Setbacks to the insurrection never depressed him, and he lived as though he were waiting for the hour to strike . . .

Needless to say, Fermín Baerga had a great influence on my Uncle Antonio. "From Fermín," he was to tell me many years later in New York, "I learned the trade of cigar-rolling and my first lessons in revolution. His stories fired my imagination. From his lips I heard the history of Narciso López and his remarkable invasions of Cuba. Those conversations sealed my fate, and the first chance I had I set out for New York."

My Uncle Antonio landed in New York early in 1857. That was the time of the big migration from Ireland. About 2 million Irish immigrants arrived in the United States in the short span of fifteen years. Hunger had driven them from their homeland, and they came ready for the worst. The most frightening misery wracked the immigrant neighborhoods of New York, Boston, and other big cities. Discrimination and police brutality were rampant. Those were the years of the "know-nothings," the years of national chauvinism and virulent attacks against the foreign-born . . . Uncle Antonio began to learn with his own flesh and blood what cruel reality the so-called land of opportunity had in store for the disinherited of the earth.

He found lodging with an Irish family and immediately set out to find work. His first job was as a cigar-roller in the Rosen, López and Co. factory, located in lower Manhattan. There he became friendly with some Spanish-speaking people, among them the Puerto Ricans Martín Castro, a black man from Santurce, Lisandro Rodríguez from Guayama, and Jesús Rodríguez from Playa de Ponce. And it was there that he had the good fortune to meet up with the Sephardic Jew Jacobo Silvestre Bresman, with whom he remained a close friend for the rest of his days.

Bresman was a real teacher to Uncle Antonio. He took him under his wing, so to speak, and in that gentle Sephardi the newly arrived young man was to find a father. With him he broadened his vision of the world and learned the roots of human conflict. With greater fervor than ever, he took the side of the workers, and he began to soak up the teachings of socialism.

Uncle Antonio hadn't been living in New York for long when he married a Puerto Rican girl from Río Cañas, Mayagüez, by the name of Dolores Betances. They made their home at 209 East 13th Street. And that apartment came to be a meeting place for exiles from Cuba and Puerto Rico.

The Civil War years in the United States passed without anything notable happening in the Antilles. But emigrants from the islands continued to arrive in New York. The Cuban and Puerto Rican community grew, one contributing factor no doubt being the growing trade between the Spanish colonies and the United States. This commercial activity had received its first impulse back in the middle of the century, and was to increase year after year. North American ships came to New York carrying sugar and molasses from the Antilles, and it was not uncommon for one young Puerto Rican or another to come ashore with every shipload. They would usually go to live on 14th or 15th Street, or down on Waverly Place. One boarding house they often used was owned by the Salvador Gely family from Patillas, and was located at 5 West 29th Street.

The residential houses in the neighborhood did not have much in the way of conveniences back then. There were usually three rooms: one served as the living room by day and a bedroom at night; there was another bedroom in the back, and in the middle was the dining room and kitchen. The flats were all lit by gas lamps. The only windows were in the front. Most of the time the only heat was from a coal stove. Few had their own bathrooms. The only place to wash was the kitchen sink.

In those years Cubans and Puerto Ricans went about their business in the big city and didn't seem to have any more pressing concerns. New Orleans, rather than New York, was still the center of Antillean exile activity. The annexationist tendency was dominant there, reflecting the interests of the Southern slaveholders.

But with the end of the Civil War and abolition, the center of emigration from the Antilles shifted to New York.

Then something happened to strengthen this trend: the failure of the Juntas Informativas sobre Cuba y Puerto Rico in Madrid . . .*

Early in July 1867, having escaped the clutches of General José María Marchessi, Segundo Ruiz Belvis, and Ramón Emeterio Betances arrived in New York.

---

*The Juntas Informativas were established by royal decree on November 25, 1865, under the Leyes Especiales (Special Laws) of 1837, which had excluded the colonies from the Spanish constitutional regime. Their purpose was to "inform" the Spanish government of the political, economic, and social conditions in Cuba and Puerto Rico.

7. New York: focal point of the Antillean revolution, and the role of the Cuban and Puerto Rican communities

The arrival of Ruiz Belvis and Betances in New York gave new life to the Sociedad Republicana de Cuba y Puerto Rico. It had been founded by a group of Cubans headed by Juan Manuel Macías and by the exiled Puerto Rican Dr. José Francisco Basora. Because of the reformist illusions encouraged by the Juntas Informativas, which had been chosen in Cuba and Puerto Rico and had convened in Madrid, the society had become moribund. But no sooner were those illusions shattered and the promises of colonial reform abandoned than the revolution came back to life. So New York turned out to be just the place for the two new Puerto Rican exiles.

Ramón Emeterio Betances and Segundo Ruiz Belvis were not unknown in the emigrant community. The former had already gained renown for medical services rendered when the bubonic plague hit Puerto Rico, and as an abolitionist. As for Ruiz Belvis, he was known for the outstanding role he had played in Madrid as a member of the Junta Informativa. The brilliant *Memoria sobre la Esclavitud* (*Memoir of Slavery*), which he wrote with José Julián Acosta, was often read in the cigar factories. His famous phrase— "We want abolition with or without indemnity"—was on the lips of every *tabaquero*.

Immediately after arriving in New York the two illustrious exiles met with Dr. Basora and formed the Comité Revolucionario. Together they signed a manifesto that ended with the following words: "Cubans and Puerto Ricans! Unite forces, work together, we are brothers, we suffer a common injustice. Let us be one also in the revolution and in calling for the independence of Cuba and Puerto Rico. And tomorrow we shall be able to form a confederation of all the Antilles!"

At this same time there appeared in the daily *New York Herald* a

48

dispatch from Havana telling of the "disappearance" of Betances and Ruiz Belvis from Puerto Rico and implicating them in a mutiny of artillerymen that had just taken place in San Juan.* The two exiles answered immediately. In the same paper, on August 2, they published a statement declaring that they did not have "the least intention to vindicate themselves before the Spanish government now or hereafter." They went on to say: "The government of the Island, proceeding in its usual arbitrary manner, decreed, without any form of trial, the expulsion from the country of several individuals of good social standing, and among them the undersigned, requiring of them a pledge of honor to go to Madrid and report to the Minister of the Colonies. We decided not to pledge our word of honor for several reasons, which in due time we shall make known, and because we think it would be mere waste of time, money, and labor to trust the good faith of such a government."

According to Uncle Antonio, Betances, Ruiz Belvis, and Basora called a meeting of Cubans and Puerto Ricans in Salvador Gely's home on West 29th Street. Among those who attended were several cigarmakers, including Flor Baerga, Lisandro Rodríguez, my uncle, and the Sephardic Jew Jacobo Silvestre Bresman. The discussion centered on the possibility of initiating a revolution in the Antilles.

Bresman questioned the likelihood of the participation of the large landholders, and underlined the need to win the support of the peasantry—the *guajiros* in Cuba and the *jíbaros* of Puerto Rico. He reported that Spain had fourteen warships in Cuban waters and that many more could be expected to arrive in Havana. The Spanish army stationed in Cuba had grown from 12,000 to 40,000 regular troops. Any plans for revolution would have to take this situation into account.

At that and subsequent meetings they mapped out an elaborate plan of action. As part of that plan, Betances left for the Caribbean, charged with the task of recruiting a landing force. Ruiz Belvis went to Santiago, Chile, arriving on October 27, 1867, to work with Benjamín Vicuña Mackenna in gathering support for the upcoming

---

*On June 7, 1867, the artillerymen of San Juan met to protest their exclusion from benefits authorized by Spain. This mutiny served as a pretext for the governor of Puerto Rico to send Ramón Emeterio Betances and Segundo Ruiz Belvis, along with a group of noted Puerto Rican liberals, into exile in Madrid. Betances and Ruiz Belvis broke the extradition order, fleeing first to Santo Domingo and St. Thomas, and ending in New York.

insurrection. Dr. Basora stayed in New York to oversee recruitment for another armed force that was to leave from the United States. This was on the eve of the Grito de Lares in Puerto Rico and the Grito de Yara in Cuba.*

To the detriment of the cause of Antillean independence, soon after his arrival in Chile Ruiz Belvis died of unknown causes in a hotel in Valparaíso. Word of his dear friend's death upset Betances greatly, but did not distract him from his revolutionary task. He went on sending clandestine messages from St. Thomas to Puerto Rico and gathering together men and arms from different parts of the Caribbean. But neither men nor arms ever saw action. The Spanish authorities learned of the insurrection and succeeded in crushing it between September 23 and the first days of October 1868.

It is known that Betances had joined forces with a group of revolutionaries from the Dominican Republic who were conspiring against President Báez. The war material he had gathered for the expedition to Puerto Rico was lost in Santo Domingo, and Betances was strongly criticized in New York.

On October 10 what came to be known as the Ten Years' War broke out in Yara. Carlos Manuel de Céspedes was proclaimed commander of the Cuban Liberation Army. This event aroused a great deal of enthusiasm among Cubans and Puerto Ricans in New York.

The revolution in Cuba seemed to have gotten off to a successful start, and the Sociedad Republicana de Cuba y Puerto Rico was renamed the Junta Revolucionaria de Cuba y Puerto Rico. J. Morales Lemus, who had been the Cuban delegate to the Juntas Informativas in Madrid, was named president. Another outstanding Cuban, Francisco Javier Cisneros, joined the Junta Revolucionaria. Dr. Basora was named treasurer and Agustín Arango was appointed director of volunteer recruitment.

The first contingent of men and arms left from Jacksonville, Florida, on the steamship *Henry Burden* and the schooner *Mary Lowell* under the command of Cisneros. But the *Burden* proved too

---

*On September 23, 1868, a group of separatists occupied the town of Lares in the interior of Puerto Rico and proclaimed a republic. The action was not a success, and its participants were imprisoned, initiating a prolonged period of political repression. The Grito de Yara took place on October 10, 1868. Its aim was to free Cuba from Spanish rule, and it marked the beginning of the Ten Years' War, which lasted until the Cuban rebels surrendered under the Treaty of Zanjón (see note p. 58).

old to make the trip, and the troops had to transfer to the schooner on the high sea. They managed to land on Ragged Island, a British holding in the Bahamas. The revolutionaries wanted to go on to Cuba, but the ship's crew refused to sail any further. They were forced to get rid of the crew and recruit a new one, all of which took so long that a Spanish patrol boat had ample time to intercept them. As a result, the British authorities took the schooner into custody, and the first military mission to Cuba ended in failure.

Meanwhile, Morales Lemus had a meeting in Washington with President Grant, at which he beseeched Grant to intervene in the conflict with Spain. This Grant refused to do, but, according to Lisandro Rodríguez and Juan Arnao, he did promise to assist the armed revolution. This report was passed on to Céspedes, who was fighting in the Cuban countryside.

The idea that the United States might help the República de Cuba en Armas rekindled the enthusiasm of Cubans and Puerto Ricans in New York. In the cigar factories, boarding houses, and restaurants there was already talk of how by next Christmas "we'll be eating our favorite stew back on our native soil."

But very different events were to transpire. Rumors of a possible United States intervention in Cuba alarmed Spanish diplomats in Washington, who denounced the Junta Revolucionaria de Cuba y Puerto Rico. Morales Lemus was summoned to the capital and reprimanded by United States authorities.

At the same time, Morales Lemus' frequent visits to Washington began to cause fears and division among the exiles. The president of the Junta was charged with "annexationism," and the revolutionary struggle against Spain went in two directions: one that had consistently demanded independence, and one that more or less openly advocated annexation to the United States.

It was around this time that women began to join the Antillean emancipation struggle. On the initiative of Emilia Casanova de Villaverde, the Hijas de Cuba, a patriotic society, was founded on February 6, 1869, at the St. Julien Hotel, located near Washington Square in New York. Fourteen women were seated around the president's table. At that meeting Sēnora Casanova de Villaverde accused the Junta Revolucionaria de Cuba y Puerto Rico of "annexationist maneuvers and betrayal of the independence movement."

For all its failings, the Junta Revolucionaria did manage to dispatch a second expedition to Cuba in May 1869, and a third by the end of the year. Both, however, were intercepted by Spanish patrol boats and only escaped by throwing part of their war material overboard. Later expeditions met a similar fate.

The insurgent army began to run short of supplies, which forced them to limit their campaigns. This critical situation generated heated discussion in the Junta. Charges were made against Cisneros, the head of the expeditions, who submitted his resignation. He was later absolved, when it was learned that the ships had been taken by surprise because of indiscretions on the part of those responsible for planning the expeditions. It became clear that Spanish agents had been able to learn dates and points of departures and had transmitted the information to their naval patrols.

At the beginning of 1869 Dr. J. J. Henna, a victim of the repression that had followed the Grito de Lares, arrived in New York. Henna immediately joined the Comité Republicano Puertorriqueño, now directed by Betances and Basora.

On October 31 of the same year Eugenio María de Hostos landed in New York. He came from Europe "sparking with rage," his soul burning with "holy fanaticism" for the independence of his country. Not long before that he had broken all this with the Spanish "progressives" in the Atheneum of Madrid. His years of compromise and discussion with Spain were over. He had come to the conclusion that the colonies would have to win their freedom "in cold blood, in the field of combat."

At Basora's suggestion, Hostos joined the editorial staff of *La Revolución,* the organ of the Comité Republicano Puertorriqueño in New York. His work for this publication was to become the subject of fiery polemics—according to Baerga, Hostos "put together and directed" the newspaper, but was never regarded as the "editor."

Hostos was aware of the bitter division between those who had consistently demanded Antillean independence and those seeking annexation of the islands to the United States. He hoped to win the confidence of Morales Lemus and the other Cuban leaders. He wanted to become the undisputed leader of the independence struggle, and worked toward that end by editing the newspaper. The mood among Puerto Rican and Cuban exiles and emigrants in New York worried Hostos. But, with his goal firmly in mind, he took up the challenge with a positive outlook. He drew up a manifesto calling on his fellow Puerto Ricans to join the revolution, and secured the adherence of several members of the Junta Revolucionaria Cubana.

In this same period a resolution was presented to the United States Congress proposing that an offer be made to Spain for the purchase of the island of Cuba. The proposal was endorsed by one of the major daily newspapers in New York. The Comité Republicano Puertorriqueño assigned Enrique Piñeyro, editor in chief of *La Revolución,* to print a response. He did so, but Hostos considered the answer "very ambivalent." The article did not make it clear that the goal of Antillean revolution was independence and instead left the reader believing that the idea was simply to throw the Spanish out of Cuba, no matter what happened after. This position led to a serious argument between Hostos and Piñeiro, and Betances and Basora had to step in to prevent Hostos from resigning. But his staying on at the paper only left a very difficult situation.

As the representative of the revolutionary government in Cuba, the Junta Revolucionaria Cubana was charged with a variety of diplomatic functions, and these tended to restrict its activities in other areas. What was needed was a forum for public discussion, a center for raising funds and recruiting volunteers, and similar purposes. It was with these ends in mind that the Club de Artesanos was created. And Hostos made use of this group to expound his ideas and to speak out against annexation.

Hostos' presence was an invaluable stimulus to the club. Cigarmakers, artisans, and laborers, both Cuban and Puerto Rican, began to fill their halls. Lectures and discussions led by Hostos were one of the main attractions. He came to be recognized as the leader of the separatist workers.

In the cigar factories the belief in the future independence of the Antilles came to life again. But the activities of the club pointed up further divisions within the emigrant community. The conservative, bourgeois, and professional elements in the Junta Revolucionaria Cubana began to encounter opposition to their plans. The animosity against Hostos intensified.

In that year, 1869, another famous Puerto Rican arrived in New York: Juan Rius Rivera. He was barely twenty years old. He joined the Comité Republicano Puertorriqueño and offered his services to Cuba. He didn't stay in New York very long: on January 19, 1870, he landed in Las Tunas, Cuba, as part of an expedition led by Melchor Agüero.

Seeking to sway United States public opinion in their favor, the Junta Revolucionaria Cubana decided to organize sympathizers in the United States. Toward this end Manuel Macías founded a group that came to be known as La Liga. Unfortunately, the new body deviated from its central aim by filling its ranks with North Americans motivated less by a desire for independence than by the hope that Cuba would be annexed to the United States. This attitude led to hostility from the Club de Artesanos, especially the *tabaqueros*. To them, the bourgeois leaders of the exiles were what they called the "aristocracy."

On February 23, 1870, La Liga sponsored a function at Cooper Union. Hostos was invited to speak and in his talk he came out against the formation of the new group. This increased the enmity of the annexationists even further. The plot thickened when Hostos presented a resolution in the Club de Artesanos urging the Junta Revolucionaria Cubana to lend financial support to the revolutionary struggle in Puerto Rico.

The positions that Hostos took separated him from Basora and even Betances. But his ideas were warmly received among artisans, as was proven by a dinner held in his honor on March 12, 1870. The feast took place at Flor Baerga's home at 227 East 17th Street. It was attended by Martín Castro, Juan de Dios Núñez, Jesús Rodríguez, Isidro Ferrer, Jesús Picón, Lisandro Rodríguez, Flor Baerga, and of course Hostos. The only one who wasn't Puerto Rican was the Jew I talked about earlier, Jacobo Silvestre Bresman.

This get-together is recalled both in Hostos' *Diario* and Flor Baerga's *Memorias*. They discussed the situation among the emigrants and the possibility of carrying the war over to Puerto Rico. They agreed to come together again, and in the course of those later meetings they debated the need to define the immediate tasks of the revolution.

At no point did Hostos tone down his campaign against the annexationists. But finally, on October 3, 1870, disgusted with himself and sick with impatience, he left New York. With Hostos gone and Betances away, and with bad news coming from the battlefields of Cuba, the newly born Puerto Rican community, divided and discouraged, lost interest in the fate of the Antilles.

8. The vicissitudes of the revolution; the war ends in Cuba, but the bright light of José Martí shines forth in New York

The reestablishment of the Republic upon the fall of the Spanish throne breathed new life into the revolutionary aspirations of Puerto Rican and Cuban exiles in New York.* But any hope that Madrid would now recognize the rights of the Antillean peoples was soon dashed, and nothing contributed more to the end of that illusion than the tragedy of the *Virginius* in October 1873.

This had to do with what was probably the largest and best-armed of the expeditions—150 men, most of them soldiers of fortune with long military experience. The ship was seized by a Spanish cruiser and escorted to Santiago de Cuba. Just about every man on the mission was summarily shot by the Spanish authorities. Even crew members were gunned down. It was such a bloody massacre that the commander of a British warship stationed in Cuban waters heard of it and asked for clemency. When the Spaniards ignored his plea, the British commander pointed the cannons of his vessel toward the city, threatening to blow it up if the mass murders were not stopped. It is said that this act saved the lives of the few remaining prisoners.

That example of inhuman repression occurred under the Republic of Castelar.

On April 22, 1874, Eugenio María de Hostos returned to New York. Betances was based in Paris and totally involved in raising

*On February 11, 1873, King Amadeo de Saboya abdicated the Spanish throne and a Republic was proclaimed. Its first president was Estanislao Figueras; he was succeeded by Francisco Pi y Margall, Nicolas Salmerón, and Emilio Castelar. The Republic came to an end in January 1874, when a transitional government was formed, leading to the eventual reestablishment of the monarchy under Alfonso XII in December 1874.

funds for the military struggle in Cuba. Basora was in St. Thomas. In New York the Club de Artesanos had gone out of existence.

But on the initiative of Antonio Molina León and Flor Baerga, new meetings were called. Hostos became part of the group, and on June 20, 1874, the first specifically Puerto Rican newspaper published in New York saw the light of day: it was called *La Voz de Puerto Rico (The Voice of Puerto Rico)*. Molina was the major financial contributor. They bought a press and the most essential typefaces. Hostos took on the direction and management of the paper.

In July there was a strike in the cigar factories, and the paper lost the economic support the *tabaqueros* had offered since its start. The only recourse was to wealthy Puerto Ricans. But no one wanted to contribute, so that less than a month after its first issue *La Voz de Puerto Rico* fell silent.

A few months later an attempt was made to bring the newspaper back to life. On September 11 a group of cigarworkers, artisans, and a few recent young arrivals from Puerto Rico got together in a meeting room on 4th Street near Second Avenue. There was some interest in setting up a new Puerto Rican committee. After a lengthy discussion, it was decided to concentrate every effort on getting the paper going again. To carry out that task a committee was named; it was composed of Flor Baerga, Jesús Picón, Antonio Molina, Silvestre Bresman, and Lisandro Rodríguez.

The group visited Basora, Henna, Mercado, and other Puerto Ricans who were in better economic straits. All of them promised to help, but not one parted with a single cent. The committee made the rounds of the cigar factories, where work had just begun again, and collected about a hundred dollars. Even that meager amount was enough to guarantee the publication of three issues. But when they arrived at the printers, they found that all of their fonts of type had disappeared. *La Voz de Puerto Rico* ceased publication once and for all.

This final fiasco had a disastrous effect on Hostos.

The news arriving from Puerto Rico was hardly encouraging. This was during the reign of Governor Laureano Sanz. The entire population was living in fear, and with good reason. Even those who dreamed of revolution expected it to come from the outside. In that case, only a revolutionary expedition capable of conquering and holding a large amount of territory had any chance of success. And that, of course, was out of the question.

This situation weighed heavily on the Puerto Rican exiles and emigrants in New York. Not only was the news from Cuba and Puerto Rico discouraging, but in those years life became difficult for the artisans and workers in New York as well. They were walking around "in rags," as Uncle Antonio would say, and for quite a few families the evening meal consisted of nothing but a "long drawn-out soup."

Uncle Antonio himself was forced to put aside his cigar knife and go looking for work in construction on the Brooklyn Bridge—a decision that almost cost him his life.

Laying the foundation of that bridge was back-breaking work. It was not easy finding men willing to take it on—only those who couldn't find a job anywhere else, which at that time meant Poles, Spaniards, and Italians . . . Not one Yankee worker, nor a single Jew, put in an hour's work on it. Thousands of emigrants died during the construction of the Brooklyn Bridge.

In the freezing winter of 1866–1867 the idea of building a bridge connecting Brooklyn and Manhattan caught fire (there's a paradox!). The East River was solid ice, so that no boats could cross. It was easier to get to New York from Albany than from Long Island. A bridge would solve the problem, and construction costs were estimated at around $7 million. It ended up costing more than twice that.

Construction began with some huge boxes made of fitted wood being turned upside down and driven into the river bed. The water was ejected with compressed air, forming air chambers into which the workmen could descend to lay the concrete and steel foundation. They had to work in nearly total darkness, breathing oxygen pumped down from the surface.

Uncle Antonio could only stand it for two days. He had no choice but to go back to cigarmaking. He and his wife agreed that their children would have to sleep together in one room so that the remaining space could be used as a factory. He borrowed a little money and bought some leaf tobacco from Hyman Sisselman, who had a warehouse down on John Street in lower Manhattan. His wife Dolores stripped stems and packed the cigars in boxes. Silvestre Bresman, the Jew so often associated with Puerto Ricans, took charge of sales and gave the business such a boost that it wasn't long before there were eight men rolling cigars in the little factory.

And that's the way people managed to stay alive. In the most difficult times cigarmaking meant salvation for my Uncle Antonio—just as it has for me.

But they had to work ten or twelve hours a day. There was no time for political or revolutionary work. Antonio Molina came by to see them now and then. He would keep them abreast of what was going on, and read to them from the newspapers. That was the only contact Uncle Antonio had with the Antillean independence movement.

The struggle was not going well in those years. The front in Cuba was beginning to weaken. In Madrid there were secret designs to put an end to the conflict. The morale of the liberation army was flagging, and reports of retreats and setbacks continued. They did not have the weaponry necessary to wage an attack on the Spanish fortresses, so offensive operations could not be undertaken. The conditions seemed right for peace to be restored.

This was the time when General Martínez Campos took advantage of the situation. The famous uprising led by Antonio Maceo in Mangos de Baraguá, in March 1878, had come to nothing. It is worth mentioning that fighting alongside the glorious lieutenant in those trying days, and showing equal courage and gallantry, was the Puerto Rican Juan Rius Rivera. But the peace at Zanjón was enforced* . . . Not until twenty years later, under the inspired leadership of José Martí, would the sparks of revolution be rekindled in Cuba.

But revolutionary energies could not be extinguished that easily. Maceo's refusal to lay down his arms was an example to the militants in New York. This was what led to the expedition aboard the *Charles Miller,* an old ship carrying a handful of men that set off from Boston in April 1875 under the command of Francisco Vicente Aguilera. Eugenio María de Hostos enlisted on this venture, determined to fight to the end in the trenches. But the ship was in such poor shape that it nearly sank and was forced to return to port. And Hostos came back crestfallen, like a beaten Quixote, to New York. Once again, plagued by depression, he struggled to raise his fallen spirits. But he could not.

---

*The Treaty of Zanjón, signed on February 10, 1878, marked the end of the Ten Years' War. It granted Cuba the same political and administrative conditions that prevailed in Puerto Rico. However, the treaty guaranteed neither political independence nor the abolition of slavery, the two main goals of the liberation struggle. It was because of this that Antonio Maceo launched the protest of Mangos de Baraguá.

The same fate awaited the mission undertaken by Antonio Maceo, when he and Ruiz Belvis traveled to Jamaica in search of aid for the revolution. The latter was to report that they only managed to "raise ten *reales* and enlist seven volunteers." There was nothing more that could be done, and what is known in Cuba as the "Little War" came to an end.

But if in the case of Cuba spirits had fallen, the insurgent movement in Puerto Rico suffered a far heavier blow. If Cuba had not been able to win its freedom after such a gallant attempt at rebellion, what hope was there for the smaller of the Antillean isles? In New York, once the initial impact of the defeat was over, agitation for Antillean independence gradually reemerged. And even in that dark hour there was no lack of men who remained faithful to the ideal of independence. Thus, on June 12, 1879, a manifesto circulated in New York, signed by Carlos García Iñíguez, Leandro Rodríguez, Pío Rosado, Carlos Roloff, Leoncio Prado, and José Francisco Lamadriz. It is declared, among other things, that "All we can demand from Spain, if we are not to be dishonored, is our absolute independence." It seemed that the struggle of the Puerto Rican exiles and emigrants in New York was entering a new stage. And that it wouldn't be an easy one.

The winter of 1879–1880 was extremely bitter. Back then they didn't plow the streets when it snowed. One snowfall piled on top of another, and the mountains of snow made the city even colder. In March the streets were still covered with snow that had fallen in December. The price of coal had gone up, and what made it worse was that it was hard to come by. Dolores, Uncle Antonio's wife, had to walk from 13th Street and Second Avenue all the way down to 8th Street by the river to buy it. Every day she would go out with the children in search of firewood to heat the house.

It was on January 3, 1880, in the middle of that bitter winter, that José Martí arrived in New York. Shortly after, it was announced that he would be speaking at Steck Hall. And in his first public appearance he captured the hearts of the Antillean exiles. His eloquence and logic were convincing. It was correct to continue struggling for the cause of independence . . . A new wave of hope began to swell in the breasts of the emigrant community.

Martí was made president of the Comité Revolucionario Cubano on May 13, 1880. The nucleus of the group was composed of Juan Bellido de Luna, Leoncio Prado, Pío Rosado, Carlos Roloff, Leandro

Rodríguez, Manuel Cruz Beraza, and Francisco Lamadriz. But the committee did not make much headway. Its newspaper, *La Revolución,* edited by Bellido de Luna, ceased publication. In the whole United States the only paper that continued to come out was *Yara,* which was published in Key West under the direction of José Dolores Poyo. Its support came from the *tabaqueros* in Key West and Tampa.

Toward the middle of the following year—in July 1881—José Martí left New York. By August, a month later, he was back again. Evidently he had reached the conclusion that New York was the most appropriate place, at that time, from which to carry on revolutionary work. From then through January 1895 Martí lived in New York, and the city served as his base of operations.

Toward the end of 1881 the Puerto Ricans in New York were a community without a head. Antonio Molina León had returned to Puerto Rico, and it was he who had kept a spirit of concern alive outside of the circles of artisans and laborers. Events of any note were few and far between in those days.

In mid-1883 an attempt was made to create a Comité Republicano Cubano, but it got no further than an initial sounding. Then a newspaper called *El Separatista* was published by J. M. Prellezó, Manuel de la Cruz Beraza, and Cirilo Publes. It folded in no time. It seems these men put forth too conservative a view for people to respond favorably to their leadership—least of all the artisan masses.

At that time José Martí was living in a boarding house at 51 West 29th Street. It was there that the Cuban patriot had his love affair with Carmen Mantilla. Separated from his wife because of profound differences, Martí struggled with that passion which caused so much talk . . . La Mantilla, my Uncle Antonio told me, was the wife of a sick old man. She, on the other hand, was a beautiful woman, a sensitive, dreamy, and romantic spirit. She moved the poet to the depths of his soul.

Martí tried to flee from his love, which may explain his disappearance in the summer of 1881. But it was too late. Uncle Antonio told me he suspected that both of them realized that it was their common destiny. But their decision was to bring them great suffering, as an incident that involved Enrique Trujillo shows.

Trujillo was a friend of Martí. On this occasion, it was his job to send out the invitations to an artistic evening. Being a conservative man, very set in his ways, he did not send one to Carmen Mantilla.

In so doing, he believed that he was showing respect for the name of Leonor Pérez de Martí, the apostle's mother, who was in the city on a visit at the time. This offended Martí, and the incident had unpleasant consequences.

Martí was fuming throughout the evening. He did not exchange one word with Enrique Trujillo, even though Trujillo read to the audience from his *Enriquillo*. The reason for his silence was no secret, and many people were whispering to each other about it. The stuffy aristocrats in attendance endorsed Trujillo's decision not to invite "Martí's lover," as they called her. Martí's political enemies used the occasion to spread sordid rumors. But to the artisans and cigarworkers, like Lisandro, Baerga, Picón, Ferrer and the others, it didn't matter whether La Mantilla had been invited or not. They weren't concerned with anyone's private affairs. What commanded their admiration were the political qualities that José Martí exemplified . . . If those relations were "immoral," Uncle Antonio told me, then down with "moralists!"

To the *tabaqueros* and artisans, José Martí's presence in New York reminded them of the days of Hostos. In the middle of 1884, Los Independientes, which was the only group then active in the city, got in touch with Antonio Maceo and invited him to come to New York. Martí spread the word and the group met. And it may be said that this visit by Maceo, who was accompanied by Máximo Gómez, sparked the first preparations for the struggle of 1895.

On October 26, 1884, a new group announced itself in the community: the so-called Asociación Cubana de Socorros. The name had been chosen in order to conceal the organization's subversive aims. José Martí was elected president, but did not accept because of differences with Máximo Gómez. Gómez was then chosen treasurer and Miguel Párraga president. The Asociación sent out a letter asking for contributions to support the resumption of the revolutionary struggle in Cuba. But only one person, Sr. Elías Sánchez, responded by sending $50 . . . Disheartened, Maceo and Gómez left for Florida.

In June 1885 an effort was made to resurrect the Asociación. At a mass meeting called for this purpose Germán Martínez and Carlos Moyano hurled insults at José Martí. They noted his differences with Maceo and Gómez and even went into the "morality" of his private life. The man they were referring to was told of this slander by some of those who attended, which no doubt motivated the publication of a leaflet that circulated throughout the Cuban and Puerto Rican community. It read, in part: "I have no other right to address myself to my fellow Cubans . . . but my deep love for my country . . . Rumors have reached me . . . that in Clarendon Hall [there was talk] of my actions . . . On Thursday the 25th, starting at 7:30 P.M., I shall be at Clarendon Hall to respond to whatever charges my fellow citizens may want to raise against me . . ." At the foot of the flyer appeared the name José Martí.

On the appointed night there was a full house at Clarendon Hall. New York had seen nothing like it since the days of Hostos. There were cigarmakers, artisans of all trades, intellectuals . . . When Martí took the stage the audience greeted him with a thunderous ovation. The wings of his enemies were clipped. When the applause diminished, that slight, delicate-looking man asked, calmly and in his deep voice, that those with accusation against him speak up. Those first words were followed by a long and nervous silence.

Finally someone at the back of the hall stood up. The speaker was a man named Manuel Rico. He began to talk, but he had no sooner started than he had a knot in his throat. He could not continue, and sat down. There followed another silence. Martí said again that anyone who wished to accuse him could do so without the slightest fear. More long minutes of silence. No one answered the challenge.

That night the man who rightly came to be recognized as the Apostle of the Cuban Revolution delivered one of the most electric speeches he ever gave in New York, and without any notes at all. He started off slowly and calmly, yet from his mouth streamed a torrent of images that lent dramatic life to his ideals and concepts. He spoke, of course, of what was closest to his soul—the freedom of Cuba and Puerto Rico. He was kind and indulgent with his critics. He was resigned to his destiny, knowing that he would have to suffer the ingratitude of other men. Only his own deeds would bring him just compensation.

When he finished speaking, the audience applauded once again. Some of those present went away feeling a good deal smaller than when they came. But the large majority, especially the *tabaqueros* and artisans, burst out into the streets filled with jubilation. They had been right all along . . . In the person of José Martí the Antillean revolution had found its foremost organizer and intellectual leader.

9. With the help of Puerto Ricans like Sotero Figueroa and Pachín Marín, the Partido Revolucionario Cubano is founded

Antonio Maceo's return to New York reawakened the enthusiasm of the Cuban and Puerto Rican community. This was demonstrated at an event held at Clarendon Hall on July 21, 1885. The veteran leader of the Ten Years' War told how he had been received by the workers in Tampa and Key West. Twelve thousand dollars had been raised, especially by the *tabaqueros,* in support of a renewed revolutionary struggle. Maceo let it slip that new expeditions would soon be sent to Cuba.

But a series of tragic events upset these plans. Once again, spirits sank and pessimism increased. The inevitable result was that serious criticism of Máximo Gómez and Antonio Maceo grew. Dissension filled the air. The revolutionary press was silent. Only one paper remained alive: the *Yara* in Key West.

Nothing had been heard of José Martí since the night of his speech at Clarendon Hall. He was ailing, but his silence was actually due to his wish not to insist on his disagreements with the leaders of 1868. In October 1887 he broke his silence by calling a celebration of the Grito de Yara. The event was held at the Masonic Temple on 23rd Street. The speakers were Tomás Estrada Palma, Enrique Trujillo, R. C. Palomino, Serafín Bello, Emilio Núñez, and José Martí.

But no lasting organization arose as a result of these sporadic activities. The decades of struggle, the war in Cuba, the many expeditions sent from the United States, the thousands of men who had been sacrificed, the vast sums of money involved—nothing had won them independence. Something was missing. It began to dawn on people, especially the *tabaqueros,* that they would have to try a new strategy.

No one seemed to know which way to turn. But some general

points were clear. No more reckless invasions. What was needed was a solid organization based among the artisans. Their propaganda would have to be broadened, able recruits won over, and the well-off creole class could not be depended on. At the same time they would have to be sure not to confine the movement to social revolution alone, as some of the *tabaqueros* wanted. The revolution had to be republican and democratic. Yet the main source of financial support was in the cigar factories. There you could find capable leaders among the talented workers from Tampa, Key West, New Orleans, and New York . . . And José Martí was aware of this . . .

On 23rd Street and Third Avenue a Puerto Rican named Domingo Peraza had opened up a drugstore. Many, many Puerto Ricans dropped in, so many that it came to be known as the Puerto Rican consulate in New York. It was the frequent meeting place of Dr. Henna, Baerga, Lisandro, Picón, Silvestre, and other compatriots connected to the Antillean liberation movement. And it was there that word of the return of Antonio Molina first reached New York.

After living in New York for a few years, Molina had decided to go back to Puerto Rico. He had settled in Ponce, where in 1882 he began publishing *El Trabajo (Labor)*. But the Spanish authorities suspended publication, and again there was no choice but exile. So there he was, ready to carry on the struggle from New York.

In December 1886 Molina, along with Baerga and Lisandro, paid a visit to Martí, who was living at 120 Front Street. The Cuban laid out a plan, which by then had been in the works for some time. The Puerto Ricans were to be an important nucleus within the revolutionary association he envisioned. Its goal would be independence for both islands.

A club called Los Independientes was organized on the initiative of Flor Baerga, Juan Fraga, Rafael Serra, and Angelillo García. Fraga was elected president and Serra secretary.

Around that time, in the middle of 1888, Flor Crombet came to New York. A Cuban of French descent, he was a close friend of Betances, with whom he had been living in Paris. He was a man of deep convictions, determined to move on to Cuba and open up a new battlefront.

Los Independientes held its first general meeting in Pythagoras Hall on July 15 of that year, with about fifty people attending. It was agreed that there was no point in continuing to improvise small military expeditions to Cuba. Instead they would work to build a large-scale campaign under competent leadership. All fund-raising would be toward this end. The exile community was tired of giving money and sacrificing men to ill-planned adventures, doomed as they were to failure.

Crombet, deeply concerned, presented his plan for immediate action. Martí, who was at the meeting, voiced his support for the more prudent politics put forth by Los Independientes. This gave rise to an altercation between Martí and Crombet. The same issue cropped up again at the commemoration of the Grito de Yara later that year.

A commotion broke out just as José Martí stood up to speak to a full house at Clarendon Hall. A group in the audience was demanding that Ramón I. Armas take the floor. He was one of Martí's adversaries. The request was granted courteously from the stage, and Armas spoke. When he finished, Martí continued, speaking in conciliatory tones. He finished his presentation to wild applause from everyone present.

That was the year that a paper edited by Enrique Trujillo, *El Porvenir (The Future),* came out. In the first issue Trujillo proclaimed his commitment to the cause of Cuban independence and to armed revolution as the means of winning it.

In October there was the usual commemoration of the Grito de Yara. That year the event had a special meaning for Puerto Ricans— for the first time since the days of Hostos one of the main speakers was a Puerto Rican. Sotero Figueroa, recently arrived from Puerto Rico, shared the rostrum with José Martí. His sincere tone and patriotic spirit moved the audience throughout his speech.

By that time José Martí had won the sympathy of the Cubans and Puerto Ricans in New York. But his financial situation was precarious. Virtually driven by hunger, he accepted a position as consul for the Argentinian government. Filling this post forced him to cut his revolutionary activities down to a minimum, which brought on renewed attacks from his enemies.

It was then that the Liga de Artesanos was founded. Its aims were mostly cultural and civic. Some of those in the organization were Antonio Molina, Juan de Dios Núñez, Flor Baerga, Jesús Picón, and Sotero Figueroa.

The Liga Antillana, a similar organization but made up of women, was also formed at that time. Its Cuban and Puerto Rican members belonged to the working class, women like Gertrudis E. de Serra, Josefa González, Dominga Muriel, Ramona Gomero, and Pilar Pivalot. It was the first such society with Cuban and Puerto Rican members ever founded in New York. It was organized by women who were related to cigarworkers. José Martí, Sotero Figueroa, Pachín Marín, Antonio Molina, Lola Rodríguez de Tió, Arturo Schomburg, Antonio Vélez Alvarado, and Flor Baerga in particular participated in its events.

It is worth mentioning that the group was completely interracial, with all its activities shared by white, black, and mulatto women. Because they were a mixed group, most of the meeting halls shut their doors to them, which is why they usually held their events in places provided by the Socialist Party or the Cigarworkers' Union. But every so often they used Hardman Hall and the Masonic Temple as well.

The Liga Antillana and the Liga de Artesanos were both bulwarks of the Partido Revolucionario Cubano. They served as centers of information and fund-raising. In no other organization was there as close a working relationship between Cubans and Puerto Ricans as there was in the Liga de Artesanos.

In April 1891 Flor Baerga had an unusual visitor from Puerto Rico. He was a young black man, just turned seventeen, who had been recommended to Baerga by a *tabaquero* back in San Juan—yet another Puerto Rican cast into exile. That beardless youth was named Arturo Alfonso Schomburg, and would in later years become one of the shining lights among black people in the United States.

In the early 1890s cultural and artistic events flourished in the Spanish-speaking community in New York. Many of these activities centered around the Sociedad Literaria, which had been founded by a group of intellectuals. In the previous decade several journals had appeared, such as *América* (1883), *El Latino-Americano* (1885), *El Avisador Cubano* (1888), *El Economista Americano* (1887), *El Avisador Cubano* (second period, 1888), *La Juventud* (1889), and *El Porvenir* (1890).

A book by Ramón Roa drew criticism from José Martí. He made reference to it in a famous speech in which he contrasted old and new pine trees.* These critical remarks in turn provoked attack from En-

---

*The book, entitled *A pie y descalso (Walking Barefoot)*, told of the hardships faced by the rebels during the Ten Years' War, in which Roa had taken part. To Martí it seemed inopportune to publish the book on the eve of a new war.

rique Collazo, who gratuitously accused Martí of "holding forth on patriotism while finding shelter in exile under the shade of the American flag." Martí responded to the insult with his usual patience. He said, "Never, Sr. Collazo, have I been a man like the one you portray. Never have I put my well-being before my duty. Never during the first war did I, poor sick child that I was, fail to fulfill my patriotic duty. . . . I am living sadly at my obscure post, because for the sake of my homeland I sacrificed my own well-being. And it's cold in this hole where I live, hardly fit for visits from anyone. But we don't have to wait until we are in the heat of battle to extend each other a hand. Rather, I would be delighted by an unexpected visit from you, at whatever place and time is convenient for you . . ."

On November 24, 1891, Martí left New York for Key West and Tampa. The *tabaqueros* gave him a warm welcome. On his return Los Independientes called a meeting at Hardman Hall. Martí gave a full account of his trip to a large audience composed mostly of *tabaqueros*. Sotero Figueroa and Rosendo Tirado, two Puerto Ricans, sat at the speakers' table.

The well-known Colombian writer José María Vargas Vila attended those meetings which, he reported, were "held on Saturdays and week nights in the large halls. The workers, silent yet filled with a kind of Indian fanaticism, would go to listen to the somber voice of the Apostle. He spoke of bright new days to come, which his eyes, so hungry for light, would never see. . . . The audience rose to its feet like a single man, their brown faces aglow with light; they stood as though transfigured by that breath of inspiration, which was like Ezekiel's as he summoned the unblessed corpses from the grave."

On that particular day, as he stepped down from the stage, Martí was greeted by a young mulatto with sparkling eyes. He had just arrived in New York from Puerto Rico, but was already well known among the cigarworkers. On various occasions he had been to meetings at the Liga de Artesanos. Now, when they saw him so close to the stage, the audience broke into applause. Shouts of "Let Pachín speak!" echoed through the hall. And this man, Francisco Gonzalo Marín, was to give his life for Antillean liberation in the battlefields of Cuba.

The year 1891 came to a close with what seemed to be a wave of spontaneous organizing, and many new clubs were founded. Right at the start of the new year, on January 24, 1892, Los Independientes held a meeting that was to set the Cuban revolution squarely on the path to victory.

It was on this occasion that Martí put forth his plan for organizing the Partido Revolucionario Cubano; the constitution and secret by-laws had already been drafted. Among the Cubans at the meeting there was Gonzalo de Quesada, Leandro Rodríguez, Juan García, and Enrique Trujillo, while the Puerto Ricans included Modesto A. Tirado, Pachín Marín, Sotero Figueroa, and Rosendo Rodríguez. Trujillo, when he had read Martí's document, proposed that it be submitted to a general meeting of the wider exile community. He also objected to the secret by-laws because he felt that they would concentrate too much power in a centralized leadership and could give rise to a dangerous dictatorship. Sotero Figueroa disagreed sharply. He agreed that the clubs that made up the party should have an opportunity to discuss the program, but he did not think that it would be right to submit secret matters to open discussion at a public meeting where enemies of the revolution might be present. This position was the one adopted.

On February 3 the Club Pinos Nuevos was founded and the *tabaquero* Federico Sánchez was elected president. The Club Borinquen was founded on the twentieth of that month. At their second meeting, the twenty-two Puerto Ricans attending chose the following as leaders: Sotero Figueroa, president; Antonio Vélez Alvarado, vice-president; Pachín Marín, secretary; Modesto A. Tirado, treasurer; and Leopoldo Núñez, Augustín González, and Rafael Delgado as members of the governing body. Betances, Hostos, and Martí were named honorary presidents. The Borinquen began its efforts with the publication of a lengthy manifesto denouncing the moves toward autonomy that followed the Assembly of Ponce in 1887.*

The first issue of *Patria,* the organ of the Partido Revolucionario Cubano, appeared on March 14, 1892. The party program was printed there for the first time, stating its primary objective of "winning the independence of Cuba and lending direct support to the struggle to free Puerto Rico." The editorial, by José Martí, was written in the same spirit: "The birth of this newspaper rests on the determination and resources of independent Cubans and Puerto Ri-

---

*The Assembly of Ponce, held in March 1887, marked the founding of the Partido Autonómico de Puerto Rico. The party's program stated as its main goal the political and juridical unification of Puerto Rico with Spain, with "autonomy" on issues of local concern.

cans in New York who are committed to contribute, unfailingly and tirelessly, to the organization of the free men of Cuba and Puerto Rico as is made necessary by the conditions prevailing on the Islands and their future constitution as republics . . ."

In April of that year a new club, Las Dos Antillas, was formed in full agreement with these principles. Rosendo Rodríguez and Arturo Alfonso Schomburg, who was still very young, were among its most prominent members. *Patria* hailed the founding of the group in its April 10 issue, and on the same day Partido Revolucionario Cubano held a general meeting in Military Hall. It was attended by people from all the clubs—Los Independientes, José Martí, Cubanacán, Borinquen, Las Dos Antillas, and Mercedes Varona— the last composed of women from both the islands. There were 173 people present in all; they constituted the membership of the party.

The presidents of the different groups met separately and, in accordance with the organizing statutes, presented candidates for the governing council. Juan Fraga was chosen president, Sotero Figueroa, secretary, and Francisco Sánchez, Emilio Leal, Gonzalo de Quesada, and Rosendo Rodríguez, council members. The general meeting ratified the selection and, quite remarkably, three Puerto Ricans held the highest positions in the Partido Revolucionario Cubano. The governing council named José Martí the party's representative and Benjamín Guerra as treasurer.

Not all of the organizations in the Spanish-speaking community were formed for political purposes. As I mentioned, there were also artistic, literary, and benefit societies. An example of the latter was La Nacional, which had been founded by Spaniards back in 1868. Another was the Sociedad Benéfica Cubana y Puertorriqueña, whose officers were announced in *Patria* in March 1892. They were Modesto A. Tirado, president; Marcos Rosario, treasurer; and J. González Mariano Rosario, Joaquín González, M. de J. González, and Juan Nieto, board members.

Other Hispanic groups active in Brooklyn and Manhattan were Círculo de Trabajadores, the Fénix social club, and La Literaria. This Hispanic-American literary society sponsored well-attended cultural activities. The first of those frequent "literary evenings," as they came to be known, was dedicated to Puerto Rico and Cuba. It was held under the direction of the Puerto Rican Francisco J. Amy. Sure enough, before the evening got under way someone suggested that the Spanish flag be hung on the stage to represent Puerto Rico. The idea was immediately rejected, but did not fail to reach the ears of José Martí, who proclaimed, when he took the floor, "When I enter this hall I come wrapped in the banners of Yara and Lares."

Some people felt that these literary activities were diverting energy away from the revolutionary cause. There were even some resignations as a result. At the same time, Enrique Trujillo was openly opposing Martí in the April and May 1892 issues of his newspaper *El Porvenir*. There he publicly presented his objections to the secret rules and by-laws of the Partido Revolucionario Cubano. He argued that they should be discussed at an open meeting. His position was rejected by the governing council of the party; the approved resolution, presented by Sotero Figueroa, condemned Trujillo for "abusing the knowledge of the secret by-laws he had gained as a member of several clubs; for seeking to discredit said by-laws outside of the clubs and in public; and for denouncing the organizational rules of the party to which he was affiliated before the enemy and at just the time when the revolutionary forces are preparing themselves for battle."

All of the revolutionary groups came out in support of the condemnation of Enrique Trujillo. And this was not the only boost to the prospect of renewed war against Spain. Showing once again his patriotism and purity of spirit, José Martí wrote to Máximo Gómez in August 1892: "I invite you to share in this task and do not fear your refusal, although I have no compensation to offer you but the pleasure of sacrifice and the likely ingratitude of our fellow men."

In August 1892 the Puerto Rican pianist Ana Otero came to New York on visit. The Sociedad Literaria organized an evening in her honor, at which she gave a piano rendition of "La Borinqueña" by Félix Astol. Vélez Alvarado praised the event in the September 3 issue of *Patria*. Along with the relevant information, he included the words of an anthem attributed to Pachín Marín. According to Pilar Pivalot, the Puerto Rican woman Pachín Marín frequently visited in New York, his poem read:

Bellísima Borinquen,
a Cuba has de seguir;
tú tienes bravos hijos
que quieren combatir.

Tu aire gentil, patriótico,
vibra en el corazón

Oh beautiful Borinquen,
Like Cuba, filled with charms,
Valiant sons are yours
Prepared to take up arms!

Your patriotic spirit
Vibrates in our soul,

y te sería simpático
el ruido del cañón.

No más esclavos
queremos ser,
nuestras cadenas
se han de romper.

El tambor guerrero
nos dice con su son
que es la agreste montaña
el sitio de la reunión.

You are most inspired
To hear the cannon's roll.

No longer slaves are we,
Trodden to the ground,
We'll burst the chains asunder,
The chains that hold us down.

The rolling drums of battle,
The warrior's mighty song,
We're meeting in the mountains,
Be sure to come along.

Máximo Gómez responded favorably to José Martí's invitation. And rather than waiting for him in New York, Martí was off to meet with the leader of the Ten Years' War in Santo Domingo. There the men came to terms. The outlook for the revolution in Cuba soared.

10. The struggle to carry the war over to Puerto Rico and, finally, the imposition of United States military force

In the United States, 1893 and 1894 were the years of great debate over the silver and gold standards. This controversy was to have a telling effect on the struggle for Antillean liberation.

The bankers and industrialists based in Wall Street regarded silver as too unstable as a standard, and set up a monopoly on gold. Farming and mining interests in the central and western United States, on the other hand, strongly favored silver and pushed for its unlimited coinage. This conflict was the center of political attention, and the two major parties advocated opposing positions—the Democrats upheld silver while the Republicans were the self-proclaimed champions of gold.

Out of this debate there arose the Populist Party, which enjoyed the backing of some sectors of agriculture, of the labor unions, and of socialist groups. This new party came out in support of Democratic presidential candidate William Jennings Bryan. But even with the million and a half votes from the Populists, the Democratic Party was beaten by the Republicans and William McKinley became the new president. The gold standard was imposed, which set United States policy all the more rapidly on the path toward out-and-out expansionism. The Antilles—Cuba and Puerto Rico—were to become the most coveted prey.

The gold standard meant a deepening of the economic crisis that had been begun in the previous year. Cigarmaking was one of the most severely affected industries. Which is why the idea of a strike began to win the approval of more and more *tabaqueros*.

Several Cubans and Puerto Ricans in New York, including Antonio Molina, Pachín Marín, and Jacobo Silvestre Bresman, founded a Comité Populista. This was the first Hispanic political group in the city whose aim was to participate in the electoral debate in the

72

United States. The committee set itself the task of guiding the *tabaqueros'* protest movement so that it would culminate in a general strike in conjunction with other national groups.

When the Spanish agents in the United States caught wind of what they might be up against, they sounded the alarm. They proposed to down the cigar factories in order to strip the Partido Revolucionario Cubano of its solid financial base. But their strategy didn't work. The *tabaqueros* reviewed the situation and decided to call off their strike, and to redirect their attention to the Antillean revolutionary struggle.

The editorial in *Patria* of August 22, 1893, had nothing but praise for the cigarworkers' actions and spirit: "If there are any fools around who still think that just because they're poor the *tabaqueros* have given up their love for freedom, that losing a table in the shop means they no longer love other men like brothers or long to secure the greatest happiness for all, and do not continue to bear vengeance on behalf of their oppressed compatriots and all that is decent and gives dignity to humankind—the *tabaqueros,* though unemployed, will turn around and stand up against anyone who thinks that by losing their jobs they have lost their honor . . ."

As Samuel Gompers reported in a publication put out by the Cigarmakers' Union, by the beginning of 1894 there were already some three thousand cigar factories in New York City. About five hundred there were owned by Hispanics—that is, Spaniards and Latin Americans. The remaining twenty-five hundred had proprietors of other nationalities, but employed many Cubans and Puerto Ricans as cigarmakers and tobacco strippers.

But cigarmaking in New York goes back to a time even before the United States won its independence from Britain. For a long time it was carried out in countless small shops set up right in the home. The Cigarmakers' Union had fought against this practice since its founding, charging that it was detrimental to the workers' health. But neither the small- nor the large-scale manufacturers shared this concern, and it was their position that tended to prevail.

The *New York Herald* came out for prohibiting cigarmaking in the home. One article even described the conditions in which the domestic cigarworker lived back then at the end of the nineteenth century, the days of my Uncle Antonio: "For the most part, families live in three-room apartments. One room—12 x 15 feet with a window facing the street—is used as the bedroom and work area. The next room is smaller, 10 x 12 feet, and serves as both a second bedroom and a kitchen. And the third room, which is smaller still (7 x 9 feet) and usually without any light, is for the children and for storing tobacco. Between these quarters and the identical apartment next door there is a hallway hardly big enough for two people. There are no fewer than 3,750 people working in those domestic cigar factories. Earnings are about $2.00 lower per thousand cigars than the prevailing rate for the larger businesses. In addition, the family has to strip the tobacco for nothing. The rent for these apartments is $7.50 to $12.00 a month."

Very often these tiny factories, especially those that were run by Cubans and Puerto Ricans, sold their cigars to tobacco stands and stores, or else directly to individual customers. But the majority operated on contract for the larger concerns. In both cases, the work was shared by the head of the family and his wife and children.

Most of the time they would use domestic tobacco. Cuban stock was only available to the large-scale factories, and imported Puerto Rican tobacco was scarce. "Pure" cigars usually had an extremely strong taste. Cigarsmokers back in those days demanded high quality and a special aroma. The cigars themselves were wrapped in decorative paper, which was adorned with elaborate designs.

In every factory there was a committee in charge of raising funds for the Antillean revolution. There were even some Spanish cigarmakers who made contributions. Each factory also had its press representative who would distribute the workers' newspapers—*Yara* and *El Proletario* from Key West, *Verdad (Truth)* from New Orleans and, of course, *Patria* from New York.

Single *tabaqueros,* and even some married ones, lived in boarding houses or with friendly families. They would pay anywhere from $3.00 to $5.00 a week for room and board. In those days Puerto Rican *tabaqueros* were concentrated in the area around 100th Street and Third Avenue, though there were some scattered in other places, such as along Morris Street. And by 1894 many of the families who were arriving from Puerto Rico were settling on Jefferson, Johnson, and Adams streets in Brooklyn.

The Partido Revolucionario Cubano was at the height of its activity. In the cigar factories and wherever else the emigrants got together, that was the topic of conversation. Even the wealthy Cubans living in New York, although they didn't contribute much, were impressed by the likes of José Martí. That frail and sickly man managed to organize fifty thousand people in support of the Antillean revolution. Martí's influence among the *tabaqueros* was so strong that on Christmas Eve 1893 they had a marvelous present for him. In the cigar factories everyone agreed to donate one day's pay. They called it El Día de la Patria (The Day of the Homeland) and the $12,000 they collected was donated to the party.

On January 15, 1894, at a meeting held at Hardman Hall, Martí gave a detailed report on the prospects for the Cuban revolution. He especially cautioned the emigrant audience about the latest moves by the autonomists. A few months later, in March, he moved to Central Valley, where Tomás Estrada Palma lived and had his school. There he met with General Emilio Núñez, who managed to make frequent trips to Cuba under the pretense of buying tobacco. The news he brought back was inspiring.

General Máximo Gómez made a trip to New York in April of that year, which was the occasion for a variety of public events and gave added impetus to the fund-raising drive. That was the time when preparations were being made for the expedition aboard *La Gonda* and *El Amadis,* in which practically the entire party treasury—some $60,000—was invested. The government in Washington seized the ships even before they left port.

Once again Spanish espionage had won out. When Martí heard about this loss of arms, he fell into a deep depression. A suit was brought against the government demanding the return of the confiscated materiel. There followed months of agony, but the work of the revolution went on without interruption.

On January 29, 1895, in New York, José Martí issued the command to rise up and take arms. His orders were conveyed to Key West by Gonzalo de Quesada. There they were passed on to Juan de Dios Berríos, who slipped the document between some large tobacco leaves and rolled a cigar, which was sent on to Juan Gualberto Gómez in Havana. In the same way, wrapped in a cigar, Martí received confirmation of the plan in New York. And a few days later he left to join Máximo Gómez in Santo Domingo.

The veteran of the Ten Years' War tried to dissuade Martí from going on to Cuba. A man like Martí was far more valuable to the revolution in exile. But Martí's soul had been bruised by all the intrigue and scheming . . . Nobody would be able to accuse him of being a sideline general! And in one of the first skirmishes, in Dos Ríos, José Martí fell in combat.

Back in New York, the Partido Revolucionario Cubano carried on under the leadership of Benjamín Guerra, a cigar manufacturer. On July 10, 1895, Tomás Estrada Palma was chosen to succeed José Martí as the party's representative. Support for the revolution came from Ramón Emeterio Betances in Paris and Eugenio María de Hostos in Santiago, Chile. And, from his home in La Ceiba, Honduras, Juan Rius Rivera put his military expertise at the service of the revolution.

Until that moment the better-off Puerto Rican professionals and intellectuals, with the exception of Betances and Hostos, had shown little or no support for the Antillean revolution. There is no evidence that they ever offered financial assistance to the revolutionary clubs, the Partido Revolucionario Cubano, or its newspaper *Patria*. But with the death of Martí, upper-class Puerto Ricans began to play a visible role in the struggle against Spain. Thus on August 8, 1895, the Puerto Rican section of the Partido Revolucionario Cubano was founded in the home of Dr. Julio J. Henna.

Leadership of the group, headed by Dr. Henna, was made up of prestigious figures from the upper class. Representation from the artisan and working classes was conspicuously absent. Men who were well known in the struggle, like Pachín Marín, Antonio Vélez Alvarado, Rosendo Rodríguez, Rafael Delgado, Angelito García, Flor Baerga, Isidoro Apodaca, I. Ferrer, José Rivera, Jesús Rodríguez, Nicasio García, Sandalio Parrilla, Arturo Schomburg, Eusebio Márquez, and Domingo Collazo—to mention some names from the registry of the Borinquen, Dos Antillas, Mercedes Varona, and Martí clubs—were nowhere to be found among the leaders of the Puerto Rican section. The reasons for this omission? Aside from their not having been invited to the meeting, readers will draw their own conclusions from what follows.

The founding of the Puerto Rican section had an icy reception among the working class, particularly the *tabaqueros*. When he became aware of this, Sotero Figueroa—who had been named to a leadership position—tried to remedy the situation. At his urging the governing body called a general meeting on December 22, four months after the section's founding. It was on that occasion, in fact, that the flag with one star was adopted as a symbol of the Puerto Rican revolution.

According to the account given me in Harlem by José Rivera, a Puerto Rican who was at that historic gathering, when Dr. Henna had finished delivering his address, Antonio Molina León asked for the floor. His name isn't even listed as being among those who attended, at least not in the records published, years later, by Roberto H. Todd. Those records do note, though, that "Molina made demands which the audience deemed to be out of order."

According to Rivera's report, which has been confirmed by Jesús Rodríguez, Sandalio Parrilla, and Flor Baerga, Molina objected to the actions of the governing body, claiming that it should only be provisional in nature and proposing that its membership be submitted to a general election. The leadership rejected the suggestion, at which point the majority of the cigarworkers got up and walked out. But the meeting went on without them.

Despite such divisions, the new wave of revolutionary activity in New York worried the autonomists in Puerto Rico. Wary that the proposed armed invasion would upset his negotiations in Spain, Luis Muñoz Rivera sent his emissary Pedro J. Fournier to confer with Dr. Henna. Fournier landed in New York in August 1895, spoke with leaders of the section, and asked for a postponement of all revolutionary action pending Madrid's response to the demand for autonomy. But the request was not granted. On the contrary, it was agreed to carry on with plans to send a revolutionary expedition to Puerto Rico.

The most important Cuban and Puerto Rican clubs affiliated with the Partido Revolucionario Cubano in New York that were active around that time were the following:

—Los Independientes: Juan Fraga, president, and Genaro Báez, secretary; 839 Fulton Street, Brooklyn

—Rifleros de La Habana: Antonio G. Camero, president, and Adelaido Marín, secretary; 2141 Pacific Street, Brooklyn

—Borinquen: I. M. Torreforte, president, and Domingo Collazo, secretary; 129 McDougal Street, Brooklyn

—José Martí: B. H. Portuondo, president, and Sotero Figueroa

—Martín del Castillo: Felipe Rodríguez, president, and Eusebio Molina, secretary; 1642 Park Avenue, Manhattan

—Dos Antillas: Rosendo Rodríguez, president, and Arturo Alfonso Schomburg, secretary; 1758 Third Avenue, Manhattan

—América: J. R. Alvarez, president, and E. M. Amorós, secretary; 231 East 61st Street, Manhattan

—Guerrilla de Maceo: Juan B. Beato, president, and Juan Fernández, secretary; 146 West 24th Street, Manhattan

—Hijas de Cuba: Angelina R. de Quesada, president, and Carmen Mantilla, secretary; 116 West 64th Street, Manhattan

—Hijas de la Libertad: Natividad R. de Gallo, president, and Gertrudis Casano, secretary; 1115 Herkimer Street, Brooklyn

—Mercedes Varona: Inocencia M. de Figueroa, president, and Emma Betancourt, secretary; 235 East 75th Street, Manhattan

—Céspedes y Martí: Petrona Calderón, president, and Juana Rosario, secretary; 2012 Fulton Street, Brooklyn

There were similar societies and clubs in many other cities, including Boston, Philadelphia, and Chicago, as well as broad-based organizations in Key West, Tampa, and New Orleans. Most of the members were *tabaqueros* and their wives and families, and artisans in other trades.

Such a vast range of organized support for the Antillean revolution was the legacy that José Martí left in the United States. His successor as representative of the Partido Revolucionario Cubano, Tomás Estrada Palma, did not have a shadow of his personal influence in the Cuban and Puerto Rican communities. Dissension between the two sectors began to grow. The establishment of the Puerto Rican section, led by Dr. Julio J. Henna, did nothing to improve these relations.

Furthermore, the plan to extend the war to Puerto Rico, the smaller of the Antilles, never received the attention it warranted. Attempts by Rius Rivera and others failed to catch on so that, following their lead, the most fervent Puerto Rican revolutionaries chose armed combat in the trenches of Cuba. Long is the list of these heroes, who to this day have never been granted the recognition they deserve.

The bombing and sinking of the *Maine* in Havana harbor on February 15, 1898, gave an unexpected turn to the revolutionary battle in the Antilles. Henna, who had all along shown annexationist tendencies, immediately set off for Washington and offered Theodore Roosevelt and Henry Cabot Lodge the support of the Puerto Rican emigrants in the plan to invade Puerto Rico. On March 21 Henna had a personal audience with President McKinley. A few days later he met with General Miles, the man who was to order the landing of troops on Guánica on July 25, 1898.

The United States army made full use of all the information provided by Henna and Roberto H. Todd—president and secretary, respectively, of the delegation. But not the slightest recognition was granted to a single Puerto Rican. As those very leaders were to state, soon thereafter, in a pamphlet in English entitled *The Case of Puerto Rico:* "The voice of Puerto Rico has not been heard. Not even by way of formality were its inhabitants consulted as to whether they wanted to ask for, object to, or suggest any conditions bearing on their present or future political status. . . . The island and all its people were simply transferred from one sovereign power to another, just as a farm with all its equipment, houses, and animals is passed from one landlord to another."

From Paris came words of warning from Ramón Emeterio Betances: "I do not want us to be a colony, neither a colony of Spain nor a colony of the United States." Eugenio María de Hostos set off from Chile for the United States. On August 2, 1898, he took part in the final meeting of the Puerto Rican section of the Partido Revolucionario Cubano held in Chimney Hall, New York. On that day it was agreed to dissolve the group, and an era in the history of the Puerto Rican community in New York came to an end.

Part 3
AFTER 1898

11. How the century began for the Puerto Rican community, and related incidents

Once the thunder of revolutionary struggle against Spain had subsided in the Antilles, the Cuban and Puerto Rican emigrant community in New York fell silent. The only groups to show any signs of activity were a few of the mutual benefit societies, and, of course, the cigarworkers' unions. There were two of them—the International Cigarmakers' Union, affiliated with the A.F. of L., and the one known as La Resistencia. Most of the Spanish-speaking *tabaqueros* belonged to the latter.

The International Cigarmakers' Union followed the basic tenets of United States trade unionism. It was opposed to the formation of a workers' party, not to mention the idea of social revolution. La Resistencia, on the other hand, regarded itself as revolutionary and advocated the principles of anarchosyndicalism. Its members did not accept the notion of a "home country." For them, *patria* only exists for capitalists. The workers have no country or, to put it another way, the workers' homeland is the planet Earth.

As anarchosyndicalists, the *tabaqueros* in La Resistencia repudiated any and all political parties, even if they called themselves socialist. But that didn't mean that they did not help the patriotic movements. In practice, though, it would seem contrary to their principles, they supported the struggle for the independence of Cuba and Puerto Rico. They justified this position in the name of human rights. They also argued that such popular upheavals provided a good opportunity to preach the idea of "one huge fatherland without borders."

In mid-1899 the socialists in New York split into two factions, the Daniel De Leon and Morris Hillquit factions. This division had its repercussions among the *tabaqueros*. The end result was that De Leon remained at the head of the Socialist Labor Party and

Hillquit and his followers founded the American Socialist Party. The Socialist Labor Party began to take on more and more narrowly doctrinaire positions, whereas Hillquit's group steered in the direction of mass politics, and quickly swelled its ranks.

Toward the end of 1899 Santiago Iglesias and Eduardo Conde came to New York as delegates from Puerto Rico to the American Socialist Party Convention, to be held in January 1900 in Rochester. For the first time in history, representatives chosen by Puerto Rican workers took part in a convention outside of the country. At that convention in Rochester Puerto Rico's cry for justice fell on sympathetic ears, and a resolution of solidarity won easy approval.

On their return from the convention, the delegates from Puerto Rico were royally welcomed by the workers' unions, which held a series of events that received a great deal of publicity. At one of those activities, organized by La Resistencia in Brooklyn, a lengthy manifesto was approved that was then widely circulated, both in New York and Puerto Rico. It proclaimed:

> The Spanish-language organizations of this city, at a meeting held on February 20, 1900, on the occasion of the presence among us of the Puerto Rican delegation, agree unanimously and enthusiastically to give to the work of that delegation all possible support within the limits of our power and intelligence . . .
>
> In the face of the close collaboration between the governments and bourgeoisies of all nations in order to oppress and exploit the workers, the working class cannot remain disunited . . . Seeing the capitalists join hands in stealing from and tyrannizing the working masses, let us unite in the common task of attaining a better lot in the present and our total emancipation in the future.
>
> Working and living under the conditions that you do, it is of little importance to Puerto Ricans whether they are governed by Muñoz or Muñiz, the Republicanos or the Federales . . .* What is urgent is that you join the Federación Regional de Trabajadores, that you struggle unceasingly and indefatigably to improve your moral, material, and intellectual conditions, and that you strive to secure higher wages, adequate food, and decent clothing . . .

---

*The reference is to the new names for the Island's political parties after the U.S. occupation in 1898. Thus on July 1, 1899, the Partido Autonomista Ortodoxo became the Partido Republicano Puertorriqueño; on October 1, the Partido Liberal Puertorriqueño was renamed the Partido Federal Americano. The Partido Republicano was led by Dr. José Celso Barbosa, while Luis Muñoz Rivera headed the Partido Liberal. Both parties advocated statehood for Puerto Rico.

The manifesto was signed by S. Monagas and Miguel Rivera for the Cigarmakers' Union, Cándido Ladrero and José López for the Escogedores, Benjamín Miranda and José R. Fernández for the Rezagadores, and Juan García and G. Quintana for the Círculo de Trabajadores of Brooklyn.*

In March 1900 Uncle Antonio and his family moved to a spacious apartment in a new building on 88th Street off Lexington Avenue. Their new home had seven rooms and cost $25.00 a month. It had steam heat and a tile bathroom. The family was in heaven, except that . . . when they were living down on 13th Street they used to buy their food in the Spanish shops along 14th Street. But their new neighborhood was mostly German and Irish, and in the Jewish stores on Second and Third avenues everything was more expensive.

One Sunday afternoon they heard a knock on the door. One of Uncle Antonio's daughters went to answer it and invited the visitors in. To their surprise, not one or two but nine people stepped into the living room, all of them looking serious. They refused to sit down and didn't even bother taking off their hats. Uncle Antonio broke the ice: "To what, might I ask, do we owe the honor of this friendly visit?"

"We come on behalf of the tenants of this building," one of them finally volunteered. "We bear no ill feeling toward anybody, but this is a white neighborhood. We have noticed that you frequently have Negroes coming to your house. People around here don't like that. We do hope that in the future you will be more careful about who you invite to your house."

The members of Uncle Antonio's family were aghast; their jaws literally dropped. "Are you saying that these people, because of the color of their skin . . ." began my uncle . . .

"See here," broke in the same spokesman, "we have not come to discuss the matter. If you wish to keep up such friendships, then you should just move out!" Uncle Antonio tried to get another word in, but the visitors promptly turned on their heels and were gone. And from that day on, not a word was exchanged with the neighbors.

Then came the first incident. Someone picked up a baby carriage that Antonio's wife had left in the hall and threw it into the street.

*In a cigar factory, the *escogedores* were those who selected and classified the cigars according to their color and quality; the *rezagadores* classified the tobacco leaves in terms of color, elasticity, and size. *Escogedores* and *rezagadores* belonged to separate units within the union.

Next a bunch of kids broke it in pieces, with all the neighbors watching. And the next day the wheels of the broken carriage were at the front door of the apartment. The day after that someone threw a rock through their front window, and a few days later they found the hallway in front of their door covered with feces. As if that was not enough, the family's mail was stolen and their gas was shut off.

Life in that house began to be unbearable. At first nobody paid any attention, but as the incidents became more and more perverse, the family, especially the women, began to get nervous.

Calling the police was useless. When they lodged a formal complaint about the disappearance of their mail, the authorities promised to investigate but never even took the trouble to visit the building. The superintendent was part of the scheme, as was the agent who managed the building. Pressure built up all around them to move out!

But Vasylisa, one of Antonio's daughters, insisted that they not submit to discrimination. One night she hid, waiting to catch by surprise whoever it was that was throwing filth on their doorstep. It was a woman; she jumped up, grabbed her by the hair, and smeared the feces in her face. The scuffle woke up all the tenants, who were outraged.

The superintendent called the police and the entire family was arrested. Morris Hillquit, the socialist leader, bailed them out of jail and went on to serve as the attorney for their defense. The trial was an uphill battle: the prosecution called no fewer than fifty witnesses, neighbors, of course. Some members of the family were exonerated, but Vasylisa was sentenced. Not only that—she was also forced to give up her job with the Board of Education because of "improper conduct." The family had no choice but to move, a few months later, over to 72nd Street and First Avenue.

At around that time Puerto Rico was passing through a very turbulent period in its history. Two political parties vied for control—the Partido Republicano, led by José Celso Barbosa, and the Partido Federal, under Luis Muñoz Rivera. With the backing of the first United States–appointed governors, Barbosa won the upper hand and Muñoz Rivera's party went into opposition. Irreconcilable enemies since the days of Spanish rule, the followers of both leaders were at each other's throats. Where the Barbosa wing held sway, supporters of Muñoz Rivera could hardly survive, and vice versa. San Juan was an example of the first case and Caguas of the second.

The so-called Republican mobs destroyed the offices of *La Democracia,* Muñoz Rivera's paper in San Juan. This attack, along with the pressing economic situation, forced the leader of the Federales—later to become the Unionistas—to flee to New York. There, on July 13, 1901, Luis Muñoz Rivera began publication of the *Puerto Rico Herald,* a weekly written in Spanish and English. Its offices were located at 156 Fifth Avenue.

Muñoz Rivera sent his paper to all the members of the U.S. Congress in Washington, to all the major press agencies, and to anyone with political influence in New York. The paper also circulated throughout the Puerto Rican community, which included at that time over two hundred noted Federals who had emigrated from Puerto Rico to escape the violence.

The manifesto of the Partido Federal appeared in the October 1901 issues of the *Puerto Rico Herald.* There the goal of the party was declared to be "that Puerto Rico become a state of the American Union, and that it be so without restrictions, just as the other states of the Federation."

It was in Muñoz Rivera's paper—in the November 2, 1901, edition—that Santiago Iglesias published an article that was to provoke serious criticism among the socialists and *tabaqueros.* Iglesias attempted to defend the A.F. of L. against the accusation that was being raised in New York and in Puerto Rico that its member unions discriminated against black workers. "The Federation," he said, "has declared openly that there can be no fraternity or solidarity among the working people if they fail to organize without regard to color or creed. . . . But, have workers of color responded, as is their duty, to this call pronounced by their fellow workers?"

"We must not confuse," he went on, "colored workers in Cuba and Puerto Rico with those in the United States. In Puerto Rico the majority are responding to the call to organize. But such is not the case in the United States, where most colored workers are the unwitting enemies of their unionized American coworkers . . ."

In the view of his critics, this position smacked of racism. Why, they asked, didn't Iglesias make the same accusation against the millions of German, Irish, and Italian workers with blond hair and fair skin who also didn't belong to the A.F. of L.? And why didn't he have anything to say about the thousands of whites of all nationalities who had served as strikebreakers on so many occasions? Is it true, they said, that the A.F. of L. declares itself, in theory, for fraternity among all workers, but no one can deny that there are unions that do not admit black workers.

A statement to that effect, signed by Schomburg, Rosseau, Apodaca, and Baerga, was soon made public.

Meanwhile, the economic situation in Puerto Rico worsened every day. The Island was still suffering from the effects of the San Ciriaco hurricane. Coffee production was reduced to a minimum. Tobacco could not even break into the United States market, and the sugar industry was only beginning.

Although the population had yet to reach 1 million, there were those who argued that "overpopulation" was the cause of all the misery. On these grounds they began to promote emigration and organize the transport of workers overseas. Uncle Antonio had among his papers a letter received by a friend of his in New York. It was signed by a Puerto Rican worker, Juanito Rivera Santiago, and dated Nipe, Cuba, August 2, 1901. It read:

> . . . there were over a thousand of us. We left Ponce at the end of July on the American steamship the *California*. We were contracted to work for the Cuba Company. Each of us carried what few clothes he had in a small bundle. More than half of us were barefoot. On board they gave us some kind of canned slop that the devil wouldn't go near. The coffee was like dirty water. . . . By the second day out nearly all of us were sick.
>
> Finally, on the brink of death, we arrived at a town called Daiquirí. . . . Little by little, some tall, fat Americans started picking and choosing among us and took on about 250 men. . . . At the next port, which I no longer recall, another 250 were picked to stay on. The rest of us continued on until we came to a city called Nipe. There were still about 500 of us. I do not know how we managed to stay alive—we hardly ate, and spent the whole time vomiting and sleeping on the floor.
>
> In Nipe, after a lot of talking and running around, a group of Americans came aboard and began to ask us all kinds of questions. They picked about 60 of us; I was one of them. We disembarked and were taken to work at a sugarmill called the Cuban Sugar Company.
>
> As for the remaining 400, almost all blacks, they weren't permitted to disembark. They said that in this country it is illegal to bring in workers on contract. I do not know what became of those poor fellows . . .
>
> I am so skinny I feel like I'm dying. I'm lucky I didn't meet the same fate as Juancho, Doña Simplicia's brother, and all the others who died and were thrown overboard in sacks . . .

Another transport of Puerto Rican workers organized at about that time was bound for Hawaii. In a dispatch from Honolulu, the *New York World* of September 7, 1901, told of the calamities endured on that expedition:

> A story of suffering and misery is told by the laborer Juan Avilés, who was brought to these isles to work in the canefields. Avilés is a boy of 18, one of the first Puerto Ricans to emigrate to this country. The agents who contracted him had promised him earnings of $18.00 a month, but once he got here they only gave him $15.00. When he became so ill that he was no longer useful on the job, they let him go . . . He spent days wandering through the city picking in trash cans for something to eat. One day he dropped dead of hunger in a doorway. They say his condition was no worse than that of others who are still working. They, also, cannot survive on what they are earning.

By that time there were already more than eight thousand Puerto Rican workers in Hawaii, and their numbers were to increase until about 1905. The man responsible for contracting those "slaves" was a certain Mr. Mature, who had his office in New Orleans. His agents in Puerto Rico were given a salary and a commission for every emigrant they got on board. The operation had the support of the governor and was encouraged by the leadership of the Partido Republicano, which considered it the best solution to the problem of unemployment and so-called overpopulation.

Some of the most unbelievable projects were conceived to "resolve" Puerto Rico's problems. One such scheme was carried out in New York in December 1901. A leaflet was circulated calling all Puerto Ricans to a meeting in Chickering Hall. No reason was given. It so happened that Gonzalo O'Neill and the *tabaquero* Julio Romero were among those in attendance. The chairman was a very well-dressed man who no one seemed to know. He talked of the misery and suffering in Puerto Rico, and of how impossible it was to remedy it. He ended by proposing that a committee be formed to petition the government in Washington to purchase land in South America or Asia in order to establish "another Puerto Rico."

No sooner had this unknown character finished speaking than Romero began a barrage of insults. O'Neill said more in the same vein . . . The man with the plan slipped out and vanished from sight.

At the end of 1901 a Latin American boarding house, Puerto Rico in New York, was established under the supervision of José D. Sulsona. Young people from various countries, including Puerto Rico, came there to live while they studied in New York. Most of them were attending St. Joseph's, a Catholic academy in Brooklyn. Among the many young Puerto Ricans, Agustín Fernández, Miguel Angel Muñoz, José Juan Monge, and Gustavo Amil studied at that school.

Around that same time Rafael Janer founded a college in Baltimore for young Latin Americans, modeled after the one run by Tomás Estrada Palma in Central Valley. The efforts of that famous Puerto Rican educator gained recognition in the Baltimore newspapers. The Puerto Rican community had a great need for that kind of acknowledgment.

More such recognition came when the Puerto Rican tenor Antonio Paoli, already acclaimed in Europe, held a recital in New York. Opening night was on April 22, 1902, in Mendelssohn Hall. He sang arias from *Tosca, Lohengrin, Othello,* and *William Tell.* There were many Puerto Ricans there, including quite a few *tabaqueros.* No one in the entire community appreciated Paoli—already known as the "tenor of kings and the king of tenors"—more than the *tabaqueros,* who had known of him from articles by Luis Bonafoux, Anatole France, and Guido de Varona, which were read in the cigar factories.

The *tabaqueros* were the boisterous claque in the uppermost tier of the Metropolitan Opera House. Everyone knows that wealthy audiences who go to the opera usually do so just to show off their fancy clothes and jewelry. It was a different story with the artisans who so admired Caruso, Tita Ruffo, Chaliapin, Frances Alda, and Mardones. The "claque," which was admitted to performances free of charge, was made up of Alfonso di Salvo, Leon Kortisky, Luigi Sabella, Tony Gualtieri, Alfonso Dieppa, and others with a whole range of national origins. Many of them knew the most outstanding opera scores by heart and had a sharp eye for the major artists. The bleachers at the Met were filled with impeccable judges. So it was not surprising that the members of the claque went to the cigar factories and to the cafés and restaurants at which the Bohemians of the time congregated.

Around the same time, too, a well-known Puerto Rican painter, Adolfo María Molina, had an exhibition on 12th Street and Second

Avenue. But unlike Paoli's recitals, this event did not attract the slightest attention in artistic circles in the city.

The year 1902 also saw the establishment of Nuestra Señora de la Guadalupe, the first Catholic church in New York City to hold services in Spanish. It was located in what was at that time the heart of the Latin community, at 229 West 14th Street.

But neither this gesture by the traditional church of the Puerto Rican people, nor the sporadic visits by a few famous artists, nor the efforts of Muñoz Rivera with his newspaper, could alter the lowly opinion in which the sons of Puerto Rico were held by the Anglo-Saxon population of New York. For the majority of Yankees, Puerto Ricans were an expendable species—an ignorant, juvenile, and uncultured people . . . Many of them think no more of us today!

12. On diatribes and insults against Puerto Ricans

William H. Hunt, the second governor of Puerto Rico—after the military government—to be named by the president of the United States, declared in August 1902: "The Puerto Ricans lack any and all capacity to govern their own destiny. The Island is nothing but corruption. The courts of law and the judges are all bribed. An honest functionary is nowhere to be found . . ."

All of this poison was printed in the New York papers. Coming as they did from such a "responsible source," such statements did serious damage to the Puerto Rican community. Some felt a need to protest, but the time was not right. And the animosities caused by the political infighting on the Island had repercussions in New York as well. Here too the Federales and the Republicanos were at each other's throats like so many dogs and cats. Partisan political loyalties were devouring the Puerto Ricans.

There were those who thought that by granting that one sole concession—American citizenship—all problems would be solved. That was the belief of Dr. Julio J. Henna, who even used his influence to get a congressman to introduce a bill to that effect. The mere introduction of the bill alarmed many sectors of opinion in the United States. The net result was that a barrage of insults came pouring down on Puerto Rico and everything Puerto Rican. The press, of course, chimed in with the implicit question as to whether it was really possible to make good Americans out of savage tribes. The bill, needless to say, never even came up for debate.

This situation gave rise to a test case which resulted in an important decision by the New York State Supreme Court that native-born Puerto Ricans arriving at United States ports were to be considered "foreigners." It was the appeal of this and similar cases to the

Supreme Court that was the origin of the famous "Insular cases."* Meanwhile, a sense of insecurity and uncertainty tightened its grip on the Puerto Rican community.

In November 1902 one of the widest circulation New York dailies, the *Morning-Sun,* published a series of articles on Puerto Rico. It had some fine things to say about Puerto Ricans, like "these people are no more than savages who have replaced their bows and arrows with guns and knives."

But racism was rampant not only in the newspapers; it permeated the workers' movement as well. The International Carpenters' Union turned down a request for affiliation sent them by the Carpenters' Union of Puerto Rico. The reason: they did not consider the Puerto Ricans to have the "qualifications to merit their becoming part of the American trade-union movement . . ." It took Samuel Gompers, the president of the A.F. of L., a lot of time and effort to get that decision overturned.

The labor movement in Puerto Rico gained added strength under the new regime. The upper classes, especially the leading figures in industry and agriculture, felt their interests seriously threatened. There followed the famous trial of Santiago Iglesias and other labor leaders, who were charged with "conspiring to raise wages." Iglesias was sentenced to three years in prison, and his comrades got a variety of other sentences. News of this outrage infuriated the workers in New York.

There began a campaign on behalf of the labor leaders and in defense of the Federación Libre de Trabajadores, which had been declared illegal by the courts.† That campaign received the enthusiastic support of Samuel Gompers, who called for the intervention of the federal authorities. Finally the Court of Appeals lifted the sentence and established clearly the right of workers to organize, demand higher wages, and call strikes.

That decision by a United States court, which overturned the

---

*The "Insular cases" were presented to the U.S. Supreme Court during the first decades of the twentieth century. Taken together, they established the political basis for Puerto Rico's status vis-à-vis the United States.

†In 1899 the Federación Libre de Trabajadores broke away from the Federación Regional de Trabajadores de Puerto Rico, which had been founded in October of the preceding year and favored reaching an accord with the Partido Republicano. The Federación Libre became the main organization of the Puerto Rican workers' movement during the next three decades.

ruling of a Puerto Rican judge and upheld the rights of workers, inspired a pro-American movement within labor's ranks. The semi-slave conditions they had suffered under Spain remained fresh in every mind. But not only that: the persecution of the first labor leaders—headed by Santiago Iglesias—at the hands of the autonomist regime of Luis Muñoz Rivera, was also too recent to forget. All of this helps to explain why the workers at that time, feeling and knowing how powerless they were before the bosses, came to seek protection and shelter within the judicial structure that the United States had recently extended to the Island. And it was this very persecution of the labor movement, in which the Republicano Barbosa and the Federal Muñoz Rivera both took an active part, that led to doubt, even in the liberal American papers, as to the ability of Puerto Rican leaders to set up a democratic government in Puerto Rico.

From time to time one of the dailies would cast us in a somewhat more favorable light. In the beginning of April 1903 the *Brooklyn Eagle* stated in one column: "The situation of the Puerto Rican workers is one of hunger, misery, and political enslavement . . . Before the Americans got to the island the averge wage was 62 cents in local currency, which is about 37 cents in gold. Today the average is between 35 and 50 cents . . . Being gold, it may seem to be worth more but it is not, since according to a study carried out by our correspondents the cost of living has risen a full 100 percent."

That year the *Brooklyn Eagle* ran more articles along the same lines. On November 7 an editorial stated: "It should surprise no one that streams of Puerto Ricans are migrating from the island and that everyone who has the chance is leaving. Cables reach us every day announcing a hundred leaving San Juan, five hundred or a thousand setting off for Yucatán, Hawaii, or some other destination. This means that they are unable to earn their daily bread in their own country. And it also means that the United States, in spite of its pledge to develop the economic life of that impoverished population, has not fulfilled its promise, nor does it see any need to do so."

This situation in the distant homeland was always present in the minds of Puerto Ricans living in New York. They would listen anxiously to everything the new arrivals had to tell them . . .

In November 1903 Uncle Antonio found out that Lola Rodríguez de Tió happened to be in New York. The renowned Puerto Rican poet was living in Cuba and had come to the city for a delicate eye operation. Uncle Antonio and his daughters Vasylisa and María Teresa went to visit her in the Hotel Audubon, where she was staying. This gracious lady was visibly moved as she received them. They were the first compatriots she had set eyes on.

Lola spoke bitterly of Puerto Rico. She had lost all hope that it would achieve its independence. The North Americans, in her opinion, were on the Island "to stay." Conditions in Cuba were hardly more encouraging. Her pessimism ran deep, and was no doubt aggravated by the eye ailment she was suffering. But then Uncle Antonio began to recall the days of José Martí and the glorious years of struggle she had lived through, and little by little her face began to light up. It wasn't long before she was reciting one of her recent poems, and with little or no urging she was at the piano playing the popular "Margarita" by Tavárez. She followed it with a medley of Morel Campos' *danzas* . . . It was well into the early morning hours before her visitors took their leave.

The surgery was a success. Days later Lola returned to Havana, hopefully spurred by a fresh burst of optimism.

And all the while Puerto Ricans continued to suffer new waves of abuse and slander. Early in March 1904 another New York daily, *The Globe,* claimed that "natives of Puerto Rico are not capable of governing themselves because they are a country that has not yet reached its maturity . . ."

Arturo Alfonso Schomburg responded. In a statement that *The Globe* had no choice but to publish, he wrote: "The Puerto Rican people have never even been consulted as to whether we wish to become part of the United States, nor on any matter bearing on our national sovereignty . . . As an independent country, we would be no worse off than the Cubans. If you wish to leave things to our free will, there will be no lack of men in Puerto Rico fully capable of leading our people in the face of whatever emergencies and dangers may confront them. Why not try it?"

Toward the end of March 1904 Samuel Gompers returned from Puerto Rico. He had made the trip at the insistence of the leadership of the Federación Libre de Trabajadores. He visited many towns, accompanied by Santiago Iglesias. On his arrival in New York he called a press conference and made such statements as: "In all my life I have never witnessed such misery, sickness, and suffering . . . The Puerto Ricans are being paid the lowest wages in the whole world . . . They are forced to work ten or twelve hours a day. Their diet is inadequate. Life is more expensive than here. The impressions I bring back from my trip are dreadful."

Gompers spoke several times about the conditions of the Puerto Rican worker at activities organized by the Cigarmakers' Union at the Masonic Hall on 23rd Street. As a result of his trip, ties between the Federación Libre and the A.F. of L. became even stronger.

In the course of these years new attempts were made to form an organization to represent the Puerto Rican, or Spanish-speaking, community in New York. The Asociación Latinoamericana, for instance, had a governing board that included Drs. Antonio González, Manuel Castillo Vilar, and Arturo Font, along with Alberto León, Francisco L. Pla, and Ricardo E. Manrique. That group sponsored several affairs to raise funds to help out needy families . . . But within a few months it lost whatever influence it had.

More promising results came out of a meeting called on May 22, 1904, by Martín Travieso, the noted adherent of Luis Muñoz Rivera. The thirty-eight people in attendance, all Puerto Rican, included Muñoz Rivera himself, as well as renowned personalities like Arteaga, Acuña, Bravo, Balzac, Blanco, Cabassa, Mario Brau, Gonzalo O'Neill, Montalvo Guenard, and Ulises del Valle . . . The purpose of the gathering was to found a nonpartisan society that would work closely with the press and the government to find a solution to Puerto Rico's economic problems.

This society never saw the light of day either.

In the hope of getting away from the harsh living conditions in the city, Uncle Antonio's family bought a small plot of land along the road that passed through Flushing. Back then the area was mostly farms. Flushing itself was little more than a group of houses along the main road. Property was cheap, so that the family was able to get two acres for $85.00.

Glowing with enthusiasm, they gradually started to build a summer house. But no sooner were they ready to put on the roof than, one Sunday, Uncle Antonio arrived with his family to find that a pile of debris was all that was left of the house. Nailed to a stake was the following sign: "Do not try to build here anymore. No niggers wanted in this town. Go back where you came from."

That was in 1905, and it was no isolated incident. Puerto Ricans were facing similar affronts in all the towns around New York City. A more recent incident took place in Elmont, on Long Island, in the summer of 1938. One of our countrymen began construction of a house on Belmont Avenue. The frame was already standing when, one night, they tore it to the ground and posted a sign with the same warning message. I witnessed that one with my own eyes, since I was living in that very town.

The size of the Puerto Rican community in New York grew considerably in the first decade of this century. Some of the emigrants moved on to Chicago and other industrial areas. There was a sizable group of Puerto Ricans in Tampa, Florida, including Manuel de Jesús Parrilla, a journalist and editor of the weekly paper *El Internacional,* as well as the working-class writer Manuel Román and the adviser to the city council Carlos del Toro.

In New York, the Puerto Ricans settled in once and for all. In the Yorkville section there was no more of the racial antagonism that had forced Uncle Antonio and his family to move from 88th Street. The atmosphere was more civil by then, especially around 103rd Street and Third Avenue.

The Socialist Party had gained wide influence in New York. Their paper, *The Socialist Call,* which was distributed everywhere, carried out campaigns on behalf of national minorities. But it was the only one that did. The other papers continued to stir up ill-feelings toward everything foreign, and were especially virulent in their treatment of Puerto Ricans. Which is why some Puerto Ricans, the better-off ones in particular, would try to pass for "Spaniards" so as to minimize the prejudice against them. There were even those who went so far as to remain silent in public. They made sure never to read Spanish newspapers in the subway or to teach Spanish to their children . . . That's right, that's what they did, I know it for a fact.

Things were different, though, in the working-class neighborhoods. There Spanish was always spoken, and on the train we read our papers for all to see. The workers were not afraid of being called "spiks." They did not deny their origin. Quite the contrary: they struggled because they knew that they were Puerto Ricans and, in a broader sense, Hispanic. That's how it was with the *tabaqueros.*

In 1912 the International Cigarmakers' Union began a movement to seek recognition of a union local made up of Spanish-speaking members. The cause was promoted by Emiliano Ramos, who held a meeting with that end in view at the Socialist section in Yorkville, located on 84th Street between Second and Third avenues. More than a hundred *tabaqueros* attended. They met several more times, but it wasn't until many years later that they achieved their aim.

In those prewar years the cigar industry was growing and prospering. There was plenty of work. The finest quality cigars were produced by Spanish-speaking artisans and by some Italians who had learned Spanish. There were many Puerto Ricans among the *tabaqueros,* and they made up the majority of the Puerto Rican community in New York.

This situation began to change as the war raging in Europe began to have an effect on the United States. In May 1914 a German submarine sank the *Lusitania;* over one thousand people died, 124 North American citizens among them. After letting up for a short period, the submarine war went on to wreak further havoc. June 2, 1918, saw the sinking of the *S.S. Carolina,* which made regular trips from San Juan to New York. Several Puerto Ricans died.

But war or no war, the emigration continued unabated. It was in those years that the Puerto Rican community in Harlem began to swell. The Chelsea area, from 26th Street down to 15th Street, was also inhabited by large numbers of Puerto Rican families, as was the Boro Hall area in Brooklyn. But the largest concentration was situated around 116th Street, which came to be known as the Barrio Latino.

In the same period business began to flourish among Puerto Ricans. This commercial development was preceded, of course, by boarding houses, the earliest type of business in the emigrant community. Next came barber shops. There were no fewer than ten by 1917—Náter's, Lasalle's, and El Chino's uptown, Lolo Torres's, Martínez's, and Rodríguez Colón's in Chelsea, and Juan Ortiz's, Rafael Lebrón's, and Peláez's in Brooklyn.

For the most part these barbers were intelligent and good people. Erasmo Lasalle was particularly memorable, a first-rate singer who was the first man to make a recording of Puerto Rican music. His shop was frequented by another great Puerto Rican guitarist, Salvador Maldonado, who performed successfully in variety shows at the time. And there was Juancito Ortiz, another barber, fine musician, and poet, who hosted many festive occasions in the Boro Hall neighborhood.

The growth of the Puerto Rican community put even greater pressure on its already strained relationships with other nationalities. The housing situation in Chelsea and over in Brooklyn was especially difficult. The condition of the residences was miserable. The best area in this respect was in the heart of El Barrio in Harlem. At that time the Jews who had concentrated there began to move out to better neighborhoods. The apartments they left behind were in good condition, and growing numbers of Puerto Ricans moved into them.

Here I must insert a very personal note: I married a Puerto Rican girl. This, of course, has nothing to do with anything, but shortly thereafter the news hit New York about the earthquakes that ravaged parts of Puerto Rico in October 1918. Puerto Ricans poured into the telegraph offices, hoping for information about their families. Then we rushed off to the post office to send whatever help we could by postal money order. All of us followed the turmoil in our country in the pages of *La Prensa*.

That paper, which came to be the longest lasting Hispanic paper in New York, began publication on June 4, 1918, although it had been coming out as a weekly since October 12, 1913. Its founder, Rafael Viera, set up his editorial offices on 87 Broad Street. For some time the editor-in-chief was the celebrated Colombian writer José María Vargas Vila. Later the job fell to V. H. Collao, under whose direction the paper became a daily. Not long thereafter it was bought by the Spaniard José Camprubí.

Thanks to the careful supervision of Camprubí and assistance from the Unión Benéfica Española, *La Prensa* established itself as a daily. Its readership expanded in the growing Puerto Rican community, and it was assured of steady revenues from advertisements. Despite opinions to the contrary, the paper made a valuable contribution to the development of the Hispanic community in New York.

In October 1918 Santiago Iglesias was back in New York, this time to begin the job of organizing the Pan American Federation of Labor. To that end he held a meeting on the seventeenth of that month at the Harlem Terrace, 210 East 104th Street. On the Thirtieth there was a larger meeting, which included representatives from Argentina, Chile, Costa Rica, Colombia, Spain, Mexico, Nicaragua, Peru, Venezuela, and Puerto Rico. Though they were all born in those countries, they were living in the United States, mostly in New York.

The meeting agreed to support the A.F. of L.'s plan to organize the Pan American Federation of Labor. It was resolved to convene a congress of union delegates from the different countries in Laredo, Texas. The idea stirred up lively debate in workers' circles in New York. The radical elements came out against it, arguing that the aim was only to use the union movements in the Latin American countries to win approval for the expansionist policies of the United States. Nevertheless, the vast majority of the *tabaqueros* sided with Santiago Iglesias.

Soon thereafter my personal life became a bit more complicated. My wife presented me with a son, and since I wasn't earning enough rolling cigars I set out to find other sources of income. With the war, the cost of living rose sharply, while cigarworkers' wages remained what they had been in 1916. Necessity forced me to move in other directions. Which is why I took up selling life insurance.

I had no fixed salary but worked on a commission. The agent received credit for the payment of premiums and new policies, and was always given a weekly allowance in proportion to his total number of commissions. Whatever balance was left was held in reserve to compensate for a decline in clientele . . . For me that line of business turned out to be pretty uncertain.

Colonial, Inc., as the insurance company was called, specialized in life insurance for workers. They assigned me to a district of the city inhabited by Hungarians, Czechs, Poles, Italians, and Puerto Ricans. I had to do my round on foot, and I can remember having to climb six flights of stairs to collect 10 cents. The two other Puerto Rican agents, José García Seda and José Martínez, were *tabaqueros* like myself. We got together and agreed to visit only Puerto Rican families.

After a few months of work a serious problem arose: the company would not give credit to the agents for policies sold to blacks. They accepted the policies, of course, but they did not grant any benefits or credits in return. As we Puerto Rican agents had been taking applications from both whites and blacks without distinction, the other agents had felt threatened and started to complain to the bosses about what they called "third-class insurance." An investigation was ordered, we, for our part, threatened to charge the company with discrimination. Finally the company decided that the risk factor was the same for black and white clients.

I did not stay at this work for long, in spite of my family's difficulties. Around that time Uncle Antonio's health began to fail. I still remember one of the last conversations I had with him. He was already bedridden when he said to me: "I have always fought for a better life for all. My beliefs brought me into continual conflict with the powers-that-be. My principles have still not won out . . ."

Soon thereafter he passed away.

13. Day-to-day life in New York and other details

In about 1918 entertainment for Puerto Ricans in New York was confined to the apartments they lived in. They celebrated birthdays and weddings and, of course, Christmas Eve, New Year's Day, and the Feast of the Epiphany. But always at home, with friends and neighbors.

There would be dancing, and between numbers somebody would recite poetry or hold forth about our distant homeland. At some of the parties there were *charangas,* lively groups of Puerto Rican musicians. But most of the time we played records. By that time Columbia Records was recording *danzas, aguinaldos,* and other kinds of music from back home.

Almost every family owned a victrola, and many even had a pianola. The fact is that once this music gained in popularity, Puerto Ricans were exploited mercilessly. Pianolas cost about $500.00, on credit. Many was the worker who wound up losing what little he earned by falling behind on his payments. Not to mention the times a family would move and have to leave their pianola behind . . . Just getting it from one place to another cost more than moving the rest of their belongings!

Those boisterous Puerto Rican parties would often disturb neighbors of other nationalities, which led to some serious conflicts and unpleasant quarrels.

And there were some less innocent events as well. In the more spacious apartments in Harlem some people threw parties on Saturdays and Sundays that weren't just family parties, but full-scale dances with a cover charge and all. And once you were in they'd take you for whatever else you had, for drinks and tidbits. Which is not the least of the shameful things that went on.

There was none of that in the homes of the *tabaqueros.*

By then there were over ten thousand Puerto Ricans living in El Barrio. The first stores and restaurants that were like those back home were opening up. Every week a new shipload of emigrants would arrive in the city. The landlords up in Harlem were making good money by charging the Puerto Ricans high rents—relative, that is, to what they were getting for their money. I remember a building on 113th Street off Fifth Avenue where, back when the Jews were still living there, apartments were renting for only $17.00 . . . When the Puerto Ricans moved in, the rents went up to $35.00.

In the winter of 1918, Manuel Noriega's theater company made its debut at the Amsterdam Opera House. Thanks to Noriega the Puerto Rican community in New York was able to see Spanish theater for the first time. One night more than two hundred Puerto Ricans attended, many of them theater-loving *tabaqueros*.

Another happy memory is of a reading by Mexican poet Amado Nervo, held in Havermeyer Hall over at Columbia University.

All this time the Brooklyn Círculo de Trabajadores, which I mentioned earlier, remained active. To give you an idea of how the Círculo got started; it was founded in the previous century and was largely made up of *tabaqueros*. They were all progressive in their thinking—anarchists, socialists, or at the very least left-wing republicans. Back then most of them were getting on in years, but their minds were young and alert, their hearts filled with optimism.

I went to the Círculo often. On any given night, in wintertime, they would get together at tables to play dominoes, checkers, or chess, or just to talk. I went from one group to another. The venerable old man Castañeda would be sitting in a corner. I can still hear him saying, "It was a shame that Martí took that rumor-mongering by Trujillo and Collazo so much to heart, and that his own pride brought him to his end in Dos Ríos. If he had only stayed on to direct and guide the revolution, Cuba today would be the freest and most democratic republic in the world . . ."

I then went to another group, where Miguel Rivera, a native of Cayey, was enthusiastically reporting the resolutions submitted by the Mexican delegation to the Congress of Laredo. "Even though the A.F. of L. accepted them," he commented, "the Yankees are sure to go on holding the Mexicans down, the same as before . . ."*

*The Congress of Laredo was held on November 13, 1918, to set conditions for the founding of the Federación Pan-Americana de Trabajo (Pan-American Federation of Labor), later referred to as the Confederación Pan-Americana (COPA). The meet-

From another group I heard cheerful laughter. I went over and found them enjoying the latest story by "El Malojero"—the "Corn Seller," as he was called—an anecdote passed on to him by Luis Bonafoux.

Making the rounds, I met up with Pepín and Anastasio Fueyo over by the Círculo's little office. They were discussing the events scheduled for that winter. I found out about a production of Guimera's *Tierra Baja* and Gorky's *The Vagabonds.* They were also thinking of staging Chekhov's *Uncle Vanya,* the Spanish version by the Puerto Rican worker Alfonso Dieppa.

Going over to the canteen for a cup of coffee, I overheard a discussion between the Spaniard José López, an *escogedor,* and the anarchist Rojas. "The Bolsheviks," Rojas was saying, "have betrayed the Russian workers. They should have set up free communities and not those iron-clad Soviets." To which López responded: "All of you anarchists have a screw loose. Only yesterday man left his wild, untamed state and already you're talking about showing them a new world, free of all restraint, and all in one fell swoop? If we are ever to arrive at a just society, you have to force men to be good and not animals."

That's what it was like in those days.

Years later I got to know a Puerto Rican cigarworker named Pedro Juan Bonit, who had been living in New York since 1913. Here is a conversation I had with him, which fills out my picture of the emigrants' life in those times.

"When did you arrive here?"

"On December 22, 1913."

"What town do you come from?"

"I was born and raised in San Juan."

"Why did you leave Puerto Rico?"

"To get to know the world. And, of course, because I thought I would be better off economically."

"Where did you live when you arrived here?"

"In a roominghouse run by Ramón Galíndez. The address was 2049 Second Avenue, between 105th and 106th."

"Was it easy to find work?"

"Immediately. There were a lot of jobs for cigarmakers back then.

---

ing, attended by representatives from the United States, Mexico, Guatemala, El Salvador, Costa Rica, and Colombia, was convened by the A.F. of L. for the purpose of stemming the revolutionary tide of the Latin American workers' movement and bringing it under the control of organized labor in the United States.

Besides, the cigar manufacturers had agents who would find them workers, and for every cigarworker they delivered they'd get $5.00. I still remember one of those agents; his name was Damián Ferrer, alias 'Batata,' or 'Sweet Potato'."

"Where was that first job?"

"In a little factory. Later I worked at Samuel I. Davis's factory on 81st Street and First Avenue. Over a hundred Puerto Rican *tabaqueros* were working there."

"Were there any other places that hired so many Puerto Ricans?"

"Many."

"And did those factories have readers like the ones in Puerto Rico?"

"Practically all of them did. In the Davis factory there were two—Fernando García, who would read us the newspapers in the morning, and Benito Ochart, who read novels in the afternoon."

"Was there any difference between the works they read here and the ones they read back in Puerto Rico?"

"Well, I think the quality of the readings here was somewhat higher. They would read books of greater educational value."

"Do you remember any of them?"

"There was *Le Feu* by Barbusse and *La Hyène enragée* by Pierre Loti . . ."

"Who paid the readers?"

"We did. Each of us donated 25 cents a week."

"Were any other collections taken?"

"Yes. Every week we also contributed to the working-class press. And then they were always raising money to support some strike movement or another."

"Were there already Puerto Rican businesses in El Barrio?"

"No. No *bodegas* or restaurants had been established yet. There were only boarding houses and a few barber shops."

"Then where did people buy plantains and other vegetables?"

"There was a Latin grocery on 136th Street near Lenox Avenue, in the middle of the black community. And as for Spanish products, you could get them at Victoria's down on the corner of Pearl and John."

"Did you know of any authentic Puerto Rican businesses?"

"None that I am aware of. But yes, come to think of it, there was a drugstore owned by a certain Loubriel on 22nd Street and Seventh Avenue."

"Do you remember any Puerto Ricans who lived near you?"

"Sure. There was Andrés Araujo, Juan Nieto, Antonio Díaz, Agustín García, Felipe Montalbán, and many more. I think that by then there were already a good hundred and fifty Puerto Rican families living on 105th and 106th off of Second Avenue."

"How about in what we now know as El Barrio?"

"No. For the most part that was where the Jewish people lived. There were only a handful of Hispanic families. In those times the Puerto Ricans were scattered in other areas—in Chelsea, and over in Brooklyn around the Armory and Boro Hall. There were also Puerto Rican neighborhoods on the East Side, in the 20's and along Second and Third avenues from 64th Street up to 85th. And the professionals and better-off families were over on the West Side, on the other side of Central Park. That's where people like Dr. Henna and Dr. Marxuach lived . . ."

"How did people get along in the community?"

"Well, each class had its own way of associating. The *tabaqueros* were the only ones who were organized collectively. There were no exclusively Puerto Rican organizations. But we *tabaqueros* did have mutual aid societies like La Aurora (Dawn), La Razón (Reason), and El Ejemplo (The Example) . . . The educational circles were almost all anarchist except for the Brooklyn Círculo de Trabajadores, which admitted workers of different ideological leanings. The trade unions were the International Cigarmakers' Union and La Resistencia . . . Where I lived there was a club called El Tropical, which had dances and where meetings were held from time to time. It was presided over by Gonzalo Torres. Over on the West Side I remember that Dr. Henna was president of the Ibero-American Club."

"What were the Spanish-language papers published here in those days?"

"*Las Novedades,* a Spanish publication put out by a man by the name of García, whom we nicknamed 'Little Priest.' And there was the anarchist weekly *Cultura Proletaria,* and *La Prensa,* which also came out weekly back then."

"Where did you buy clothes for the first time when you got to New York?"

"I got them from Markowsky, a Jew who had a store downstairs in the building where I lived. A lot of *tabaqueros* bought things there on credit."

"Were there any notable racial differences among the Puerto Ricans?"

"Not among the *tabaqueros;* for us there were no problems of race or religion. But when it came to the so-called better-off people, some of them were even more prejudiced than the Americans."

"How much were your earnings back then?"

"At Davis's I was averaging about $30.00 a week."

"And what were your expenses like?"

"For a room, food, and clean clothes I paid about $10.00 a week."

"Did anyone play *bolita,* or lottery?"

"Yes. I've been told that game started back in 1870."

"What about problems between Puerto Ricans?"

"There would be a fight now and then, but never anything serious."

"What kind of parties did you have?"

"We celebrated Christmas, New Year's, and the Feast of the Epiphany in people's homes."

"Was there much concern over the situation in Puerto Rico?"

"Of course."

"Would you like to go back?"

"Don't make me sad. I've been back twice and if I could I'd be off again tomorrow."

News from Puerto Rico at the end of 1918 and the beginning of 1919 told of widespread misery and of strikes that crippled the country. Thousands of agricultural workers went out on strike, and many were persecuted and beaten. The *tabaqueros* also had frequent work stoppages. And on top of that there were the victims of the earthquakes . . . *La Prensa* called for donations from the public to help those struck by the catastrophe. Angered at the lukewarm response of its readers, it published an editorial complaining of the lack of charity in the Hispanic community. A lively debate ensued, involving Luisa Capetillo, Gabriel Blanco, and other writers of note.

The most widely discussed position was the one Luisa held. She openly blamed the people in power for the miserable living conditions in Puerto Rico. She called for making progressive people in the United States aware of this situation, and ended by saying that "Tyranny, like freedom, has no country, any more than do exploiters or workers."

I should say something about that great Puerto Rican woman. At that time Luisa Capetillo was employed as a reader in a cigar factory. She belonged to the leadership of the Federación Libre de Trabajadores and took part in meetings and strikes all over Puerto Rico. She could rightly be called the first woman suffragist in the Antilles.

Aggressive and dynamic by temperament, she was devoted body and soul to defending the rights of workers and the cause of woman's liberation. She came to New York from Havana, where she had created a scandal by showing up in the streets dressed in culottes, which only the most advanced women at that time dared to wear.

The last time I spoke with Luisa was at a boarding house she ran on 22nd Street and Eighth Avenue. She worked interminable hours and always looked tired. But that didn't stop her from using every chance she had to propound her revolutionary and strongly anarchistic ideas to her boarders. Nor did that prevent anyone from eating very well at her place, because aside from her enthusiasm for the revolution, Luisa had a great love for cooking. And as that noble woman from Puerto Rico never cared very much about money, everyone who came there hungry got something to eat, whether he could pay for it or not. Needless to say, her "business" was in a constant crisis, and she was often hard put even to pay her rent.

Younger generations, especially women in our own day, should know of Luisa Capetillo and her exemplary life as a tireless militant. It is a story of great human interest. I do not know what became of her after that meeting.

Meanwhile, thousands of Puerto Rican workers continued to land in New York. The apartments of those already here filled up with family, friends, and just anyone who was down and out. The number of Puerto Ricans climbed to 35,000. According to statistics kept by the International Cigarmakers' Union, there were over 4,500 Puerto Ricans enrolled in its various locals around the city. But the majority of the workers lacked a skilled trade, and made a large labor supply willing to take on the lowest paying jobs in New York.

No serious effort was made to organize the community and fight for its civil rights. The groups that did exist, as I have pointed out, had no other purpose than to organize dances. The only exception was the Club La Luz, located on the corner of Lenox and 120th Street, which in addition to dances would hold occasional cultural evenings.

In early 1919 the first issue of *El Norteamericano* circulated among us. Published by the South American Publishing Co. at 310 Fifth Avenue, that weekly became very popular in Hispanic homes. But it did not last long.

Around the same time the great Spanish novelist Vicente Blasco Ibáñez visited New York. He gave three lectures at Columbia, the first and most controversial on the subject of "How Europeans View America."

But the only event really worth remembering, the one that had a lasting impact on the Puerto Rican community, was the Floral Games sponsored by *La Prensa.** This was, in fact, the most outstanding event in the Spanish-speaking community in New York since the turn of the century. The nominating judges were Federico de Onís, Orestes Ferrara, Pedro Henríquez Ureña, and the North American Hispanist Thomas Walsh.

Prizes were awarded on May 5 at an event held in Carnegie Hall. All of the Spanish-American peoples were represented. At no other event did I ever see so many beautiful women—Mexican, Spanish, Dominican, Cuban, and Puerto Rican. First prize went to José Méndez Rivera, a Colombian poet who received the Flor Natural prize. The Dominican writer M. F. Cesteros won another prize. And as for the Puerto Ricans in the audience, all of us left happy. A young Puerto Rican poet had been given Honorable Mention for his poem, "Yo soy tu flauta." His name: Luis Muñoz Marín.

---

*The Juegos Florales, or Floral Games, are a long-standing tradition in the Spanish-speaking world, going back to the late Middle Ages. The Juegos Florales generally included a beauty contest and a poetry contest; the prize flower often went to the best poem in praise of that year's beauty queen.

Part 4
THE 1920s

14. Political campaigns, the decline of tobacco, and the Great Depression

The first political campaign in New York in which Puerto Ricans participated was the Alfred Smith campaign of 1918. Around seven thousand Puerto Ricans registered to vote, the majority in the first and third electoral districts in Brooklyn. A major force behind the drive was the Club Democrático Puertorriqueño, the first organization of its kind inside the Democratic Party of the United States. It was founded and directed by two Puerto Ricans, J. V. Alonso and Joaquín Colón.

During that election campaign other Hispanic groups were established in Harlem. They were set up not as independent clubs, but in affiliation with the local Democratic Club. There the outstanding Puerto Rican leaders were J. C. Cebollero and Domingo Collazo— the latter was recognized by Tammany Hall as the representative of the Puerto Rican community.

But the vast majority of Puerto Ricans in New York did not exercise their right to vote. It was no easy matter to go down to the Board of Elections and register. The officials would question the applicant in order to intimidate him. That kept a lot of Puerto Ricans away from the ballot box. Besides, most Puerto Ricans felt they had "nothing to get out of American politics," that "it didn't concern them." And that was the general attitude for many years thereafter, until Fiorello La Guardia and Vito Marcantonio entered the city's political life.

Neither of the political parties, Republican or Democrat, showed any real interest in winning the support of the Puerto Rican people. While their campaigns were in high gear, of course, some of their propaganda reached the Puerto Rican neighborhoods, but they did nothing to register voters. To this very day, so many years later, those parties have nearly the same attitude.

The drive to unionize Puerto Rican workers was facing similar problems. For the most part Puerto Ricans worked in nonunion shops. Sewing shops and restaurants, in particular, were filled with Puerto Ricans. But the unions in those lines of work didn't do a thing to recruit them. Furthermore, carpenters, bricklayers, tailors, and barbers who came from Puerto Rico were not admitted as members of the A.F. of L. unions.

In fact, not until the cigarmakers began to wage their union battles did unions in other trades show any interest in Puerto Rican workers. And that didn't happen until into the 1920s. Shortly before that, the first union to break through that barrier within labor, after the International Cigarmakers' Union, was the Furriers' Union.

The first committee of the Socialist Party to be made up of Puerto Ricans—and it enjoyed a long and active life—was formed in 1918 by Lupercio Arroyo, Jesús Colón, Eduvigis Cabán, Valentín Flores, and myself. Further on there will be ample opportunity to say more about those comrades.

Around that time there were a few Puerto Ricans in New York with nationalist ideas, but they were not grouped together in any one organization. Only somewhat later, under the spiritual leadership of Vicente Balbás Capó, did they go on to found the Asociación Nacionalista.

The heated political campaign gave rise to rivalries among some of the Puerto Ricans who were leaders in the Democratic Party. A battle followed over "leadership of the colony," as it was called back then. While there can be no doubt that those people were struggling for the good of their fellow countrymen, envy and divisiveness doomed every collective effort to failure. As a result, pessimism and frustration were everywhere.

In 1919 a trying period for the Puerto Ricans began. When the Great War in Europe ended, the war industries in the United States were shut down. With the conversion back to a peacetime economy, Puerto Ricans were among the first to find themselves out of work. And while incomes fell, rents and the cost of living in general were on the rise.

That year also saw the political persecution of socialists and any one else suspected of sympathizing with the Russian Revolution. Anyone and everyone who voiced the slightest criticism of the system was labeled "Bolshevik." Many notable figures found themselves in prison for their pacifist and anti-imperialist ideas. Such was the case with Victor Berger, the U.S. Congressman elected on the Socialist Party ticket who was sentenced to ten years in prison. Eugene V. Debs, the party's outstanding leader, was also found guilty, and hundreds of other labor leaders from all over the country met the same fate.

The wave of repression was extended to Puerto Rico. Striking *tabaqueros* in San Juan sent two of their leaders, Ramón Barrios and Alfonso Negrín, to Cuba in search of assistance and support. Both were arrested upon landing and charged with being "anarchists." The International Cigarmakers' Union and the Socialist Party appealed to Washington, and through the intervention of the United States embassy in Havana they were set free.

On February 23 the New York dailies published a story that had an immediate effect on the Hispanic communities of the city. The headlines in one paper announced, "Uncover Plot to Assassinate President Wilson, 14 Hispanic Anarchists Held."

Among the various anarchist circles in New York there was one that went by the name of Los Corsarios (The Corsairs). Its membership included some *tabaqueros,* but the majority were dockworkers and sailors, some of them Puerto Rican. The group published a newspaper, *El Corsario;* contributors included Marcelo Salinas, Pedro Estuve, J. de Borrán, Maximiliano Olay, Ventura Mijón, and other Spanish, Cuban, and Puerto Rican writers. The paper circulated widely among Spanish-speaking sailors, dockworkers, and miners in several industrial centers across the United States.

The "muchachos" ("boys") of El Corsario, as their friends called them, would meet at 1722 Lexington Avenue near 107th Street. That was the newspaper's editorial office. One Sunday afternoon, when the group's entire membership came together to begin distributing the papers, they realized they were surrounded by about fifty policemen and federal agents. The paper was confiscated and they were all arrested on charges of conspiring to assassinate President Wilson, who was due to return from Europe at about that time. Only one Puerto Rican, Rafael Acosta, was among those detained.

There were vehement protests against the arrests, and a prisoners' defense committee was set up. But this time the struggle did not last long. After a few preliminary hearings, the defense lawyers succeeded in getting the charges dropped. Even that did not prevent the Spaniards involved—and they were the majority—from being deported back to Spain.

Puerto Rican political activity picked up in the course of that year. The *tabaqueros* initiated several demonstrations against the imprisonment of Eugene V. Debs, who started serving his ten-year sentence on May 13. In July a massive strike brought cigar production in New York to a standstill, and the strike soon spread across the United States.

That strike had a special meaning for Puerto Rican workers. An indirect result of that struggle was that many other unions came to recognize the important role that Puerto Ricans can play as workers. It was then that they began to organize Puerto Rican confectioners, bakers, hotel and restaurant employees, and workers in the needle trades. We finally began to enjoy wages and hours equal to those of workers of other nationalities.

Another significant outcome of the cigarmakers' strike was that for the first time Puerto Rican delegates to union meetings participated on an equal footing with representatives and leaders of other nationalities. Several of our countrymen, whose intelligence and militancy had earned them the respect of the leaders of the major national unions, served on the strike committee. Some of the many who played distinguished roles were Santiago Rodríguez, Angel María Dieppa, Rafael Acosta, Lupercio Arroyo, Eduvigis Cabán, Enrique Plaza, Rafael Correa, Ceferino Lugo, Domingo García, A. Villanueva, Tomás and Valentín Flores, and Angel Cancél.

It was in those days that the Puerto Rican nationalist movement first emerged in New York. What sparked it off, indirectly, was a statement by Antonio R. Barceló, who had replaced Luis Muñoz Rivera as leader of the Partido Unionista. He declared to the press: "We are aware that the United States needs Puerto Rico for strategic reasons, because of the position our Island occupies at the entry point to the Caribbean and opposite the Panama Canal . . . What we are asking for is a government that will allow us to manage our own affairs. Give to our people the right to elect their own governor by popular vote, and allow all government officials to be elected or appointed in Puerto Rico . . ."

Such pronouncements from the man who was supposed to represent the cause of independence and who led the party that included independence in its program were regarded as signs of "humiliation and surrender" by those who had begun to call themselves national-ists. They came together to organize a protest demonstration, and they have remained together ever since.

The economic depression hit hard in 1920. Traditionally, the *tabaqueros* had been the highest paid workers in the Puerto Rican community. But now their relative prosperity came to an end. Handmade cigar production was the sector most severely affected by the crisis. There was only a demand for cheap cigars, and the tobacco companies began to mechanize production and lay off the workers they no longer needed.

Inevitably this transformation of the industrial process led to head-on clashes between workers and bosses. Manufacturers in New York began to move their factories over to New Jersey and Pennsyl-vania. There they taught the trade to women, thus dropping the price of labor still further. In spite of all this, over two hundred independent factories producing choice cigars remained in New York.

Spanish-speaking workers, along with Jews and Italians, orga-nized a new union which we called the Trabajadores Amalgamados de la Industria del Tabaco. Local chapters were established in several cities, and we started *The Tobacco Worker,* a newspaper published in Spanish and English. The editorial staff was made up of the Cuban W. Rico, the Jew Sam Sussman, the Italian Cayetano Loria, the North American J. Brandon, and me, who served as the repre-sentative of the Puerto Rican *tabaqueros.*

Our organizing activity, of course, brought us into conflict with the International Cigarmakers' Union of the A. F. of L., which was attempting to hold back the mechanization of the industry by offer-ing concessions to the small factories. The *amalgamados,* as we called ourselves, condemned this policy and advocated the organization of the workers in the newly mechanized factories.

The fact is, though, that the age in which the *tabaqueros* were an important factor in the economic life and trade union movement in the United States was drawing to a close. Mechanization left many Puerto Rican *tabaqueros* no choice but to set up little workshops, known as *chinchalitos.* Unemployment also dispersed them. Even so, as we shall see, the *tabaqueros* still contributed to the betterment of the Puerto Rican community in New York.

In 1920, at the beginning of the harvest season, workers in the sugar industry in Puerto Rico staged a widespread general strike.

Serious confrontations between workers and police occurred at several points on the Island. In the U.S. newspapers, the North American corporations, especially the Aguirre Refinery, roundly denounced the workers as "revolutionaries" and "bandits" and called on Washington to intervene with repressive force.

In New York, the *tabaqueros* organized numerous acts of solidarity with the strikers. To counteract the sugar corporations' propaganda, they issued reports to the press, news agencies, and the U.S. Congress, giving the real story. This task was undertaken by Lupercio Arroyo, Pedro San Miguel, Jesús Colón, the socialist leaders Algernon Lee and August Claessens, and Luis Muñoz Marín . . . This was the first time Luis Muñoz Marín took an active part in the workers' struggle.

In August 1920, at the behest of the Puerto Rican legislature, Alfonso Lastra Chárriez stopped over in New York on his way from France with the remains of Ramón Emeterio Betances. At the request of Dr. José J. Henna, the ashes of our illustrious patriot were placed in City Hall so as to give the Puerto Rican community an opportunity to pay their final tribute. Representatives from Mexico, Cuba, the Dominican Republic, and Haiti paid their respects, and countless workers filed past the urn with deep veneration. Finally, Betances' remains were returned to Puerto Rico.

Back then there were many Hispanic actors and singers around the city—Eduardo Fort, Pilar Arcos, and Carlos Blanc, to name a few—who had great difficulty getting public performances. In many ways, the times simply weren't right.

I should mention that the times were no better for me personally than they were for most other *tabaqueros*. When the Trabajadores Amalgamados de la Industria del Tabaco was founded, I accepted a job in the leadership, with pay. Aside from being editor-in-chief of the paper, the *Tobacco Worker,* I also served as mediator between the bosses and the workers. This latter task was extremely difficult because of the changes taking place in production. It meant, on the one hand, defending the interests of the workers, without at the same time forcing the factories to move to other cities. Many of my problems were with well-meaning comrades who failed to understand the magnitude of the changes taking place in industry. In time I was exhausted by the endless debates and the fruitless battle—totally illogical, in fact, from the socialist point of view—

against the machines that a handful of people were trying to impose. So I resigned, and joined the huge army of unemployed.

All of my attempts to find a job proved fruitless. When three months had gone by and I was still out in the street, I had to send my wife and daughter to stay with her family. I stayed in the apartment, but I would get back late at night and sneak out before the sun was up so as not to cross paths with the superintendent. All to keep up the search for work that couldn't be found.

In the course of the day I would usually stop by the cigar factories. Some friends would always have a "smoke" for me, so that I wouldn't be without cigars for myself, but all I did was to sell them in the bars along the way. I usually went to the ones that had a "happy hour" where if you bought a beer you could help yourself to free food. But you had to watch out and not go back to the same place twice in one week or you'd be taken for one of the long line of vagabonds who were also making the rounds. You were always running the risk of being thrown out into the street by the seat of your pants.

One day as I was looking through the window of a pizzeria on 34th Street, watching an Italian cook make spaghetti, my rib cage showing through my empty stomach and my mouth watering, I looked up and read a sign on the building next door. "Strong men needed for work outside of the city." I made a leap for the door and went in.

The job, I was told, was in Pennsylvania. They were paying 75 cents an hour and guaranteed you a five-day week. There was even a chance to work Saturdays and Sundays if you wanted . . . I took the job right there on the spot!

But my heart (and stomach) sank when they then informed me that each applicant had to pay his own travel expenses and put down a $7.50 deposit in advance. All of those hired were to be at the main hall of the train station at five o'clock Monday morning. At six sharp the special train would leave for Pennsylvania.

The agency had advertised the jobs in glowing terms in all the papers. A lot of workers showed up, but many of them walked away downhearted because they didn't have the money. I left, but was determined to get the money somehow. Some friends helped me out, and that night I didn't even go back to the apartment. I headed straight for the train station. Nor was I alone: some three hundred others had done the same thing, and all of us, including about fifty Puerto Ricans, spent the night there.

Five A.M. came and went. Then it was six, seven, eight, nine, and still no one from the agency showed up. A few of the workers went over to the dispatch office and asked about the special train to Pennsylvania. No such luck!

No one knew anything about it. You can imagine how indignant we were, and we headed for the nearest police station. A clerk came. There would be an investigation . . . Needless to say, nothing ever came of it.

The whole thing was a trick. And I was back in the streets, this time with mild suicidal tendencies.

15. New organizations, an old rag business, and back to cigarmaking

The year 1922 was especially hard on Puerto Ricans in New York. There seemed to be more people crammed into apartments than ever. As I recall, there were at least a dozen people—men, women, and children—in every room. I even knew of cases where three couples had to live in the same place. I can also remember families that worked it out so that the men would sleep during the day and the women at night. And in spite of this, new emigrants kept arriving from Puerto Rico.

That year there was almost total unemployment among Puerto Ricans. I knew men—honest, law-abiding citizens—who had to resort to bootlegging. Many were the families who stayed alive by selling rum under the counter. The other recourse was the numbers. Yes, *la bolita* was a means of survival for quite a few "bankers" and countless numbers runners.

People went to bed hungry and dreamed of numbers and symbols. Books for interpreting dreams, or *la charada* as they were called, could be found in nearly every home. In the Puerto Rican neighborhoods it was not uncommon to hear people in the streets saying, "Lend me your *charada*. I had this weird dream last night." "Well, try playing 033."

Whenever a family had to move out of its apartment they would use a hand cart. Beds, couches, and cots were usually all the furniture they had. Sometimes there would also be a rickety old table and some chairs. And, of course, there were kitchen utensils.

The buildings where Puerto Ricans lived were never painted. Broken windows were never repaired either, so that they had to fill the holes with pieces of cardboard or old rags. The only time there was any heat or hot water was the night before the landlord came around to collect the rent. Garbage collection in those neighbor-

119

hoods was irregular at best. In fact, it's amazing that tuberculosis, prostitution, and delinquency were not more widespread than they were, and that, in spite of everything, Puerto Ricans did manage to survive under such unfavorable conditions.

An extreme example, but by no means an isolated one, was the case of Salustiano Miranda, whose family I happened to know. The husband, his brother, and his wife and children were living in a cellar which you could only get to by going down a dark stairway. The place had been a coal drop. I had to grope around in the dark to find my way. The quarters were lighted by gas. There were no windows, and behind a thin wall was the boiler, which provided hot water for the building. Over in one corner there was a mattress covered with old newspapers and a tattered blanket . . . The following is my record of one conversation I had with Sra. Miranda:

"How long have you been in New York?"

"My children and I arrived last summer. My husband and my brother-in-law came two years ago. They sent for us later, when they had enough to get us here."

"And where is your husband?"

"He's out with his brother looking for work. The factory where they were working closed down six months ago."

"Where are you from?"

"We are from Utuado. From the country . . . We had a little land off the highway to Adjuntas. But we lost it and went to town. From there we moved on to New York."

"And how did you end up in this cellar?"

"The janitor is from Utuado . . . You know, he sneaked us in."

The other Spanish-speaking communities were in the same straits, but at least they had some assistance from their embassies. The Spaniards pressured Madrid to send a ship so that the worst off among them could return to Spain. With the aid of their government, over two thousand Spaniards left New York. Mexico helped out its own, too, and made it possible for Mexicans who wanted to return to do so. People at the consulates also set up cheap cafeterias in several large cities. That's how tough things were for the emigrants.

A new attempt was made to form an organization that could fight on behalf of tenants and for improved medical services. But no meaningful result came of this effort.

In those years some of the leading Puerto Rican intellectuals in

New York were Rafael Torres Mazzorana, Luis G. Muñiz, Cordero de la Fuente, Gadea Picó, Antonio González, Alfonso Quiñones, Gonzalo O'Neill, J. Cruzado, Domingo Collazo, and Fiol Ramos. Some of these men took part in the founding of new societies, but they always seemed to turn their backs on the working people. For the most part they rejected socialist ideas and did not side with the workers' struggle.

One of the organizations that was established was the Alianza Puertorriqueña led by Gonzalo O'Neill. That group, along with such others as the Club Latinoamericano and the Club Betances came together on December 2, 1922, at Wadleigh High School to form the Liga Puertorriqueña. That was the first serious effort to set up one unified grouping for the entire community. The leaders were O'Neill, J. Rodríguez Sanjurjo, and R. Pabón Alves. Although their members attended in large numbers, none of the leaders of the artisanal societies was elected to office.

On September 3 the newly founded Asociación Nacionalista called a meeting to organize a demonstration against the then-governor of Puerto Rico, E. Montgomery Reilly. The Partido Unionista, headed by Barceló, came out strongly against excesses committed by the governor, while officials of the Partido Republicano and socialist leader Santiago Iglesias came to his defense.* The meeting, held at the Waldorf Astoria, was well attended. Working-class leaders like Lupercio Arroyo, Gabriel Blanco, Ceferino Lugo, and Julio N. González were present, but when they went to speak those chairing the meeting denied them the floor. A minor scuffle ensued, and the group withdrew. But the meeting went on as planned, and shortly thereafter a demonstration was held against the governor, whom people had nicknamed "Moncho Reyes," a takeoff on "Montgomery Reilly."

On November 20 it was announced that Gov. E. Montgomery Reilly would be arriving in New York. He was to be accompanied by Santiago Iglesias and the Republican leaders Roberto H. Todd and Carlos Toro. They were en route to Washington, where they

---

*E. Montgomery Reilly was charged with a wide range of breaches of established legal and political procedures, particularly his appointment of government officials without consulting the president of the senate, at that time Antonio R. Barcelo, head of the Partido Unionista. Reilly's decisions and policies also showed a blatant favoritism toward the Partido Republicano and the Partido Socialista—to the disadvantage of the Partido Unionista.

planned to petition for certain government reforms. On the following day they were greeted at the pier by a picketline organized by the nationalists. The authorities tried to blame the protesters for a fire that was set on board, causing the ship to sink right there at the dock. But they couldn't come up with any proof to back up the charge.

A number of Puerto Rican groups—or at least groups where the majority of the members were Puerto Rican—emerged at this time: the Club Demócrata Hispanoamericano, the Asociación Puertorriqueña, started by Manuel Negrón Collazo, and the Club Caborrojeño, founded and headed by Ramón Pabón Alves.

And what was my life like in the meantime?

Well, I was going through hard times, to say the least. But one day an opportunity turned up where I least expected it. I had a few friends of Italian background, cigarmakers by trade, who thought highly of me. One of them, Gaetano Scime, had given me the overcoat, and the shoes for that matter, that I had worn the previous winter. Many were the times I eased my hunger in that generous family's home. The Scimes, by the way, came from Sicily. They had emigrated to Argentina toward the end of the last century, and from there had moved on to Tampa, Florida, where they had learned cigarmaking. Later on they came to New York. It was in their friendly home that I came to meet another Sicilian, Tony Di Angelo Pope. He made ends meet by dealing in rags, and his business had grown beyond all expectation. Being illiterate, like the rest of his family, he needed someone to do his bookkeeping . . . "Well, here's your man," I said.

And there I was, a ragpicker and bookkeeper. Good old Puerto Rican vanity would not allow me to tell my wife the nature of my occupation. Born to the lesser "aristocracy" of one of our small towns back home, she might have felt ashamed. But I myself was happy as could be.

I would leave my apartment at four in the morning and pick up Tony, who would be getting the horse-drawn cart ready. His trusty nag had bells tied around its neck which would ring all along the route, announcing that the ragman was passing. We would start at 72nd Street and West End Avenue and end up at 110th Street and Riverside. That was the area where people of means lived, and there were always good deals to be made. Aside from that, Tony also had his regular clientele: the building supers and the domestic help had all kinds of clothes to sell, especially women's wear. Tony had a reputation for paying better than any other ragdealer.

I found out how prosperous the business was as soon as I started taking an inventory. Tony owned a few buildings in Flushing that he used to store the clothing. His wife and daughters, along with some hired women, would go through the goods and separate them into three piles: unusable, average, and first-rate. Items in the latter two categories were mended and ironed, and then sold, mostly to neighborhood stores. The rest were bartered away to other dealers.

The business paid off in more ways than one. Every day they would find something of value in those discarded rags: money, jewelry and so forth. It should also be noted that many of those garments belonged to persons recently deceased, and that some of the other goods they sold had not been acquired in the most honest of ways. But in that trade there was no room for scruples.

I kept the accounts in order—having mastered that trade—and each week I would give the boss a report on sales and bank deposits. Every now and then he would buy another rundown building and land in the Flushing area. When I started working for him he took over a printing company and appointed one of his relatives manager. In no time that business was flourishing too.

I was very happy with my $35.00 a week plus carfare and lunch (cooked by Tony's wife). On top of that, I was due for a bonus at the end of the year.

I renewed my studies and began to prepare for the entrance exams for the State University of New York. I felt fine, worked like a dog, and had no desire to lose my job. But the devil is always lying in wait to sow the seeds of discord.

Tony was a relatively good man. But he had nothing on his mind but his business, and was quite narrow-minded. He exploited his family mercilessly, even though he was already rather rich. He didn't allow his daughters the slightest diversion. There were five of them—he had no sons—the eldest in her thirties and the youngest nineteen. They didn't even go to the movies. They spent their days, even holidays, in the warehouse going through the clothes, mending and ironing. They saw to the chores around the house, cooked for the hired help, and even had to look after the horse, two cows, and some sheep they kept on some land near the warehouse.

The family dressed in whatever old clothes arrived. Sometimes, when her husband wasn't looking, the mother would pick out some good dresses for her daughters. To Tony, that was an extravagance. . . . Except for two cousins, I was the only person those women had anything to do with. If the mother asked, I would sometimes buy things for the family when I went into the city. She would always warn me not to let Tony know about it.

At first those harmless favors did not alarm Tony. But it wasn't long before I began to detect signs of hostility from him, and I came to realize that he was giving me things to do that would keep me away from the house. Having to take care of those other tasks, I wasn't able to keep the accounts up to date. Saturday was my day off, so I had Friday afternoons and Sundays to bring the accounts up to date.

And Tony wouldn't leave me alone for a single moment. He would bring me my food in the improvised office. But I must say that with all that he never once subjected me to ill treatment. On the contrary, he not only gave me a $100 bonus at New Year's, but raised my pay as well.

The women of the family, though, became aware of the new situation. The mother and daughters thought I must be displeased with them for some reason. But they lived in fear of the man of the house, not daring to approach me to ask what was wrong. Days went by, until one Sunday . . .

The father was busy with some buyers in the warehouse. The mother, seeing that it was getting on to noon, sent the youngest daughter in with my lunch. At the very moment that the girl was coming into my office, Tony appeared. Without uttering a word, he slapped her across the face, led her forcefully to his wife, and started a scene. When he came back to the office I gave him the final balance, and informed him that he should find someone else for the job because I had found work in the city. The truth is I just couldn't go on witnessing such paternal tyranny.

Tony knew the real reason for my resignation. He said that he didn't want his wife and daughters to get mixed up in the affairs of the business. He swore that he had full confidence in my honesty and suspected me of nothing. He went so far as to offer to rent an office right there in Flushing so that I could work free from disturbance. And because of the convenience of the job, and what was for those times an enviable salary, I decided to stay on. I took the opportunity to ask that he free me of the task of accompanying him when he went out to buy rags. He agreed.

With its new office, the business continued to prosper. In fact, that's where all business was transacted. I only communicated with the family by phone, and exclusively on matters relating to the business. But then the women started to bring up other topics; they wanted to know what had happened. I always gave them the same answer—that the business was growing and a new office had become indispensable.

One afternoon Tony's youngest daughter showed up unexpectedly at the office. She was all dressed up, wearing lipstick and nail polish and the best rags the streets had to offer. To tell the truth, she was very attractive. But frightened as I was, I could only ask her, "Who told you to come here?"

"My poppa called on the phone to say that he was staying in the city until later. And while he's not around I want to go to the movies. I've never been to one. You have to go with me."

"Does your mother know you've come to get me?"

"No. I told her I was going over to my girlfriend's house and would be back before poppa gets home."

"You shouldn't lie to your mother."

"I just don't feel like putting up with so many prohibitions. My mother and my sisters can go on being slaves, but not me!"

"But this isn't the best way of going about it. Call your father . . ."

"You don't know him! If I say anything to him he'll only beat me."

"But what about your cousins?"

"They're all afraid of him! Well, come on, it's getting late. Will you take me to the movies or not? Because if you won't come along, I'll go by myself."

"Don't get me wrong. I . . ."

I could hardly get the words out. Before me stood temptation, but all I could think of was my job.

"So, I'll go alone," she exclaimed, and ran down the stairs.

I soon realized that I had been saved in the nick of time: at that moment Tony appeared. He had overheard the whole conversation from the hallway. Boiling with rage, he stormed in and said, "You are a loyal friend. I like men like you."

Almost crying with anger, he turned on his heels and was off after his daughter.

I had no trouble imagining what would happen, and within a few minutes my worst fears were confirmed. The father gave his daughter a serious thrashing, and when her mother tried to step in he gave one to her too. The hapless lady made the mistaken assumption that I had informed her husband of their daughter's imprudence and castigated me bitterly on the phone. The whole mess dragged on for several weeks. Finally I couldn't stand it any longer and quit . . . I hardly need add that I left with a pain deep in my soul.

I had again spent a few weeks out of work when one night at a meeting of the Socialist Section I met Amalie and Frank Lotarius, whom I hadn't seen for some time. When they learned of my economic situation, that kind couple from Czechoslovakia offered to lend me some money to set up a small cigar factory. I would have two years to pay them back, with no interest on the loan . . . I accepted.

In partnership with Henry Havidon, a Jewish socialist, I opened a workshop—it wasn't much more than that—at 342 West 42nd Street. I worked at the bench and Henry sold the goods. That was the arrangement. But it wasn't long after we got the operation going that my partner lost all interest in selling cigars. A bachelor pushing fifty, he struck up an acquaintance with a woman of some means. And the more attention he paid to the lady, the faster the business went downhill. There was no choice but to sell it—before going completely bankrupt, that is.

The money I got from selling out was barely enough to pay off my original loan. Meanwhile, things didn't go any better for Luis Piérola, who bought the place, except in one sense: the owner of the building wanted to terminate the lease and Luis thought he'd come out ahead because of the fact that he was relieving the man of his debts. Wouldn't you know it but two months later we found out that the owners of the building had sold it for a fat sum, and had paid each tenant $10,000 to leave. On that very site they constructed the McGraw-Hill Building, one of the best along 42nd Street.

Months later, as we stood watching the building go up, Piérola said to me, consolingly, "Bernardo, my friend, you can't make a silk purse . . ."

16. Dissension, internal conflict, and Puerto Rico comes out the loser

The problem of the political status of Puerto Rico was an intensely controversial issue among Puerto Ricans in New York in 1922. In January Antonio R. Barceló passed through the city on his way to Washington. He was going to defend the Campbell Bill, which was pending before a Congressional committee. The bill called for making Puerto Rico into what was called a "Free Associated State," similar to what came to be established years later at the urging of Luis Muñoz Marín.

The Federación Libre de Trabajadores and the Partido Socialista—and of course Santiago Iglesias—were opposed to the projected bill. Iglesias, in fact, had said in a recent speech that what they were talking about was "neither a state, nor free, nor associated." Playing with words as usual, he claimed. "Puerto Ricans should demand complete sovereignty for their country. I, and the working people whom I represent, are partisans of the state, and we are against the kind of 'state' being proposed because it cannot compare, by the furthest stretch of the imagination, with the autonomy of the British Commonwealth . . ." In line with this position, the A.F. of L. worked in opposition to the Campbell Bill in Washington. Support for the measure never materialized.

The Asociación Nacionalista held an assembly at 153 West 33rd Street at the beginning of February. The meeting was presided over by J. Meléndez, and others in attendance included Rafael Torres Mazzorana, Vicente Balbás Capó, Octavio E. Moscoso, and Alfonso Quiñones. It was concluded that the provisions of the Campbell Bill were inferior to the autonomy Spain had conceded in 1898. The only acceptable solution, they agreed, was complete independence.

That same group later sponsored an evening to honor the anniversary of the death of José de Diego.

127

There was another commemorative act, though one much more modest in scale, held at about that time. A group of us—*tabaqueros* and workers in other trades—organized an evening in memory of Pachín Marín. The idea of honoring Francisco Gonzalo Marín, our valiant poet who had died in Cuba during the revolution, came from Alfonso Dieppa and Domingo García. Let me say a few words about the first of these two men.

Dieppa, who was mentioned earlier in this chronicle, was an excellent Puerto Rican. A sailor in the merchant marine, he had traveled to all parts of the world, spoke several languages, and had written many works of prose and verse. Being a modest man, he never had any of them published. The only one to become known was his adaptation of Chekhov's *Uncle Vanya,* which enjoyed a very successful run at the Círculo de Trabajadores in Brooklyn.

At around that time Dieppa was putting the final touches on a book about what the United States would be like in the year 2000. To judge from what I heard, it was a piece of what would later be called science fiction. Unfortunately, nothing more was heard of the book or its author. In fact, after the event I am referring to Alfonso Dieppa disappeared from New York.

A large number of old *tabaqueros* who had personally known Pachín Marín attended our commemoration. Domingo Collazo gave a brief account of Marín's life in New York before he left to take up arms in the battlefields of Cuba. He presented the following portrait of the hero: "Pachín was slightly larger than average in build. He had an elegant bearing and a magnetic appeal, without any sign of arrogance. He was modest of word and in his relations with others, unmistakable and unforgettable from the first time you saw him. He had a distinct gift for making a favorable impression. He was a black Lord Byron . . ."

Santiago Iglesias and Bolívar Pagán spoke at a rally held at the Harlem Terrace in defense of the governorship of E. Montgomery Reilly. Many socialists—Jesús Colón, Guillermo Vargas, and myself among them—repudiated that position. We understood that it adversely affected our struggles in New York, and we were therefore not inclined to provide a haven for the opportunistic designs of Iglesias and the Partido Socialista of Puerto Rico.

In April there was an unfortunate incident that crushed the hope that a unified group might represent the Puerto Rican community. The Liga Puertorriqueña, headed by Gonzalo O'Neill, affiliated itself with the Democratic Party. Its leadership justified the action in a long-drawn-out manifesto, which stated: "If we are to live with the American people, if we are to become part of this Great Republic, we must not, given our aspirations, sit around and vegetate, or act like a bunch of robots. No, we must act like conscious human beings . . . and show that we possess qualities that make us worthy of being considered valuable political allies . . ."

But this move to a partisan political position was repudiated by many members of the Liga. Their opposition was vocal at a meeting held in the Liga headquarters at 600 West 125th Street. Gonzalo O'Neill presided, and opened the meeting with a speech justifying the affiliation. The audience heard him out patiently, but as soon as he had finished the hall erupted: everyone wanted to speak, some in favor and some against. Finally J. Ortiz Lecodet got the floor and reminded the group that it had been formed as a merging of different organizations. He added, "The purpose of this alliance was to create a civic, cultural, and benefit society to which compatriots of all parties, ideologies, and learnings could belong . . ." He challenged the authority of the leaders to adopt such a partisan measure unilaterally.

Joaquín Colón went on in the same vein, pointing out that there already was a Club Demócrata Puertorriqueño in Brooklyn. He argued that the Liga was supposed to be a different kind of organization, with a much broader purpose and composition. Gonzalo O'Neill and his backers became more and more isolated from the rest of those present. And the meeting came to an end without any formal consensus.

Subsequently, the leadership of the Liga—O'Neill, Sasport, José Martínez, Alfonso Quiñones, Ramón Pabón Alves, and others—founded a committee of the Democratic Party. But after a few meetings it was clear that they did not have the support they had hoped they had.

Before long, still another organization emerged, the Alianza Obrera, under the leadership of Lupercio Arroyo, Jesús Colón, Eduvigis Cabán, Guillermo Vargas, Catalino Castro, and Luis Muñoz Marín. Its aim was to foster the unionization of workers and to set up a headquarters for the defense of Puerto Ricans, regardless of political affiliation.

Meanwhile, Gonzalo O'Neill gave up the presidency of the Liga and was succeeded by Luis G. Muñoz. An advocate of unity, he called a meeting, which was very well attended. But although everyone favored this position, there were serious differences as to the direction that should be taken. Representatives of the Asociación Nacionalista, for example, claimed that any such group was pointless if it did not uphold the independence of Puerto Rico. Members of the Alianza Obrera, on the other hand, argued that membership should be "by everyone and for everyone," and that the Liga should not assume partisan political positions. The discussion went on for several hours, and it was finally agreed to appoint a committee to study the differences and come up with some points of unity to present to the next meeting. The committee was named, but it was unable to come to any agreement. Thus this second effort to establish a group representative of the Puerto Rican community also ended in failure.

Quite a few Puerto Ricans continued to identify with the Democratic Party, and called meetings in Harlem and in Chelsea. In those and in other parts of the city Democratic Clubs made up of Puerto Ricans arose. Finally, a Federación de Clubs Demócratas Puertorriqueños of New York was established.

On Labor Day in September 1923, the Alianza Obrera held a rally at the Harlem Terrace that was attended by over a thousand people. The president, Eduvigis Cabán, gave the floor to Torres Mazzorana and Santos Bermúdez, who used the occasion to launch a broadside against Santiago Iglesias, the Partido Socialista, the A.F. of L., and even the Alianza Obera itself. Torres Mazzorana condemned all of these organizations as "societies without heart and soul." He charged that they did not have "a feeling of nationality or love for matters of the spirit," and that "all they demand for the workers is a piece of bread." He accused those who belonged to the Federación Libre de Trabajadores and the A.F. of L. of being "opportunists." Santos Bermúdez went on to denounce Iglesias, Gompers, and other labor leaders, calling them "swindlers who are betraying the interests of the workers."

These speeches put the audience in an uproar. But the president protected the speakers and made sure they were not interrupted. When they finished, however, President Cabán made it clear that they had abused the good faith of the chair since they were not scheduled to speak at the meeting. These were Prudencio Martínez and Luis Muñoz Marín, who followed Torres Mazzorana and Santos Bermúdez to the rostrum and contradicted everything they had said.

Toward the end of the year there was a meeting of "men without a homeland" in New York, a group of Puerto Ricans who had explicitly refused to accept United States citizenship when it was imposed by the Jones Act in 1917. It is said that between two hundred and three hundred people took this position. Sixty compatriots attended the meeting, which was held in a restaurant at 104th Street and Columbus Avenue. The U.S. Supreme Court had recently stripped them of all their civil rights. They thus became outcasts even from their own country, Puerto Rico.

One of those present, Osvaldo F. Torres, suggested that they appeal to a Latin American country to give them the opportunity to found a "colony." This was agreed to, and a commission was named to pursue the matter further. Mexico extended a hand to those "without a homeland" and invited them to settle there. When Santiago Iglesias heard the news through the Pan American Federation, he sent word to these Puerto Ricans that he wished to speak to them. They accepted, and another meeting was held for that purpose.

Iglesias was received with animosity, and even outright hatred. But he listened calmly to their scathing remarks. In response he stated: "I do not share your views about American citizenship. I firmly believe that Puerto Rico will be able to carve out its political and economic destiny much more readily by being part of the United States, as long as all of us work together to achieve rights equal to those of other American citizens. I admire your courage, idealism, and the love you have for your homeland, but what you plan to do is absurd and misguided. Even if you go on opposing my ideas, you will do more for Puerto Rico by living in New York or there on the Island. . . ." He then promised to put in a word with his friends in Congress, urging them to introduce a bill that would restore all the privileges due them as American citizens. Whether it was that gesture or just the good humored way he endured their angry outburst, Santiago Iglesias certainly managed to calm those noisy "expatriates."

After the Alianza Obrera, the most important organization in the life of Puerto Ricans in New York in those days was the Puerto Rican Brotherhood of America, which had been established on November 3, 1923. Among its founders were Antonio Dávila, Eusebio Cruz, Juan Valderrama, Juan Carreras, Aurelio Betancourt, Jacinto Paradís, Juan J. Matos, and Faustino Dorna. Its first executive board included Rodrigo del Manzano, president; Tomás Gares, vice-president; Juan Carreras, secretary; and Vincente Rolón, treasurer. Manzano was succeeded as president by Julio Pietrantoni, followed by Felipe Gómez.

Luis Muñoz Marín and Santiago Iglesias attended that year's A.F. of L. convention, held in Portland, Oregon. The most important thing about the delegation was its resolution denouncing the crimes of Venezuelan dictator Gómez, which was presented to the meeting by Muñoz Marín. That motion paved the way for a series of meetings between Venezuelan exiles and leaders of the A.F. of L. in Washington. The result was a petition calling on the U.S. government to sever diplomatic relations with the tyrant.

At that convention of the A.F. of L. three resolutions were discussed that departed from the usual order of business: a resolution to form a labor party, to reorganize the trade unions along industrial lines, and to recognize the Union of Soviet Socialist Republics. The more liberal, socialist, and radical delegates argued in favor of these positions. But after heated debate the conservatives won out and the three resolutions were overwhelmingly rejected.

It is worth mentioning that on their return home, the Puerto Rican delegation stopped off in San Francisco, where the local Liga Puertorriqueña gave a party in honor of Santiago Iglesias and Luis Muñoz Marín.

The beginning of 1924 found the Puerto Ricans caught up in still another political fracas. The Resident Commissioner in Washington, Félix Córdova Dávila, proposed a bill in Congress calling for, as one newspaper put it, "a form of autonomous government" for Puerto Rico. "No longer," the newspaper went on, "would anyone need to cherish the dream of independence if the form of government being asked for is made law." The Puerto Rican Legislature named a joint committee that was to lobby for the bill in Washington. The committee included Santiago Iglesias. In New York there was a group of Puerto Ricans who bitterly hated Iglesias, men such as Luis G. Muñiz, J. Rodríguez Sanjurjo, Antonio González, Rafael Torres Mazzorana, Alfonso Quiñones, and José Martínez. Claiming to speak in the name of the Puerto Rican community, this group sent a message to the Secretary of the Interior demanding that Santiago Iglesias not be recognized as a member of the committee. It charged, among other things, that he "had been a dangerous agitator with radical tendencies," that he used "incendiary Communist and Bolshevik propaganda," and that he "constitutes a genuine threat to the welfare and tranquility of Puerto Rico." The secretary's response was that he "could not decline to receive a representative officially appointed by the Legislature of Puerto Rico."

Opposition to the attack on Santiago Iglesias came from other corners as well. In the name of the Federación de Clubs Demócratas Puertorriqueños, J. V. Alonso and Joaquín Colón, also condemned the vicious attack. Reaffirming their "impartial" position, they declared that although it was perfectly acceptable to criticize political leaders in Puerto Rico, "We consider it poor judgment on the part of these gentlemen to discredit any Puerto Rican who is in this country on an official mission. We will not tolerate it in the case of Iglesias," they concluded, "any more than we would tolerate it if it were directed against Barceló."

The Congressional Committee on Insular Affairs began its hearings on the bill and Muñiz and his group asked to be heard. Luis G. Muñiz and Rafael Torres Mazzorana were called to testify. The former declared that "even the limited political abilities of the Puerto Rican leaders have been used to support corruption." He asked Congress to conduct an investigation. Torres Mazzorana, for his part, stated that "the people of Puerto Rico are neither ready nor able to exercise the vote," and that for that reason "Puerto Rico should not be granted any extension of self-government or autonomy."

In the course of his statement Torres Mazzorana claimed to represent "the eighty thousand Puerto Ricans living in New York." In answer to questions from one of the members of the committee, he admitted that he did not have credentials from any existing organization. And Córdova Dávila, another member of the committee, subjected him to a rigorous questioning, implying that the man before them was using the threat of his role as publisher of a newspaper in New York to blackmail the committee . . . As he left the hearings, Torres Mazzorana announced that he intended to take Córdova to court. But he never carried out his threat.

At one point in the questioning the following exchange occurred between a committee member and the witness.

"How long, Mr. Mazzorana, have you been residing in the United States?"

"Five years. I am a registered voter in my electoral district."

"You have lived here such a short time and think you are qualified to elect the governor of New York State, yet you do not consider the people of Puerto Rico capable of suffrage . . ."

Testimony supporting the bill came from Lupercio Arroyo, representing the Alianza Obrera, and J. V. Alonso on behalf of the Federación de Clubs Demócratas.

The reaction to the testimony of Luis G. Muñiz and Rafael Torres Mazzorana, both in New York and Puerto Rico, was violent and tumultuous. This was particularly true when, at the end of the hearings, it was announced that the secretary of the interior had asked Congress "not to give Puerto Ricans the right to elect their governor because they are not able to live up to that responsibility . . ."

Muñiz and Mazzorana had triumphed . . . *against* Puerto Rico!

17. The "third party," an underwater job, and the sweltering summer of 1926

Life was no easier on me than on my fellow countrymen. In January 1924 the second of my children was born, a daughter . . . After selling my little shop I had been unemployed for several months, working a day every so often in this or that friend's little factory. Otherwise, I made cigars secretly in my own house. Things were so bad that I was ready to take on whatever work I could find.

One day I discovered that they were looking for "a strong man who wasn't afraid of work" down at a plant that produced antiseptics. I ran right down to apply for the spot. The man who saw me looked me up and down, asked me a few questions, and handed me a form to fill out. I signed on the dotted line, and it was like a slave contract: miserable wages, long hours, and the slightest complaint about an accident and you're out . . . In those days, and under those conditions, you had to put up with anything.

Before I started to work they showed me how to dress. First I had to put on a pair of rubber boots that went up above my knees. Then I'd get into the overalls, also all rubber, that covered my whole body. Then I covered my head with a hood made of the same material, with holes for my eyes and nose. And finally, I'd pull on my big leather gloves.

Once I was dressed they sent me down some stairs to the cellar. Down there they had a huge wheel crisscrossed by hundreds of thin metal pipes spurting out water under high pressure. With one hand I was supposed to grab dirty bottles as they came down on a moving belt, take those bottles that had already been washed off the wheel, and put the dirty ones on. Nothing to it, right? The only problem was that the damn wheel was spinning around so fast that you didn't have a chance to breathe. And all of this was to be done under a constant stream of water!

That damn job must have been invented by the devil. My arms never stopped moving. Even with all the gear I had on, I was soaked to the bone. The workday was from seven in the morning until five in the evening, with a two-hour break for lunch. The pay: $3.00 a day.

I spent many months of my life down in that cellar meant for frogs, dreaming of the emancipation of the working class. Even so, the truth is that they were days of glory compared to what the majority of my countrymen were going through. In the course of that year, 1924, unemployment in New York rose to half a million, and there were reported to be over 5 million unemployed nationwide. Needless to say, there was no unemployment insurance of any kind.

Young emigrants kept arriving from Puerto Rico full of high hopes and plans, only to find themselves facing a very hard reality. Their willpower shattered and, embittered by circumstances, they easily fell into crime. It was in April of that same year, in fact, that the first case of armed robbery carried out by a Puerto Rican in this city was reported. Félix Munet, the son of a distinguished family from Ponce, held up a commercial establishment at 532 West 22nd Street. He was carrying a gun, and made off with $3,000.

Not that there weren't other such lawless acts. And from that moment on the words "Puerto Rican" were associated in all the major papers with some kind of crime. That's when they started to build on all the prejudice against us, and to rationalize suspicion and discrimination.

In 1924 Puerto Ricans took a great interest in political issues in the United States. They were especially active in the presidential campaign.

A new force had emerged on the political scene—the "third party" of Robert M. La Follette. His bid for the presidency won the backing of the American Socialist Party. The leadership of the A.F. of L. soon announced its official support as well. East Coast liberals, farmers from the mid-West, organized workers, the national minorities—all united in the progressive movement behind La Follette . . . A spirit of victory filled workers' circles across the country.

In New York, our Alianza Obrera called a rousing rally in support of the La Follette campaign. At a later date we held another large meeting, this time with the participation of Fiorello La Guardia, who was later to become mayor. A campaign committee was named, made up of Lupercio Arroyo, Jesús Colón, Cabán, Félix León, Luis Boveda, Valentín Flores, Luis Muñoz Marín, and myself. The first thing we did was to organize a series of rallies, in all the Puerto Rican neighborhoods.

The La Follette campaign was directed against the concentration of capital and the monopoly of the bankers and industrialists over the economic resources of the nation. La Follette took a stand against imperialist expansion and the exploitation and domination of the weaker nations. He spoke out for better living conditions for the workers, the protection of agriculture, and the creation of new sources of employment. La Follette was expected to get at least 9 million votes. But that estimate turned out to be very optimistic. A.F. of L. locals failed to respond to the call from the leadership, so that the "third party" movement's showing at the polls was not what its militant campaigners had hoped for. Among the large mass of voters, the tendency to vote for one of the traditional parties won out.

One anecdote from the campaign that is worth retelling was when the campaign staff asked Santiago Iglesias to recommend a speaker for a rally they were organizing in Brooklyn. He suggested Cayetano Coll y Cuchí, who had been a member of several political parties in Puerto Rico and was at that time flirting with the Partido Socialista. The recommendation was not to our liking, and we decided to attend the rally to dispute the speaker if that proved necessary. But to our surprise crafty old Cayetano delivered a speech with great social content. None of us could have outdone him.

Muñoz Marín and I accompanied the speaker back to Manhattan. In the subway we had the following exchange:

"Tell me, *compañero* Cayetano, have you always held the ideas you expressed so well this evening?"

I threw the question at him directly, knowing that in Puerto Rico he had been one of the most outspoken opponents of the socialists.

The man didn't bat an eyelash. He looked at me squarely, turned to Muñoz Marín, and, fixing his sharp gaze back on me, responded with that cunning lawyer's aplomb for which he was so well known: "My good friend, if in years past, and especially in Puerto Rico, I had dared speak as I did tonight, I surely would have died of hunger, or would be wandering through the world with no country of my own to return to."

That was how all the intellectuals and professionals thought and acted, with very few exceptions. And if some of them, at least, could now express their ideas with a stronger sense of humanity, much of this was due to the efforts of the Federación Libre de Trabajadores and the Partido Socialista. At that time the FLT had 236 member locals, and assets of $150,000. The Partido Socialista, in turn, had received 59,817 votes in the 1920 elections in Puerto Rico, had elected one senator and four representatives, and enjoyed a majority on the boards of nine municipalities. It stood out as the party of the future, so that sympathetic professionals and intellectuals could ally themselves with it without having to worry about dying of hunger.

Around then I took up my studies again, this time at the Cooperative College that had been set up on 115th Street by the Socialist Party and the trade unions. Quite a few university professors and public-school teachers taught classes. They were paid a token salary, and the cost of the courses was shared equally by all of the students. The school offered preparatory courses for the general entrance examinations given periodically by the State University of New York.

Thousands of Jews got their training in the liberal professions at the Cooperative College, and a small number of Puerto Ricans also began to recognize the opportunities it could open up for the working-class people. Four of our countrymen took classes with me: Lorenzo Mercado, Modesto Seda, José Machuca, and José Verdiales. The last of these became a pharmacist, and later joined the International Brigade that fought to defend the Spanish Republic. But I lost track of that brilliant compatriot.

Meanwhile I continued at my underwater job washing bottles. What kept me going was the dim hope that by continuing my studies I could accumulate enough credits to get me into law school. But life, it seems, had other things in store for me.

In that year, 1924, the Puerto Rican community lost one of its most illustrious citizens, Dr. José J. Henna, who died on February 2 at the age of 76. Henna, who along with Hostos and Betances had embraced the struggle for revolution in the Antilles, spent fifty-five years in this city. He arrived here, an exile after the Grito de Lares, in 1869. He had returned to Puerto Rico only two years before, having graduated from medical school in Paris.

Aside from his revolutionary activities Henna was a renowned physician and man of science. He was loved as a doctor throughout the Latin American, French, and Chinese immigrant communities. He was a highly cultured man who, in addition to his native Spanish, spoke perfect English and French. He could also get along in Italian, German, Portuguese, and even spoke a smattering of Chinese. He was versed in painting, sculpture, and music.

Henna was dean of the Spanish-speaking doctors in New York. He was on the medical staff of Bellevue Hospital, was a founder of the French Hospital, and a member of the board of the Metropolitan Museum of Art. The French government made him a Knight of the Legion of Honor, and he was honored and decorated by several other countries as well. The funeral services for that famous Puerto Rican were an occasion of deep mourning. Thousands of his countrymen filed past his coffin, as did countless South Americans, Frenchmen, North Americans, and Chinese . . . It was a tribute to his great achievements.

And while we're talking about Dr. José J. Henna, tribute should also be paid to another man who represented the Antillean revolution—Juan Rius Rivera. In the following year, on September 24, 1925, news of his death arrived from Honduras, where he had been living. When we heard of this new loss we organized an event in his honor at the Partido Socialista offices in Chelsea on 26th Street and Eighth Avenue. Domingo Collazo was asked to deliver the eulogy.

Collazo traced the broad outlines of Rius Rivera's life. He recalled that in 1870, at twenty-two years of age, Rius Rivera had landed in Cuba with General Agüero. In recognition of his impressive military ability and boundless courage, he was given a high rank. He carried out the campaign in Oriente, along with General Calixto García. For his service in Holguín he was promoted to Comandante. At the end of the Ten Year's War he joined up with the great Antonio Maceo, the Bronze Titan, in the protest of Mangos de Baraguá.

When José Martí called for the resumption of the armed struggle, Rius Rivera answered, and even attempted to extend the revolution to Puerto Rico. When that proved impossible, he assumed command of an expedition to Cuba. He was captured by the Spaniards and sentenced to prison in Ceuta. By the end of the war he had advanced to the rank of general.

An old North American seaman named Albert Sheridan was also at the memorial. He had come to know Rius Rivera when he was a member of the crew of the ship used for Rius Rivera's final landing in Cuba. He recalled the dangers of that crossing . . . His vivid account moved the audience deeply.

The continuing attempts to establish new groups in the Puerto Rican community came from several different points on the political spectrum. In July 1924, for example, the Junta de Defensa de Puerto Rico was set up under the direction of Domingo Collazo, J. Monge Sánchez, Ernesto Andino Cepeda, Luis Battistine, J. A. González, and Antonio Gotay. Within a short time, however, it dissolved.

Then, in September, the community's elite convened at the Waldorf Astoria and founded the Casa de Puerto Rico. Its governing board was made up of Dr. Ruiz Arnau, Gonzalo O'Neill, Martín Travieso, Pedro Rodríguez Capó, Esq., R. M. Delgado, Manuel Argüezo, Dr. López Antongiorgi, Dr. Arturo Martínez, Luis V. Rivera, Esq., Ulises García Sandoval, José P. Echandía, Dr. Janer, and F. González Acuña. This was the cream of the crop . . . But there is no record of their ever having accomplished anything, and they certainly never built as much as a single shack.

Some time later, in May of the following year, a number of Puerto Rican writers and journalists in New York decided to hold a literary dinner. As they put it in the invitation, their aim was to "set things right in the world." With that end in view, José G. Benítez, Rafael Torres Mazzorana, J. Rodríguez Sanjurjo, Francisco Torres López, Ramón Gadea Picó, José Sangado, Jorge Pastor, Ramón Mínguez, Carlos Fernández, R. Villa, Antonio González, and Luis G. Muñoz met at La Bohème, a restaurant on the corner of 120th Street and Seventh Avenue. The group was founded, without a doubt . . . But from all indications it soon discovered how hard it is to change the world, and its ambitious plans never came to anything.

There were other Puerto Ricans who turned their attention to electoral politics, especially the Democratic Party. There were over two thousand Puerto Rican votes for Congressman Sol Bloom in the 19th District in Manhattan. During his campaign Bloom had shown great interest in our problems. After winning the election, though, he made a statement to Domingo Collazo, the New York correspondent for *La Democracia*. When one community group demanded an explanation, Representative Bloom was forced to deny that he had ever made such a statement . . .* That incident caused much

---

*This refers to statements attributed to Sol Bloom on a visit to Puerto Rico in April 1925. Commenting on the movement for increased political autonomy, Bloom compared the Puerto Rican people to "little children who refuse to take their medicine but in the end are obliged to obey the prescriptions of the doctors and their parents." The episode, including the protest by Puerto Ricans in New York, was reported in *La Prensa* (April 7, 1925), and other newspapers.

dissatisfaction among Puerto Rican voters and led many to wonder if they could ever expect anything from a Yankee politician if this was the behavior of one who claimed to be liberal.

It was in Brooklyn, rather than Manhattan, that Puerto Rican affiliation with the Democratic Party advanced farthest. The Democratic clubs helped to ease many of the problems faced by the emigrants—tenant problems, legal aid, compensation for injuries on the job, medical services, and so on. The clubs also organized parties, dances, and sports activities which were attended by large numbers of Puerto Ricans. In fact, it was the local Democratic Party leaders who set up the first Puerto Rican baseball team in New York, the Puerto Rico Stars.

From the time of the Club Agüeybana and the Club Rius Rivera, at the height of the Antillean Revolution, there were no new Puerto Rican organizations in Brooklyn until 1917, when Julio Díaz, Rafael Osorio, and Jesús Colón began to form political and cultural groups. J. Castro López, José Avilés, Ricardo Portela, Carlos Tapia, Pedro Tejada, Joaquín Barreras, and many others contributed to that effort.

A large number of attempts to establish different kinds of societies occurred in 1925, the most effective and lasting being the founding of the Club Caribe Democrático in Manhattan, on the initiative of J. V. Alonso. It functioned along the same lines as the clubs in Brooklyn. As we shall see, El Caribe—as it came to be known—performed many valuable services on behalf of the Puerto Rican community in New York.

During this time the Alianza Obrera was as active as ever. Toward the middle of 1925 we held a rally at which Prudencio Rivera Martínez, the labor leader from Puerto Rico, delivered the keynote speech. The event was part of our campaign to promote the organizing of Puerto Rican workers, increasing numbers of whom were entering the hotel and restaurant industries, garment factories, and the service industry.

Such was our plight as we entered 1926. Summer that year was steaming. Our people lived in the streets, and singing and laughter were heard everywhere in El Barrio and across Harlem. The sidewalks were filled with groups playing checkers and dominoes. Others would make their way, laughing and joking, toward the lake in Central Park. On every other corner the men who sold *piraguas,* or snowcones, did a thriving business . . . Raspberry, *guanábana,* (soursop), and vanilla ices! It was the Puerto Ricans who brought the *piragua* to New York.

It was July 28. Suddenly the noisy gaiety of the afternoon was silenced. People scattered in all directions. Mothers who had brought their children to the park for some sun took them in their arms and hurried away. All the people swarming the streets vanished in a matter of minutes. The tables where the men played were abandoned on the sidewalk. Doors and windows were slammed shut. And in the darkened apartments the talk was of the killed and wounded.

All of a sudden mobs armed with clubs had begun to attack Puerto Ricans with a fury. Several stores owned by Puerto Ricans had been attacked. The sidewalks in front of the *bodegas* were covered with shattered glass, rice, beans, plantains, and tropical vegetables. A *piragua* cart was broken to bits on the corner, the gutter littered with broken bottles . . . Terror gripped El Barrio.

Not until later did anyone know for sure what had happened. The first attack had left more than fifty people wounded, some critically. When word got around the Puerto Ricans reacted. Some armed groups took to the streets to prove their manhood . . . Only then did the police show up, supposedly to restore law and order.

That sweltering summer of 1926 was a fiery baptism for the Puerto Rican community in New York.

Top: American Tobacco Company cigar factory in Comerío, Puerto Rico, during first part of the century. At right, women and children strip tobacco leaves. *Bottom left:* Workers in San Juan sign up to work in U.S. armaments industry during World War I as government officials watch. *Bottom right:* Migrants arriving from Puerto Rico in the late 1940s, when most came by plane.

Top: Liga Puertorriqueña baseball team in 1935. (Photo courtesy of José Ramón Giboyeaux)
Middle: Banquet at the St. George Hotel in Brooklyn in the 1940s. Fourth from left is Doña Antonia Denis, organizer of the Comité de Damas and many other Puerto Rican organizations during the 1930s and 1940s. (Photo courtesy of José Ramón Giboyeaux) *Bottom:* Liga Puertorriqueña outing. Bernardo Vega is in the back row, middle. (Photo: Jesús Colón Papers, Centro de Estudios Puertorriqueños, Hunter College, CUNY)

Top: Meeting of the Logia Puertorriqueña of the International Workers' Order in the 1940s. Jesús Colón, fourth from left, headed all the Hispanic lodges. *Middle:* A party to celebrate a baptism, 1927. (Photo: Jesús Colón Papers)

Top: Some of the many progressive Spanish-language newspapers in New York that Bernardo Vega contributed to. *Bottom left:* Arturo Alfonso Schomburg, 1874–1938. *Bottom right:* César Andreu Iglesias, the editor of the *Memorias* and a close friend of Bernardo Vega's, at a rally in the 1960s. (Photo from Georg Fromm, *César Andreu Iglesias: Vida y obra* [Río Piedras: Huracán, 1977])

Top left: Jesús Colón addressing a Puerto Rican rally in New York City during World War II. At left is Evelina Antonetty, a community activist and today the leader of United Bronx Parents. (Photo: Jesús Colón Papers) *Middle left:* Fiorello La Guardia and Vito Marcantonio. *Top right:* Vito Marcantonio arrives in Puerto Rico to defend Pedro Albizu Campos in 1935. *Middle right:* A demonstration for low-cost housing in the 1940s. (Photo: *Daily World*) *Bottom:* East Harlem rally supporting independence for Puerto Rico. (Photo: *Daily World*)

Top left: Bernardo Vega in San Juan in 1948. (Photo courtesy of Olympia Colón) *Top right:* Bernardo Vega and Jesús Colón at Bernardo Vega's house on Long Island in the mid-1940s. (Photo: Jesús Colón Papers) *Middle left:* Bernardo Vega confers with Juan Mari Brás, general secretary of the Movimiento Pro Independencia de Puerto Rico (MPI) in 1965. (Photo courtesy of Juan Mari Brás) *Bottom:* Bernardo Vega, far left, with Juan Mari Brás and other leaders of the MPI during a street march in Río Piedras in the early 1960s. (Photo: *Claridad*)

18. A year of personal disaster with a happy ending

To the last person, the Puerto Rican community was up in arms. The Puerto Rican Brotherhood took the initiative and called all groups to a meeting.* Blas Oliveras, head of the Brotherhood, presided. He informed those present of the protest that had been lodged against the city and state, and ended with a fervent call for unity. After some discussion, it was agreed to call a community meeting. It was held a few days later, on August 9, 1926, at the Harlem Casino. Thousands of people attended.

By that time most people had a pretty clear idea of what was going on. The real cause of the aggression was a rivalry that had developed between Jewish and Hispanic businessmen. Some of the stores owned by Jews were in financial trouble, and their proprietors resented the growing number of Puerto Rican and Hispanic *bodegas*. They had contracted with thugs to spread fear among Puerto Rican businessmen.

The *New York Times,* the *Daily News,* and the other New York dailies, including the Jewish *The Day,* sent reporters to the meeting at the Harlem Casino. After the speeches, it was agreed to found a unified organization. The goals of the Liga Puertorriqueña e Hispana, as it was called, were to be: "Unite any and all Hispanics . . . Represent the community before the authorities . . . Serve as a benefit society . . . Maintain an educational center and information office . . . Carry out campaigns urging Puerto Ricans to vote . . . Work for the economic, political, and social betterment of Puerto Rico . . . Not to serve as the tool of any party . . ."

A board of directors was chosen immediately: Blas Oliveras be-

*The Puerto Rican Brotherhood of America was founded in Manhattan on November 2, 1923. Its program called for a broad range of reforms on behalf of the Puerto Rican people in the United States and on the Island.

came president; J. V. Alonso and Pedro San Miguel, vice-presidents; José González Benítez, secretary; J. M. Antonmarchi, assistant secretary; J. M. Vivaldi, treasurer; and Lupercio Arroyo, Cayetano Arrieta, Carlos M. Fernández, Ricardo Irigoitá, Enrique Alegría, and N. Viques, members of the board. The latter three were Argentine, Spanish, and Central American respectively.

The protest from the community was very effective. Tension continued for several weeks, but although there were a few altercations in the streets none were of major significance. And then calm and good judgment returned. *The Day* and the other Jewish newspapers ran editorials condemning the disturbances. And as for us, there wasn't much we could do but defend ourselves.

The perverse intentions of those who had initiated the conflict were not encouraged in the Jewish community. Nor did most Puerto Ricans allow themselves to be misled by those among them who tried to stir up old antagonisms. Blas Oliveras, Pedro San Miguel, Lupercio Arroyo, J. V. Alonso, and the other leaders of the defense movement always called for harmony and neighborly goodwill.

So at least one good thing came of that sweltering summer of 1926: the Liga Puertorriqueña became a large organization, representing the entire community.

That year also saw the founding of the Ateneo Obrero, of which I was president. Some of the other founders of the organization, which was for those interested in literature and the arts, were Sabino Vázquez, Jesús Colón, Juan Rovira, Emilio Fariza, Manuel Flores Cabrera, and Juan Bautista Pagán, all Puerto Ricans, as well as people from other national backgrounds. Our common aim was to support and broaden the ideas of the Alianza Obrera along clearly defined cultural lines. We were interested in setting up an educational center which would counteract the widespread tendency among Puerto Ricans in New York to consider their stay a temporary thing and to continue to believe that they would eventually return to the Island. We were well aware that a new generation of Puerto Ricans was being born and raised in the city, and that they demanded our close attention. It was important to help them learn their cultural origins. And, as will be seen, we did accomplish some of this.

Once again the news arrived of a plan to organize the large-scale emigration of workers from Puerto Rico to Arizona and New Mexico. In September the newspapers were publishing reports like, "Large contingent of Puerto Ricans brought over to work on the cotton plantations refuse to work for 50 cents a day. More than a hundred men, women, and children, having deserted the fields, are now living in total misery . . ."

Thus history was to repeat itself once again. The Puerto Rican workers, defying their swindling bosses, preferred to bear their misery with dignity. Some perished. Others were rescued by the Puerto Rican community in San Francisco. Still others managed, with great hardship and sacrifice, to find their way to the homes of relatives in New York.

For me personally, 1926 was a total disaster. When I finished my preparatory courses, I registered at the university. But paying tuition was too difficult; I couldn't come up with all the fees. I had no money. I had no job. My health was poor and my mood unsettled. I would have to give up, once and for all, whatever hope I had of acquiring a profession.

Thanks to my job washing bottles, I came down with an acute case of sinusitis. I had to miss work and, without giving me any notice, they replaced me. And on top of that—when it rains, it pours—my married life was becoming increasingly intolerable, and I finally had to end it. Separated from the love of my two children, who were the light of my life, I began a period of great sadness. Such was the disastrous downfall of a dreamer.

I spent my days wandering aimlessly around the city, bereft of all hope and ambition and feeling more despondent every day. My thanks for helping me to find my way out of that abyss go in large part to Joe Slavin. Joe was a comrade from the Young Socialists whom I hadn't seen in years. We ran into each other in the street and Joe, seeing my state of mind, dragged me to an appointment with his father, a prestigious doctor. With meticulous care, he opened up my sinuses to alleviate my sinusitis. Little by little I regained my health and with time my spiritual scars also healed . . . I decided to make a fresh start, as though I could begin my life all over again.

Marcelo Mendoza, a *tabaquero* from my hometown of Cayey, gave me a job at his little factory at 53rd Street and Eighth Avenue. In those days the streets between Sixth and Ninth avenues followed the curve of the elevated train line and were a filthy slum inhabited mostly by North American blacks. That whole neighborhood, down to Times Square, was riddled with speakeasies. It was prohibition: contraband and bootlegging were rampant.

The blacks, and poor people in general, used to patronize the bars on 53rd Street between Eighth and Ninth avenues. What they consumed went by the name of *maplé*—denatured alcohol. The more luxurious clubs, which were always hidden, were located near Broadway, on 52nd Street between Seventh and Eighth. One of them, owned by a Frenchman by the name of Louis, was especially famous . . . The owners of those establishments never seemed to have last names.

Louis' place took up the spacious basement of a building that you entered through an unobtrusive little cafeteria facing onto 52nd Street. At the back was a hallway with a door that seemed to open out onto a backyard. The clientele had to show some identification before they were allowed to go any further. An underground passage led to an adjacent building. That was the way out to 53rd Street. Thus the customers would go in on one side and leave by the other, so as not to cause any suspicion.

A large basement room was decorated with a certain amount of luxury. The walls were draped with curtains, not only for appearance's sake but also to cushion the noise. A band played all night. There was a floor show, as well as a dance floor. At one end, there was a bar, where ten and sometimes twenty bartenders would serve liquor from all over the world. At every door, and standing beside some of the tables, were men armed with billy clubs. Some had their hands in their pockets. Needless to say, they were standing guard.

I got to know the place because I used to go there to sell cigars. To give you an idea of how the patrons squandered their earnings, 10 cent cigars would go for $1.00. A glass of cognac was $3.00. As for women, they came in all nationalities. There were also young homosexuals, who cost twice as much as the women. I tell you, it was like in an old novel: every sort of vice could be had for the asking.

At the beginning of 1927 a subcommittee of the Puerto Rican Brotherhood conducted a study of the situation faced by Puerto Ricans living in New York. Their report, which was published in the Brotherhood's official bulletin, included the following: "The population of the [Puerton Rican] colony now exceeds 100,000, concentrated in the following areas: between 14th and 30th streets, from east to west, 10,000; from 90th to 116th streets, east of Fifth

Avenue, 20,000; between 110th and 125th, west of Fifth Avenue over to Manhattan Avenue, 40,000; over in Brooklyn around the Navy Yard, along Columbia Street, and the surrounding area, 25,000."

The same study found that there were fifteen Puerto Rican organizations in the various neighborhoods. As for voters, it stated that 5,000 had registered, 2,000 of these in the 19th District. Some 400 Puerto Ricans were reported to be employed in federal agencies in New York. A final piece of information was that there were approximately 200 grocery stores and over 125 restaurants owned by Puerto Ricans.

I believe that the information contained in the report was fairly accurate, although I remember that around the same time the New York Mission Society estimated that the number of Puerto Ricans living in New York was more like 150,000. The *New York Times* then published a figure of 200,000. As for registered voters, I believe that report's estimate was low.

In January classes began in the Ateneo Obrero. There were classes in English, political economy, sociology, and the history of the labor movement. Those in charge of the courses included Spencer Miller, August Claessens, and Emilie Bartok, socialist professors who volunteered their services.

Around that time socialist and progressive circles in New York were organizing to protest against the invasion of Nicaragua by the U.S. Marines. People were beginning to refer to César Augusto Sandino as the defender of his country. One of the activities in this campaign was the appeal the Alianza Obrera made to Fiorello La Guardia, whose district included our Barrio Latino. La Guardia was asked to take a public stand denouncing this imperialist act. And he did so.

Another momentous event that had us all up in arms was the trial of Sacco and Vanzetti, which was taking place up in Boston.

On June 6 there was a work stoppage to protest the death sentence handed down on those two proletarian martyrs—more than half-a-million workers in the New England states alone. Many cities across the country witnessed similar actions. In New York there was a huge demonstration that ended at Union Square. I was designated as the speaker representing Puerto Rico.

Toward the end of that year the Centro Obrero Español was formed. It included not only Spaniards but Latin Americans and

Puerto Ricans as well. Some of its founders were Ricardo Martínez, Miguel Cruz, Manuel González, Domingo García, Alfonso Machado, J. Fernández, and the Sephardic Jews Alberto Moreau, S. Fidias, and Leon Slavin.

Those were the years when the American Socialist Party was on the decline. Eugene V. Debs had died. The Communist Party/ U.S.A. was formed. A deadly conflict raged between the two parties, while each was also torn apart by internal struggles.

The Liga Puertorriqueña held several events over the course of 1926. One was an exhibition of pictures of the most illustrious Latin American, and of course Puerto Rican, figures. The Brotherood sponsored a lecture on Hostos by Antonio S. Pedreira at Columbia University. The Liga also organized an event to honor the legislative commission headed by Antonio R. Barceló for its efforts to introduce reforms on behalf of Puerto Rico.

That year also saw the emergence of several newspapers that represented the Puerto Rican community. Two *tabaqueros,* Guillermo Vargas and Carlos Cosme, published *El Machete Criollo. Metrópolis* was published by Alfonso Lastra Chárriez. And Ramón La Villa started a weekly of light humorous reading, which he called *Gráfico.* It was *Gráfico* that took on the greatest importance, and was to last for many years.

Partisan electoral politics once again sowed seeds of discord in the Puerto Rican community. The Republican Party ran a Puerto Rican, Víctor Fiol Ramos, for the city council seat in the 17th District. Many Puerto Ricans lived in that area, and the Brotherhood announced its support for the candidate. This gave rise to heated controversy. One side maintained that if a party nominated a Puerto Rican, this was enough to merit the backing of the entire community. Others, including the leadership of the Liga Puertorriqueña, held the opposite view: they claimed that it was unacceptable for a party machine, without the participation of the voters, to name a Puerto Rican just because he was Puerto Rican.

The polemics raged for several months. Even though the more recognized Puerto Rican groups refused to support the candidate, large numbers of Puerto Ricans went ahead and voted for him. But we were still far from seeing one of our kind win an elected office, whether as a Republican or a Democrat—or on any other ticket for that matter.

Around that time my physical ailments began to act up again. Dr. Slavin recommended a change of climate, and prescribed a trip to Arizona or Colorado. Under no condition, he stated, should I work in a cigar factory. Nothing irritated my sinus condition more than tobacco. What strange ideas our doctor friends have!

In any case, I was obliged to seek another type of work. And so, after thinking about it, I finally decided to become a salesman and began to walk the streets with samples from some of the cigar factories. Not getting very far, I suddenly had the idea of selling tobacco by the branch. By a stroke of good luck, I struck up relations with The Schwartz Tobacco Leaf, a Jewish-owned company located at 197 Water Street. In three weeks I made my first sale, which amounted to over $2,000, and from then on my sales were never under $5,000 a month. I became the firm's star salesman. For the first time in my life I came into some big money.

With this change in my economic situation my physical and spiritual condition took a turn for the better as well. I went back to dreaming, and to idealistic projects, and on March 20, 1927, I bought the weekly *Gráfico* from Ramón La Villa.

You must not simply take my word for it that *Gráfico* was the best paper in the Puerto Rican community so far. If you have any doubts, just go to the New York Public Library and have a look at their collection. I am confident—and proud—that that publication served Puerto Ricans, and all Hispanic people, well. We launched campaigns for better economic, political, and social conditions. Our editorials—which appeared in Spanish and English—addressed problems of housing, crime, inadequate services, civil rights, culture, and the arts. We defended the goals of the Puerto Rican struggle, and spoke out against dictators like Juan Vicente Gómez in Venezuela and Gerardo Machado in Cuba. No case of discrimination agaist a Puerto Rican was not condemned in the pages of *Gráfico*. In a word, it served, within its limited means, as a faithful eyewitness for the Puerto Rican community in New York.

Some of our most outstanding writers wrote for *Gráfico*. Most memorable were Cayetano Coll y Toste, Antonio J. Colorado, René Jiménez Malaret, Muna Lee de Muñoz Marín, Jesús Colón, Rafael Torres Mazzorana, Juan Bautista Pagán, Erasmo Vando, and Antonio González. Of those who assisted in its publication, I want especially to mention Ramón La Villa, Eugenio Nogueras, Francisco

Colón Berdecía, Simón Jou, Tomás Gares, Alberto O'Farril, Carlos M. de Castro, Enrique Besteiro, Luis Torres Colón, and Manuel Flores Cabrera.

The publishing venture cost me dearly. But it was well worth it, since it was a solid and lasting attempt to provide our community with a disinterested and independent mouthpiece. Unfortunately, there were still many squabbles and much hostility among the leaders of the organized groups, each of which was intent on entering the field with its own patched-together journalistic endeavor. Thus we continued to lack a spirit of unity and a genuine national consciousness. Yet, in spite of everything, we moved forward.

19. The consolidation of El Barrio, and new pages in its history

By now the Puerto Rican neighborhood extended from Lexington Avenue between 96th and 107th streets over to the beginning of the Italian section on First Avenue. Through this entire area, life was very much like what it was back home. Following the example set by the *tabaqueros*, whites and blacks lived together in harmony. There were many Hispanic *bodegas*, barbershops, and butchers. Branches of green plaintains hung in the store windows, and the sidewalks were lined with food and vegetable stands. In the stores and in the streets, all you heard was Spanish.

But the other national groups living in the area resented the constantly growing Puerto Rican population. For them the way of life of the *boricuas* was scandalous, and relations among the different nationalities were fraught with tension. Women would often clash while shopping, and at times the fights in the neighborhood bars would become serious. After the disturbances up in Harlem, this situation got even worse.

Hardly a day went by that a Puerto Rican child didn't come home from school with a black eye. Mothers lived in constant fear. The schoolchildren, of course, fought back. And it would have remained a squabble among children had racism not reared its ugly head. But it was not long before the adults began to step into the fray. One day—June 14, 1927, to be exact—on the corner of 96th Street and Third Avenue, a grown man kicked a young boy named Luis Berríos. An on-duty policeman who was standing nearby laughed it off, as though it were a joke. But at that moment a fellow Puerto Rican, Juan Sabater, happened to be passing. Ignoring everyone else, he jumped on the aggressor as though he were stomping out a raging fire, and he didn't stop until the man was carted off to the

151

hospital. Only then did the cop step in: he arrested the Puerto Rican on charges of felonious assault!

In a matter of minutes the news spread through the neighborhood. Whole groups of irate *jíbaros* poured into the streets to stand up for their kin, and this prevented the conflict from becoming even more serious than it was.

The many groups in the Puerto Rican community immediately met and agreed to mount a vocal protest against the city authorities. Another well-attended meeting was held at the Harlem Terrace. Some of the speakers were J. V. Alonso, J. N. Ocasio, Rafael Rivera, Luis Torres Colón, Alfonso Lastra Chárriez, and Blas Oliveras. There was an appeal for peace and tolerance, but everyone agreed that any further aggression had to be met in like manner.

This firm but calm approach had a positive effect in the neighborhood. Those who had shown ill will toward Puerto Ricans quieted down, or simply moved out. Our countrymen made it clear that we were in charge in that part of town.

The Puerto Rican community had its bad types, of course, like any other community. The fact is, though, that so many lowlifes of other nationalities—many stowaways from the Latin American countries—had wound up in El Barrio that there had been a considerable increase in crime and vandalism. And the sad thing is that these people were usually taken for Puerto Ricans.

Which is not to say that our countrymen never engaged in illegal activities. But there is evidence that we were accused of more crimes than we actually committed. I exposed this injustice in *Gráfico* after studying all the police reports filed between 1930 and 1933 having to do with hold-ups and robberies.

Unfortunately, this slander against our people not only served to give us a bad image; what is perhaps worse, it undermined our own regard for ourselves as Puerto Ricans. Like any people, all of us born in Puerto Rico, and our descendants here in New York, must do all we can to preserve our heritage as people of good will, as well as that quality which has always distinguished the best of our kind: our dignity.

Washington had stepped up its campaign of aggression against Nicaragua. The press was filled with horror stories about the "gang of bandits" down there, and about their ringleader, César Augusto Sandino. Socrates Sandino, the leader's brother, was in New York at the time and met the slander campaign head-on. North American liberals, progressives, socialists, and communists made common cause with the Nicaraguan people.

One of the many protests against the invasion was a large rally held on February 19, 1928, at the Labor Temple on 14th Street and Second Avenue. The principal speakers were Scott Nearing, the well-known author of *Dollar Diplomacy;* Leon Ganett, editor of the *Nation;* John Brophy, president of the International Mineworkers' Union; Juan De Jesús, president of the Philippine Club; Ricardo Martínez of the Unión Obrera Venezolana; H. C. Wu of the Chinese Writers' Society; and the author of these memoirs in his capacity as editor of *Gráfico.* After this event the struggle against the invasion of Nicaragua took on a new dimension.

Shortly afterward, while visiting New York, Santiago Iglesias spoke at an event held by the Liga Puertorriqueña without once mentioning that act of United States imperialist aggression. Not only that, he even praised Washington's policies toward Latin America. The socialist labor leader's attitude was bitterly and widely censured by leaders of the Puerto Rican community in New York.

Meanwhile, Puerto Ricans were beginning to show greater militancy at the workplace. An example was when they brought all work to a halt at a button factory in order to back up their demand for better pay. And they got what they wanted, even without the support of the recognized unions. In fact, the A.F. of L. locals still treated the struggles of Puerto Rican workers with indifference.

That year the Republican Party won the election and Herbert Hoover moved into the White House. At a time when Nicaragua was being invaded by the Marines, Haiti was under military occupation, exports from the Dominican Republic were rigidly controlled, Cuba was being dominated through the Platt Amendment, Puerto Rico was being subjected to a process of assimilation, and Colombia was bleeding from the wound of Panama—at such a time the newly elected president chose to pay a goodwill visit to the countries of Latin America. This served to heighten anti-imperialist sentiment in progressive circles throughout the hemisphere, and especially in New York.

In the large hall of the Park Palace, right in the heart of Harlem, a public debate was held between students from the Universidad de Puerto Rico and Columbia University on the subject of United States intervention in the Caribbean. Our team was made up of Antonio J. Colorado, Gabriel Guerra, and Vicente Roura. The jury was composed of Columbia professors Fernando de los Ríos, William Shepherd, and José Padín, and the president of the Hispanic Chamber of Commerce, Eduardo López.

The young men from the United States made an able showing, but the jury, with the support of the audience, decided in favor of the Puerto Ricans. Our team proved superior both by virtue of the position it took and the brilliance of the arguments it put forth. "Unless it declares war," we held, "the United States has no right to intervene in the Caribbean."

At around the same time the case of a Puerto Rican sentenced to die in the electric chair gripped the community. It concerned Félix Ostolaza, who had been convicted of murder in the first degree. Had it not been for the intervention of several organizations, especially the Federación Puertorriqueña de Clubs Demócratas, Ostolaza would have suffered the death penalty. But thanks to the work of some good lawyers, it was proved that the accused man had acted in self-defense. And so we saved our compatriot from the electric chair.

When the news reached New York of the destruction caused by the San Felipe hurricane in Puerto Rico, a relief campaign began immediately. Aid was sent to the victims through the Red Cross. To raise funds we held an artists' festival at the Star Casino. Fiorello La Guardia offered us his wholehearted cooperation. I still remember when Pedro San Miguel, Alberto Hernández, and I went down to visit him in his offices.

"Godo di vederla"—"Pleased to see you"—he said in Italian when we stepped into his private chambers. "Voglia scusarmi un momento"—"Please excuse me for just a minute."

He was on the phone, and could only say hello. But once he hung up he turned his attention to us, saying in English, "Forgive me for making you wait. I am at your service."

"We came to ask for your cooperation on behalf of the hurricane victims in Puerto Rico. We would like to organize a cultural festival . . ."

We needed to say no more.

"That's a wonderful idea!" And, reaching for the phone, "Things like this have to be taken care of now, not later."

While we were still there he made a few calls, and finished by saying, "The place and date are already worked out. We'll pay a nominal fee for the hall. As for artists, you will have the best playing on Broadway this season. Hispanic artists I leave up to you. It'll be a show like there's never been in Harlem before."

That's what La Guardia was like. I might add that the event was fantastic. All of the artists performed for free. Once the few costs were paid, all the proceeds went to the hurricane victims in Puerto Rico.

Fiorello La Guardia enjoyed great support in the Puerto Rican community. As soon as he was named Republican Party candidate for mayor, the Puerto Rican Republican organization pledged its support. The leaders of that group were R. Villar, Juan B. Matos, Fernando Torres, Frank Torres, Francisco M. Rivera, and Felipe Gómez.

As time went by the main areas where Puerto Ricans lived changed, both in location and social composition. By 1929 the old neighborhood on the East Side, made up mostly of *tabaqueros,* had moved up toward Harlem, and El Barrio was finally consolidated as the heart of the Puerto Rican community in New York.

Living conditions, far from improving, grew worse and worse. Once a building was occupied by our countrymen, no more maintenance was done on it. Garbage collection also became inadequate, and the whole neighborhood gave the impression of being totally neglected. Living quarters, which included cellars and basements, were packed with people. Men, women, and children shared what little room they had with rats, cockroaches, and garbage.

El Barrio took on its own distinctive features. There arose a culture typical of that common experience of people fighting for survival in the face of hostile surroundings. In the long run, that culture was to bear fruit in its own right.

Small pharmacies and *botánicas* sprang up throughout the neighborhood. There wasn't much difference between one and the other— *boticas* and *botánicas.* Both dealt in herbs like lemon verbena, sage, and rue, and they even carried pieces of the devil's claw . . . Doctors, witches, druggists, mind readers, dentists, spiritualists, palm readers, all shared the same clientele. Misery always seems to breed superstition, and when there is no hope of getting out of a life of poverty, dreams are the only consolation left. This helps explain the role of religion, in all its popular forms. It also helps explain why there was so much gambling, as is always true of destitute communities. And, of course, there was dancing.

Scores of groups competed in organizing dances, and personality and beauty contests. Young women, especially, were drawn to that kind of flashy show. But the worst thing about these activities wasn't that they were all so frivolous; it was that many of them were really just a front used by a whole range of good-for-nothings to win favors and make profits. Some of those hustlers would set themselves up as president or secretary-treasurer of some nonexistent organization whose only service was to line the pockets of its founders. A few such groups were, no doubt, on the level. But there were a lot of "coronations," with some naive little backwoods girl as "queen," that were organized by operators who would "clean up," as they would say, a few hundred dollars in the process.

At those festivities there were often little skits, supposedly funny, in which the characters were always *jíbaros* from Puerto Rico. The skits would consist of a few ridiculous scenes where some fool would think he was a comic actor just because he had a peasant's hat on his head and came on stage in patched-up pants playing *maracas*. There was always someone in the audience who would protest. But that's what people wanted. And I should also point to one notable exception: Erasmo Vando, a versatile actor, who with his group "Los Jíbaros" staged performances that did capture the genuine flavor of Puerto Rican peasant life.

The events sponsored by the Centro Obrero Español, which had become a focal point for many social concerns, were quite different. Many groups were organized at the center, including the Liga Anti-imperialista Puertorriqueña, which was headed by Domingo García, Antonio Rivas, Sandalio Marcial, Concepción Gómez, Angel María Dieppa, and José Santiago.

That group put out the paper *Vida Obrera (Workers' Life)* as part of its union organizing drive. One fruit of its effort was the organization of a Hispanic branch of the Amalgamated Restaurant and Cafeteria Workers' Union; its founding director was Pablo Martínez.

As for the arts, I must point especially to the founding of Puerto Rico Literario. Some of our fellow countrymen, who in the course of their lives achieved things of some note, set up this society in June 1929. It defined its aim as "cultivating Spanish letters, promoting an interest in study, and upholding the faith of Puerto Rican youth in the cause of independence."

We met at the public library branch on 115th Street, in a little office graciously put at our disposal by our compatriot Pura Belpré, who was a librarian. Registered members of the group were soon to excel in many different areas of Puerto Rican life and letters. Francisco Acevedo was a pioneer in radio broadcasting in San Juan. Lorenzo Piñeiro, also a journalist, later became a lawyer and an outstanding leader of the Partido Independentista Puertorriqueño, which he represented in the U.S. Senate. Max Vázquez was an outstanding journalist and writer; Bartolo Malavé, a lawyer; Rafael Mariotta, another journalist; René Jiménez Malaret, an essayist; Juan Bautista Pagán, a journalist and author; Luis Hernández Aquino, one of the foremost poets of his generation; Erasmo Vando, an actor . . . That was the group, then, with whom I had the honor of sharing some of my fondest hopes and dreams.

At around that time Rafael Hernández was making the rounds in New York. These were his bohemian days, when he was hard at work. His song "Lamento borincano" began to fill the air in El Barrio . . . We were on the eve of the most serious economic depression ever to hit the United States of America.

Part 5
THE DEPRESSION YEARS

20. Two reprehensible but timely events in my life

In El Barrio and throughout Harlem, every day seemed to be a holiday. The streets were filled with people twenty-four hours a day. Unemployment was rampant. Hardly a day went by that one Puerto Rican family or another didn't have its furniture dumped into the street. The struggle against eviction was on.

But our people didn't seem to be too upset by the economic depression. The fact that the crisis extended clear across the country made it a little more bearable for people who were used to living at the edge of misery. Pulling the belt one notch tighter didn't seem to make that much of a difference.

The *bodegas* had more and more uncollectable debts. According to the police, the crime rate had doubled: armed assault, robbery, prostitution, rum-running and, of course, *la bolita,* that poor people's lottery that builds up your hopes while a handful of "bankers" rake in the big money . . . It was at that time, in New York City, that Rafael Hernández composed his immortal song, "Lamento borincano."

My own situation had gone downhill. The tobacco warehouse where I was working went bankrupt. To my deep dismay I had to end my journalistic adventure at *Gráfico.* I once again fell into the army of the unemployed, which by then numbered in the millions. I went back to making cigars and "hawking" them without a license for whatever price I could get. But I had to cut that out too. There were so many *tabaqueros* doing the same thing that there was no market.

At that point in my life I found myself forced to become involved in two disgraceful activities. The first had to do with the numbers racket.

In the summer of 1929 I was living with my sister. Abandoned by her shameless tyrant of a husband, my dear sister, who had a baby son, was going through one of those trying times in life. To make things worse, she was also very sick. So I came to her aid, and we put together what little we had to make ends meet.

Just about every day I'd be out in the streets early in the morning hoping and dreaming that some miracle would come my way and change my fortunes. I remember walking from 115th Street all the way down to 59th Street and across the south end of Central Park. By noon I was down near my friend Mendoza's little factory. I arrived just as he was getting ready to go out for lunch. He invited me to join him, and I of course accepted.

Then we went back to the shop and continuing my free ride I set to work making up a batch of cigars to take with me. That's what I was doing when I was suddenly faced with the opportunity of landing a good job, and maybe even the chance to get rich quick. It happened like this:

The apartment next door to Mendoza's little cigar factory was the headquarters of a man named Francis, a black man who was one of the kings of the numbers racket in Harlem. He had more than half a dozen people working for him, each earning $100 a week. All he did was go over the lists his "runners" brought him every day. Together they made up a network that extended through all of Harlem and El Barrio.

The winning numbers would be announced at 3 o'clock in the afternoon. Going over the lists took the two previous hours, and once the people working there had started there was no communication with anyone outside. No one was allowed to leave until it was all figured out and the winners announced.

But somehow, no matter how tight the system, someone would learn the lucky number ahead of time, and people had time to play it before it was announced. Sometimes those last-minute bets would clean out the bank and Francis would be threatened with ruin.

Well, that afternoon the "banker" was at Mendoza's and started to complain bitterly of his troubles.

"They're robbing me blind," he whispered confidentially, "and I don't even know how they do it."

And for some reason it entered my head to ask him, "Tell me, Francis, how much would you pay someone to find out how they do it?"

"Jesus, I'd give him a fat reward, and a good job to boot."

"I'll look into it," I said, not bothering to give it much thought since all I could think of was my poor sister and her little boy.

I went through his office with him. Then I watched his employees as they worked. For the entire time they were going over the lists, all telephone lines were disconnected. The windows were closed— some of them were in any case permanently boarded up. There was no communication between the people inside and the street. No one was permitted to move until he had finished his job. It was a tough problem indeed.

I stood watch in front of the building. For a few days I just hung around on the sidewalk, smoking absentmindedly. More than a week went by and I still didn't have any idea how to unravel the mystery. From time to time I would try to imagine how much money Francis would give me once I got to the bottom of the "robbery," as the banker called it. Among other things, I planned to get married again. Whether that was my main incentive or not, I started to feel like Sherlock Holmes.

Every day at the same hour I would see a boy going through the streets selling magazines. "*Life, Vogue, Mercury*!" he'd shout. He'd reach the corner and then turn and go back down the same side of the street, calling out the same words at the top of his lungs. One day I noticed that he was carrying some other magazines but that he only called out the names of those three. "Ah, hah!" I said to myself. The next day I bought the three magazines from him. The boy resumed his customary route up to the corner, and then started back toward where I was standing. Then I heard him shout out the names of the magazines I had just bought from him . . . "The mystery is solved!" I exclaimed to myself.

I felt it was solved when I saw that the boy went on calling out the same magazines at the top of his lungs even though he had sold the only copies he had. On the following day I had Francis stand watch with me. And when the boy appeared and was about to start hawking his magazines, we grabbed him and shoved him into Mendoza's.

The kid had copies of ten different magazines, and Francis bought all of them. The boy seemed very nervous and wanted to hightail it out of there. But we didn't let him go. Francis interrogated him, offered him money, and finally he spilled the beans . . . Each magazine, he confessed, stood for a number. Usually he would have ten of them, from one to zero. The three that he called out, in order, indicated the number that had come up that day, and there was still time to place bets on it. It turned out that it was Francis' nephew who had thought up the trick.

That same day Francis gave me $500 and offered me a job paying $100 a week. I accepted the reward but turned down the job. I must admit that to this very day my hands still burn from having accepted that money. I had helped save one of the powerful hustlers in Harlem from ruin. The necessity of the moment had forced me to do it, but under no circumstances was I going to take the job. I had always condemned that kind of "business."

It should be pointed out, though, that quite a few Puerto Ricans made money as "bankers" in the numbers racket. I won't mention any names so as not to cause their families any embarrassment. But the truth is that even among those noted "personalities" who were commissioned to go to Washington to lobby for Puerto Rico there was always a "banker" or two. I mention only one of them, known as the "Crazy Cuban," who was one of the organizers of an inaugural party for Governor Theodore Roosevelt at the Park Palace . . . All of them, of course, preached morality and a good life.

Shady deals and unscrupulous transactions have always flourished in New York City. For the most part, the city has been governed by swindlers and racketeers, protected by Tammany Hall. It hardly comes as a surprise, then, to see "bankers" in the numbers racket in high political and social positions. A good number of Puerto Ricans and other Hispanics began to show that they, too, had the talent and know-how to make the most of the situation, which is why so many people have the idea—born out by the facts—that every new wave of immigrants produces its own mafia.

Now it happens that one of the strongmen in the budding Puerto Rican mafia was someone I knew very well, and he was always trying to prove to me what a good friend he was. When he found out that I was in bad straits, he offered me a job. Seeing the negative look on my face, he went on: "It's a nice little job, but mind you it has nothing to do with gambling. I know a cabaret where they're looking for someone to brighten things up. You like to crack a good joke . . . It would be a perfect spot for you."

"It has never occurred to me that I'd be any good at that."

"Well, I'm sure you'd be a big hit. I always read your 'fool stories' in *Gráfico*. Stories like that would be just the thing to introduce the floor shows."

"You know I can't stand that kind of entertainment."

"Don't be silly! You don't have to get mixed up in anything. You'd go to the cabaret to work, that's it. Look here, I happen to be a silent partner in a place up here in Harlem. I will have my agent pay you $40 a week, plus all you can eat and drink. You go down there Friday night, after eleven, and give it all you've got!"

The offer made me think. Turn down $40 a week, plus food and drinks on the house, when I was so hungry I was swallowing my tongue . . . After mulling it over deep down inside, I set my reservations aside and showed up at my new job on the day indicated.

The so-called nighttime café was located—as that type of establishment usually was—in a basement on a street in El Barrio. A married couple, who weren't Puerto Rican, acted as hosts. The clientele was mostly older men, little dandies with money, and a few professional types. The place, I might add, was well protected by the police, who could always count on their "share." So at least it was safe around there.

The dancers in the floor show were women of all different nationalities; they seemed to have come with their husbands, but the men with them were actually their pimps. They would dance half naked, and the most popular number was the "pajama dance." Between numbers, the customers would make their easy "pick-ups"—as I think people call it nowadays.

I worked there for three months. I performed the variety-show numbers: one show at midnight and another at 3 in the morning. In the middle of my routine I would always tell a story. I guess they liked my performance, since I always got tips. Quite a few times men and women would show their appreciation by asking me beforehand to dedicate that night's story to them. Financially I did all right, but I got more and more disgusted at that dungheap of a place. One night, without giving it much thought and without saying goodbye to anybody, I decided never to set foot in that dive again . . . And so I was out of work all over again.

But with the money I had earned during those two experiences disgusting as they were), I paid off all my debts. I never liked owing anything to anybody. Which may be why I always had a reputation of being well off. The reason is that I didn't go around crying about how poor I was. One thing I know is that our friends who have money don't have anything to do with us when we're down and out.

By the same token, I've always believed that an empty stomach and empty pockets don't go well together. And then, especially in a big city, a man is twice as badly off when he's not only hungry but goes around wearing a dirty shirt with no jacket or tie. Nothing is less likely to bring about a change of fortune than wearing misery on your face. Which is why I made a habit of dressing that much better the worse off I was financially.

Like the nobleman in the story, I was back to walking around New York with a toothpick in my mouth.

In spite of President Hoover's rosy promises, the economic depression in the United States couldn't be plugged up with one hand. Following Hoover's ridiculous advice, the unemployed in the streets of the big cities resorted to selling apples. Others called for mass action, but the police smashed their demonstrations.

On February 11, 1931, over sixty thousand unemployed rallied at Times Square demanding jobs. The city government unleashed waves of mounted police against them. In Washington, meanwhile, violence was also used to silence the clamor of the unemployed veterans . . . In New York alone seventy-five thousand poor people signed up for assistance at the police stations.

But the government offered no aid of any kind. The public assistance program had gone bankrupt. Under such conditions it is no surprise that crime and immorality were rampant in all poor neighborhoods.

This situation produced a whole crop of shysters and crooks who fed on Puerto Ricans and blacks whenever they fell into the clutches of the law, whether they were guilty or not. Needless to say, the rich racketeers and their agents, the fat cats of the gangs, were never bothered by the police. And the reason is obvious: "police protection" could be arranged for a price.

All of this corruption began to come into the open as a result of an investigation conducted by the district attorney's office. Harlem and the surrounding areas were the center of attention. Hundreds of witnesses came forward to testify against the swindlers, who included politicians, lawyers, and bailbondsmen. Among other things, they uncovered a racket dealing in birth certificates from Puerto Rico.

That was a thriving business in those times. The evidence showed that there was a network connecting San Juan, Havana, and New York. Criminals of all kinds and descriptions came from many countries disguised as Puerto Ricans—and so it was Puerto Ricans who ended up suffering abuse and prejudice. According to one estimate, over fifteen hundred people, mostly professional criminals, purchased Puerto Rican birth certificates. They went for $500. Which is why on one single day the New York newspapers ran the following headlines: "Gangs riddle Harlem children with bullets . . ." "Armed man guns down businessman in Harlem . . ." "Hoodlums hold up Hispanics in Harlem . . ." "Crime wave in Harlem . . ." "Mother kills two children and commits suicide in Harlem . . ." "Hold up store-owner in Harlem . . ." "Large number of Hispanics arrested for giant jewel theft . . ." "Round-up of number runners in Harlem . . ."

And so forth and so on.

21. Luck smiles and I make money, without for a moment abandoning the struggle

Just as the economic situation was getting increasingly serious, I had a stroke of good luck that seemed like a fantasy come true. After the job in the cabaret I went back to rolling cigars in a little factory owned by my friend Manuel Samalot. One day I got a phone call from one of the creditors of the tobacco company where I used to work and which, as I mentioned earlier, had declared bankruptcy. The man wanted to see me immediately. Thinking he might have an offer to make me, I rushed right down to his office. The first thing he had said was, "I would like to enter into partnership with you and open a tobacco-leaf warehouse in Harlem."

"And what happens if I don't have a penny to my name?" I exclaimed.

"That's not necessary. I'll put up the capital and the credit, and you your ability as a salesman."

"Sounds all right to me. But how do I stay alive while the business is getting off the ground?"

"You will receive a salary so that you can live regardless of what happens to the business. If at the end of the first year there are any profits, we'll divide them equally between us."

"I accept."

"Okay. The first thing to do is find the right location. Here's a check for $1000 . . . Open an account in the nearest bank in the name of our partnership."

In those days vacant buildings were a dime a dozen anywhere in Harlem. I found a splendid site on the corner of 117th Street and Lexington Avenue. And I got down to work with all the devotion that can be imagined.

The business grew by leaps and bounds. I set up a long-term credit plan for all of the small cigar factories. I sold leaves to unemployed *tabaqueros* who were producing on the side. Since I agreed that they could pay me small amounts each month, many, many of those *chinchaleros* became my clients. Every month I would pick out at least one honest worker and help him open up his own factory. Sometimes I'd go so far as to pay his first month's rent. I soon became one of the main suppliers in the retail leaf-tobacco business. And this was a time when the wholesale tobacco warehouses were overflowing with tobacco, with no way of getting rid of their stock.

By around November of our first year in business I was handling a surprisingly large number of accounts. Once again I was into big money, this time as a partner in my own firm. And from one day to the next, almost without being aware of what I was doing, I embarked on my second matrimonial voyage.

Of my personal life I shall say nothing, as that is of little importance. I want to bring this chapter of my life as a thriving businessman to a close, even if I have to cover it rather quickly. Suffice it to say, then, that our competitors felt threatened by my aggressive approach. They waged an out-and-out war against me, and tried to drive me out by going to the government and accusing me of selling goods to "bootleggers" who worked without licenses. Then came the investigations and lawsuits. The upshot was that profits were cut to a bare minimum and our partnership was left with nothing but a stack of debts we couldn't pay. We resolved to pay off our creditors, which we did. And so, after that brief era of abundance, I was back in the ranks of the penniless.

But don't think that I was completely out of the struggle while I was managing the tobacco business. My own warehouse, in fact, served as a center for discussing battle plans against the Machado dictatorship in Cuba. A clandestine group founded with that end in view, called the Legión de la Flor Roja (Legion of the Red Flower) met at my place. Some of those who took part were the Cubans Andrés Garmendía, Prudencio Fernández Trueba, Alvaro Moreno, General Alemañy, Olivín Zaldívar, and J. Medina Reyes, Sabás Vega from the Yucatán, the Dominican Tulio Cestero Burgos, and myself, a Puerto Rican.

In the spring of 1931 we concentrated on an effort that was being made to send an armed expedition to Cuba. A ship and ample military supplies had been purchased, and over 150 volunteers awaited orders to set sail from New York. Our group was defeated, though, when it came time to select the commander of the expedition. I was anything but pleased when General Menocal was named to head the revolt against Machado.* It seemed to me that this was nothing more than replacing one bigwig with another, and I resigned. But even then I continued to help organize the armed expedition.

The plans were upset by Machado's spies, who revealed our preparations to the American authorities. Some of the volunteers, including most of the leaders, were arrested. Only thirty-three men made it to the ship, which was anchored outside of United States waters. The rest never made it.

Nevertheless, despite all the problems, the expedition managed to land in Cuba. Machado met it with a sizable army. The revolutionaries fought bravely but were defeated. Three of those who came out alive were members of Flor Roja: Montiel, Alvaro Moreno, and Sabás Vega.

On February 3, 1932, the Democratic Party presidential candidate addressed the nation in the first of what were to become his well-known fireside chats. The working class, and the American people in general, listening on their radios, were impressed by Franklin Delano Roosevelt's reassuring words. In simple terms he described what he proposed to do, if elected, to return the country to prosperity. He would launch large-scale public-works projects, giving jobs to millions of unemployed people; he would have the government take the initiative in exploiting the vast sources of hydroelectric power; he would bring together the best brains the country had to offer . . . That speech, and the many that followed, spread a spirit of optimism across the United States.

By that time 15 million workers were unemployed. New York was one of the cities most seriously affected. The winter of 1932 was particularly harsh, and in the middle of February the whole city was blanketed in snow. Around twelve thousand men were hired by City Hall to clean up the streets. Many Puerto Ricans jumped at the opportunity to make some money, and what a sight it was to see

---

*Mario García Menocal (1866–1941) was president of Cuba from 1913 to 1921. A leader in the fight for independence from Spain, he later became a conservative politician. As president he initiated a "businessman's" government that was widely criticized as corrupt and arbitrary. In 1931 he led an abortive revolt against Machado, after which he went into exile in the United States. When the Machado government fell he returned to Cuba, running unsuccessfully for president in 1936.

them all wrapped up in rags, their necks covered with old news-papers, swinging their shovels and shivering to the bone.

It is worth noting that between 1930 and 1931, twenty-five thousand suicides were reported in New York, a figure which included thirty-five Puerto Ricans.

The wave of protests continued unabated, even after the authorities called out the police and the army (as in the veterans' demonstration in Washington) to put down the masses. But all the force and all the beatings, far from quelling the demonstrators, only stirred up public opinion even more. All progressive people lined up behind Roosevelt.

But when the Democratic Party won the election in November 1932, the Puerto Ricans in New York lost their strongest ally in the U.S. Congress, Fiorello La Guardia. As mentioned, he was running on the Republican Party ticket, and the avalanche of votes for Roosevelt brought with it the victory of the Democratic candidate in El Barrio, J. J. Lanzetta.

At about that time, the Liga Puertorriqueña became increasingly inactive. Many of the old members and some of the leaders wanted the group to move in directions more in tune with the current situation. This gave rise to the founding of the Club Eugenio María de Hostos, whose first board of directors was composed of Jesús Colón, Alberto Rivera, Isabel O'Neill, María Alamo Cerra, Manuel Flores Cabrera, Juan Rovira, and the author of these memoirs.

The intensification of the social struggle breathed new life into radical organizations in the United States, especially the Communist Party. The Communists began to play a leading role in the trade unions and in organizing the unemployed. In the poor neighborhoods they organized rent strikes and headed the struggle against eviction. In Harlem and El Barrio, too, the influence of the Communists—whose ranks included many blacks and quite a few Puerto Ricans—was becoming more and more evident.

It was around this time that an unfortunate incident stirred up conflict between Puerto Rican Communists and nationalists. To the nationalists, all Puerto Ricans—no matter where they found themselves—were supposed to dedicate their enthusiasm and support to the struggle for the independence of their homeland. They even went so far as to insist that Puerto Ricans who became involved in the immediate social struggles in New York were betraying their primordial patriotic duty. In their view, *boricuas* in New York were not emigrants but "exiles," and their only thought should be the redemption of our native soil and their prompt return to Puerto Rico.

Puerto Rican workers, and especially the Communists and their sympathizers, rejected this position. Although there was no argument about the need to fight for Puerto Rican independence, they did not accept that this should involve folding their arms and doing nothing about the exploitation being suffered by Puerto Ricans in New York. Such conditions gave the immediate, practical struggle a high priority.

As long as these opposing points of view remained matters for debate, no major problems arose. But soon Puerto Rican nationalists and Communists began to challenge each other's positions at some of the rallies held in the streets of El Barrio. Speakers would be interrupted by questions from the crowd, which led them to accuse each other of "wrecking" the rally. Next thing you know some of them got involved in street fights, which degenerated further into a series of personal encounters. In one such squabble a young Puerto Rican, Angel María Feliú, a nationalist, was fatally wounded—and the crime was attributed to the Communists.

Neither group, of course, had any criminal intentions. The unfortunate event was the result of heated feelings on the part of individuals. But for a long time thereafter it held back the growth of the social struggle among Puerto Ricans and all Hispanics in New York. And needless to say there were those who wanted to seize the opportunity to play up the incident by firing up ill feeling and destroying the unity of the people.

President Roosevelt hadn't completed his first year when it was already clear that more than simple emergency measures were needed to put the country's economy back on its feet. The debate between conservatives and progressives became more intense. Whatever new legislation the White House sent to Congress was attacked by the reactionaries. New Deal forces had to expand their base of popular support. The labor movement began to take an increasingly radical posture. Unionization of workers in heavy industry was in full swing.

At the same time, new political forces were appearing on the scene. One very significant example was the establishment of the Fusion Party, which united progressive Democrats and Republicans behind Fiorello La Guardia's candidacy for mayor of New York City. On September 29, 1933, the Fusionists nominated a Puerto Rican, J. M. Vivaldi, to run for the state assembly from the 17th district.

The Fusion Party established an Hispanic division, based in Harlem. The leadership included Vivaldi, Enrique Torregrosa, Víctor Fiol, Salguero Font, Florencio Ruiz, Antonio González, Félix Caro, J. D. López, Miguel Collazo, and Luis Caballero.

Meanwhile the trade union struggle of Puerto Rican workers continued to grow, especially among hotel and restaurant workers and in the needle trades. Many of our countrymen were employed in those lines of work, and during the year they held several work stoppages and mass pickets.

The Harlem section of the Communist Party put up candidates for the state assembly and city council. These candidates won the support of the Liga Antiimperialista Puertorriqueña, the Centro Obrero Español, and several labor unions.

Heading up the Fusionist forces, La Guardia carried out an extremely effective electoral campaign. He kept his rivals in the traditional parties constantly on the defensive. He campaigned in the poor neighborhoods and explained what measures he would take if elected mayor. To the surprise of all the local newspapers and to the shame of Tammany Hall, the Fusionists swept the election by a margin of over 200,000 votes. And thus began Fiorello La Guardia's reign in City Hall.

The newly founded Club Hostos quickly became the center of many activities, including classes in Spanish and in Hispanic culture for children and young people, and a vast number of lectures and meetings. Filiberto Vázquez, for example, gave a talk on the "Foundations of the Nationalist Struggle in Puerto Rico," and Max Vázquez gave one on "Russian Literature Before the Revolution of 1917"—which gives an idea of the kinds of topics that were discussed at the club.

The Junta Nacionalista also sponsored a number of public events, one of which concerned the Congreso Estudiantil Inter-Americano being held in Costa Rica. The event centered around a report delivered by the delegate of the students from Puerto Rico, Francisco Pagán Rodríguez.

An equally active group was the Liga Antiimperialista Puertorriqueña. The Cuban intellectual Leonardo Fernández Sánchez, one of the most admired orators of the time, came to speak in its hall. The theme of his speech was Puerto Rico, and particularly the relationship between the agrarian problem and sugar production.

In May 1933 a famous incident occurred between the multimillionaire John D. Rockefeller and Diego Rivera, the Mexican painter. Diego Rivera had contracted to paint a series of murals in Rockefeller Center, for which he was to be paid a small fortune. The artist presented an elaborate plan of the project, which was accepted. But after he had finished his first mural, Rockefeller hit the ceiling when he recognized a picture of Lenin stretching out his arms to clasp hands with a Negro and a soldier. The leading representative of U.S. finance capital demanded that Diego Rivera paint something else; this, in his opinion "was not a work of art."

Diego refused of course. The whole city was talking about the controversy. A huge picketline was organized in front of Rockefeller Center. But the millionaire would not give in. The mural ended up being destroyed by that "great patron of the arts." Diego Rivera's principled stand won admiration throughout the world.

Meanwhile, the Roosevelt years did not seem to bring many changes in our Island's fortunes. Our hope that, with the New Deal, governors with somewhat greater intellectual and administrative competence would be appointed were destroyed by bitter reality. The first to receive the appointment, strictly for the support he mustered in Florida during the election campaign, was a certain Gore. No sooner had he taken office than, on a visit to his home state, he declared that "independence would bring ruin" to Puerto Rico. If Puerto Rico were independent, he went on, it would lose free entry of its sugar into the United States. Florida would be the beneficiary, since it would be able to take the Island's share of the sugar market. For that reason, he extended an invitation to the large landowners in Puerto Rico to move their sugar plantations and mills to Florida. He not only ranted and raved along these lines, but he even went so far as to suggest the massive emigration of Puerto Rican workers to Florida. We protested against that idea in New York, and even got a campaign going in Puerto Rico. Our position caught on, and the hair-brained scheme never got off the ground.

Another public act that was to prove damaging to Puerto Ricans was committed by the First Lady, Mrs. Eleanor Roosevelt. On her return from a well-publicized trip to Puerto Rico in April 1934, she spoke at a benefit held in her honor by the Women's Trade Union

League in New York. She told of the deep impression the dire poverty she found on the Island had made on her, and went on to say: "Tuberculosis is widespread everywhere, just as it is in the Puerto Rican community here in New York . . . I assume that none of you will be hiring any of them in your homes, but however careful we may be in rearing our children, they can still come into contact with one of those sick people in the streets or in the schools. And tuberculosis is an extremely contagious disease . . ."

Those were her words, spoken without malice and with the best of intentions. But the consequences, at least in the short run, could only hurt Puerto Ricans, especially those living in New York. Thousands of us were working in restaurants and cafeterias, and came into contact with food that was served to the public. The chances of finding, and of holding onto, jobs in that kind of work became dimmer than ever. It was even harder on all the Puerto Rican women working as domestics and nursemaids. And so, to add to the usual discrimination, the population was led to fear that our countrymen would infect them with tuberculosis!

"Isn't that something. Even when they try to do us a favor, they only bring more harm to Puerto Ricans . . ." That's what I said to myself, and I decided that we had to do something about it.

22. Of how even the best of intentions can sometimes do more harm than good, and other events

The correlation between tuberculosis and Puerto Ricans established by Mrs. Roosevelt after her trip to Puerto Rico had immediate, and prejudicial, consequences. The New York City Department of Health tightened its restrictions on the little cigar factories where so many of our countrymen worked, whether as owners or as employees. Countless domestic workers lost their jobs, and so did those in hotels and restaurants. The real or imaginary danger was used as an excuse not to promote Puerto Rican workers and to condemn them to menial jobs as dishwashers and the like.

We were quick to respond to Mrs. Roosevelt's ill-advised words. At the time I was chairman of the Club Hostos and president of the Liga Puertorriqueña, and in those capacities I sent the First Lady a telegram informing her of the distressing result of her statements. She either didn't—or didn't want to—understand, and brushed aside our objections in rather angry terms.

The newspapers, both in New York and San Juan, reported our protest, labeling us "ingrates" for failing to appreciate "the humanitarian lady's show of generosity." Needless to say, it was people whose children would not be affected by the consequences of Mrs. Roosevelt's statements who repudiated our position! But I refused to be intimidated, and carried on my press campaign with comments like, "The portrait offered by Mrs. Roosevelt is not favorable; on the contrary, it is damaging to us . . ." "Anyone who has taken the trouble to study the impoverished conditions in which our people live knows full well what it is that caused it . . ." "We sons of Puerto Rico did not come here because we wanted to. We live in New York out of necessity. Our problems cannot be solved by doing what Mrs. Roosevelt has done and portraying Puerto Ricans as a racial group afflicted with contagious diseases so that a few charitable Americans can give us alms while the rest—the majority—do nothing but insult us . . ."

Shortly thereafter something happened that, unfortunately for us, only confirmed our worst fears about what Mrs. Roosevelt's remarks might lead to. There were several religious groups that recruited children from the Puerto Rican community to attend their summer camps. Around six thousand Puerto Rican children were able to enjoy a week or two of summer vacation in the country in upstate New York. Churches of all denominations, especially in El Barrio, signed up the children, giving special consideration to the neediest families.

Now it happened that on May 22, 1934, a letter was received by the Reverend Joseph Haviland, who each year sent a large number of Puerto Rican children from his parish to the church's summer camp. The letter read as follows: "Dear Mr. Haviland: Your communication of May 16, addressed to the Gould Foundation, has been submitted to our office, as we are presently making arrangements for the children's accommodation in the summer camps. I understand that most of your children are Puerto Rican. Such being the case, I regret to inform you that the Gould Foundation will not be in a position to accept them this year, as we have been asked not to send any Puerto Rican children. Sincerely yours, Edith May Holmes, Director of Applications."

The letter was sent by nothing less than the Federation of Protestant Welfare Agencies.

As soon as the news broke, the Liga Puertorriqueña called a mass public demonstration. Practically every social, political, and religious group in El Barrio showed up for the planning meeting.

It was agreed to hold a rally in the form of a public hearing at which the accused would be the Gould Foundation and the religious agencies that practiced such harsh discrimination against Puerto Rican children. The Park Palace was jammed with people as the hearing began. It fell on me to preside over the tribunal. The first thing was to select a jury composed of twenty-three delegates from various labor and religious organizations. The distinguished lawyers Jacobo Bohana and H. Tower were named as judges. León Abramaguer, Esq., acted as defense attorney on behalf of the accused institutions, and the Reverend S. Martínez of the Hispanic clergy as "friend of the court." And arguing for the prosecution, as district attorneys acting for the Puerto Rican community, were H. Brideman, Julio Medina, and Jesús Colón. All of the accused were duly informed of the trial and invited to name their defenders should they desire to do so.

As you can imagine, the event turned out to be very dramatic, and held the interest of everyone present. Need it be said that the prosecution's argument convinced the jury—as well as the audience—that the attitude toward Puerto Rican children shown by the Gould Foundation and the religious agencies had been "abusive, discriminatory, and cruel." Those institutions were ordered by the court to "issue a public retraction of that vicious and inhuman attitude and to give to the Protestant congregations in El Barrio the opportunity to send their children to summer camps, as has been the case in the past . . ." And indeed, the convicted agencies responded favorably and corrected their behavior.

Around that time I took an apartment at 1644 Park Avenue. On the fire escape, just outside the kitchen window, the previous tenant had left five clay flower boxes with a few withered plants in them. Being a *jíbaro,* and loving plants as I do, I started to give them some water, hoping that they would spring back to life. And that's what happened, so that before long my kitchen window was decorated by five lovely plants.

Everyone who came to visit was filled with admiration for "my garden," as I called it, stretching the term somewhat. The truth is that I didn't have the slightest idea what kind of plants they were. I was just hoping for the day when they would bloom . . . They did in fact produce some seeds, which I gave away to my visitors.

One friend I took into the kitchen to admire my plants was Francisco Colón Berdecía, who worked in a drugstore in El Barrio. The moment he saw the plants he exclaimed, "Do you know what you're growing there?" I told him that I had no idea.

"Well, I strongly advise you to pull them up and burn them. That is *cannabis indica,* or, as they call it around the neighborhood, *la grifa . . .* It's marijuana!"

My wife became very nervous. And so did I. In those days they would often search your house for the evil weed. And if they came after me, who in the devil's name could I convince that I had cultivated those plants in complete ignorance? I took my friend's advice: I uprooted them and set them on fire.

Marijuana dealing was already very widespread in New York. Aside from what was imported, it was also grown in homes and backyards. The dealers would mix it with dried oregano and roll cigars and cigarettes that were three parts oregano to one part marijuana. This "homegrown" product would sell for less than the imported kind.

As president of the Liga Puertorriqueña and chairman of the Club Hostos, I continued to press for the unionization of Puerto Rican workers. But despite interest on the part of the workers themselves, the leading officials of the A. F. of L. unions proved indifferent, if not actually hostile. Among the women working in the needle trades, a spontaneous movement arose in which the Puerto Rican rank-and-file of Local 22 of the International Ladies' Garment Workers' Union appealed to the top leadership—in a letter signed by 187 members—to authorize the formation of a local for Spanish-speaking workers. The same thing had been done earlier with Italian workers so as to facilitate organizing among them. The executive council of the International effectively killed the proposal by refusing to put it on the agenda.

Another such spontaneous organizing drive arose among workers in several cardboard box factories, where there were also a lot of Puerto Ricans. A work stoppage began in one plant and soon spread to others owned by the same company. There were quite a few scuffles between strikers and scabs. Spanish-speaking workers, mostly Puerto Ricans, who made up over half the workforce, were loyal to the strike. Many were arrested and beaten by the police. Nevertheless, the strike was fairly successful.

In January 1935 we received news of a strike called by the dockworkers in San Juan. Simultaneous strikes hit the sugar industry across Puerto Rico. In several places there were violent clashes between workers and guards hired by the companies. The news sparked a strike solidarity movement in New York: we formed a united front of several labor union federations, some civic groups, the Harlem Section of the Communist Party, and the Junta Nacionalista de Puerto Rico en Nueva York. This movement proved to be significant for several reasons: not only did it lead to a rapprochement between the Puerto Rican nationalists and the labor movement, but it also helped overcome the hostilities that Feliú's death had provoked between the nationalists and the Communists in New York.

One of our major acts was setting up a picketline supporting the strike in front of the shipping companies that transport cargo between San Juan and New York. Protest letters were sent to the authorities in San Juan and in Washington, and messages of solidarity and support went to the striking workers. At several places in the city committees were formed to collect aid for the strikers.

This mass effort in support of the strikes in Puerto Rico had positive results. The coming together of the different organizations opened up the possibility of closer collaboration in the future, which in turn broadened the horizon of the Puerto Rican independence struggle. The impressive parade that took place on September 14 of the same year in the streets of Harlem and El Barrio was one sign of this. The massive turnout was a result of the wide range of organizations that took part: from the Harlem section of the Communist Party, the Junta Nacionalista, and the Asociación Pro Independencia de Puerto Rico, to the Unemployed Councils, the International Workers' Order, the Centro Obrero Español, and the Church of the Seventh Day Adventists.

On March 21, 1935, Harlem was hit by a major riot. It was sparked off by the arrest of León Rivera, a young boy accused of stealing from the Kress store on 125th Street off Lenox Avenue. Several women who witnessed the event thought Rivera was a black American, although he was of course Puerto Rican, and rushed out into the street to protest the abusive manner in which the private guards (whites, of course) made the arrest. Hundreds of people gathered around the women, anger flared, and rocks started sailing through the store's windows. Violence spread throughout the neighborhood and lasted for several hours. When order was finally restored, Harlem looked like a city in ruins and was in a state of siege.

The roughing-up of the young boy by the guards and the women's outburst was like pulling a cork, and all of the pain and suffering of the black people rose to the surface. There were thousands of businesses in the area, all of them run by whites. In none of them—from the largest to the smallest—was there a single Afro-American person working. Discrimination was rampant, and was all the more abusive and humiliating because Harlem had the greatest concentration of blacks in New York City. The refusal to hire Negroes, even in businesses largely patronized by them, and at a time when the most severe unemployment was among black people—who, on top of all that, also had to pay higher rents than whites—made racial discrimination all the more disgusting.

Fortunately, Fiorello La Guardia was mayor of New York at the time. As soon as he heard about the riot, he went up to Harlem himself, restrained the police—who thought they could solve the problem with billy clubs—and stated publicly that black people were victims of a grave injustice. He called a meeting right there on the spot, spoke in conciliatory tones, and pledged the resources of the city government to alleviate the most pressing problems afflicting the Negro population—immediate assistance, jobs, and so forth. His quick action prevented a repetition of the violence.

That riot of March 21 seemed to strike panic into the managers of companies operating in Harlem. From then on, nearly all the stores began to hire blacks for menial work. The recently established "relief agencies" recruited blacks to conduct some of their investigations, and employment became available at the Board of Education and in the Police Department. These were some of Fiorello La Guardia's achievements during his first term in City Hall.

If anything taught the Puerto Ricans—including white Puerto Ricans—what life is like in the United States, it was the awareness of discrimination. As we have come to see, racial prejudice takes on many different faces. One form it took, around that time, was exemplified by the New York City Chamber of Commerce. Claiming that it needed to determine the "intelligence quotient" of Puerto Rican children, it sponsored a series of experimental tests. After administering the exam to 240 students, the Chamber announced in the papers that Puerto Rican children were "deficient" and lacked "intellectual development."

That "experiment" provoked a protest from groups representing the Puerto Rican community. In a message to the Chamber of Commerce, we proposed that they name a committee of teachers, to include representatives of our community, that would draw up an examination to be administered to an equal number of Puerto Rican and North American children. We were certain that our children would not come out any worse as far as natural intelligence is concerned. But the Chamber of Commerce showed little or no interest, and turned to other matters. Our suggestion was never followed up.

By that time the Puerto Rican community had spread out considerably. In addition to El Barrio in Harlem, thickly populated neighborhoods had sprung up in the Bronx, Washington Heights, and on parts of Long Island. The owners and managers of apartment buildings actively resisted this Puerto Rican expansion. In many cases, especially up in Washington Heights, they refused to rent to families who had come from Puerto Rico, which is what gave rise to the Comité de Defensa de Derechos de los Hispanos. Its membership included such prominent figures as Drs. E. Verges Casals, Max Ríos, and Vando de León, and attorneys Enrique Sarabals and Carlos Rodríguez.

In 1935 I reached my fiftieth birthday. I had been in New York for nearly twenty years. Counting my years of struggle in Puerto Rico, it could be said that I had spent no fewer than thirty years striving to "improve the world" . . . The truth is that I was feeling tired, and for some time the desire had been gnawing at my insides to retire to the country and live in peace and quiet.

I had wanted to found a broad educational movement, with the Liga Puertorriqueña as its base. And we had done some good work. Courses were offered on a variety of political and social topics, and there were also many Spanish classes. But as time went on they began to dwindle in size. In fact, the organization itself lost many of its resources. Membership dropped and we were hardly able to keep up with the financial cost of the educational program. To make matters worse, there were internal differences, so that each meeting was stormier than the last. A rather pointless rivalry formed between the Brooklyn and Manhattan branches of the Liga, and a split was not long in coming. And so the time had come when, finding myself without any help and caught in the middle of pointless battles, I decided to resign.

Thus began a new chapter in my life. I had bought a house in a rural spot out on Long Island, and I decided to work the land. It will soon be seen how long that partial withdrawal from the struggle was to last . . . In the meantime, major changes were at work in the Puerto Rican community, at least as far as politics were concerned.

In the elections of 1934 a new man, of Italian background—a young lawyer named Vito Marcantonio—defeated J. J. Lanzetta, who had snatched the Congressional seat from Fiorello La Guardia. As he was now in City Hall, La Guardia's former post in Washington—which included representation of El Barrio—was filled by Marcantonio. It is no exaggeration to say that with that event a new age began for the Puerto Rican community in New York.

23. Vito Marcantonio, "champion of the poor" and advocate for the Puerto Rican people

On October 1, 1934, at the Vulcan Restaurant on 116th Street and Third Avenue, a dinner was held in honor of Vito Marcantonio. He was thirty-two years old at the time. The dinner was given on the initiative of a number of clergymen, including Joseph Haviland, Robert McLean, F. B. Aparicio, Arturo Salguero, E. Paz, José Franco, Elías Mason, and J. Stark, Protestant pastors from different churches in Harlem. At that event there were pledges of support for the young lawyer's candidacy for the United States Congress. After a moment of prayer, the Reverend Haviland rose to give Marcantonio the blessing of all present, proclaiming him the "champion of the poor."

At the age of eighteen, while still in high school, Vito Marcantonio had led a tenants' strike in Harlem. On graduation from law school, he became Fiorello La Guardia's campaign manager. When La Guardia was replaced by J. J. Lanzetta, and later ran for mayor, Marcantonio decided to win back La Guardia's old district.

Though nobody thought Lanzetta was in Congress for the sake of Puerto Rico and our countrymen, his candidacy was supported by some Puerto Ricans, such as Dr. Cesteros, Juan I. Matos, Laura Santiago, Dr. Antongiorgi, and attorney Pesquera—in other words, those who represented the tiny professional and bourgeois elite. Marcantonio, on the other hand, got his backing from the organizations in El Barrio, the small churches, the workers, and a sprinkling of left intellectuals.

Despite strong opposition from the old-line leadership, Marcantonio won the Republican Party nomination and launched an all-out battle against Tammany Hall. He enjoyed the enthusiastic support of La Guardia and his Fusion Party. And after a fierce struggle he carried the 20th Congressional district by 247 votes.

From his first day in office, Marcantonio took on a work load fit for an entire regiment. His offices and campaign headquarters, located at 247 East 116th Street, were swarming with people at all hours of the day. No fewer than six languages could be heard: Italian, Spanish, Polish, Hebrew, Hungarian, and English . . . Men and women, young and old, would show up with problems of citizenship, health, public assistance, accidents, housing, immigration, and the thousand and one other day-to-day worries that afflict the poor. And there was Marcantonio with his secretaries, each from a different national background, the champion of all of them, doing everything he could to alleviate their difficulties.

Even during the most grueling sessions of Congress, Marcantonio always found time to get back to New York, so that even if only on Saturdays and Sundays, he was there at the service of his constituency. He always played an active role in Congressional debates, too, and had the best attendance record. For him no human problem was too small. Listen to this story as one example.

One night a girl came up to me in the street. She was a young Puerto Rican, and seeing how skinny she was, I could only assume that she had had very little experience as a streetwalker. I struck up a conversation with her, and aside from the usual tall tales that are an obligatory part of that profession, her story sounded quite real to me. When I asked her why she hadn't applied for relief, she said, "I filled out the papers over six months ago and they haven't even sent anyone out to investigate."

Learning that she lived alone with her mother, who was sick, I asked her to take me to her house. We went up a broken-down stairway that gave off a foul smell. The building had no heat or hot water. There were no bathrooms in the apartments. The tenants had to use the sanitary facilities out in the hall, and there was nothing sanitary about them, judging from the stench coming from the broken pipes. The whole place was like a pigsty.

The young prostitute had told the truth. In fact, she had only told me half the story, since she had not mentioned her two- or three-year-old child. We found him playing with some filthy cards when we got to the apartment, which consisted of no more than a fairly clean little living room and a kitchen. On a bed against one wall I made out the figure of a woman—or rather, a heap of bones— wrapped in a few theadbare blankets. She told me that this was her mother; the woman made an effort to sit up, but she was unable to do so.

I gave her a little money to buy some food and I left, overwhelmed with sympathy and seething with anger.

The next day I went to see Marcantonio and told him what I had seen. Before I had even finished talking, he grabbed his hat, which was hanging on the back of a chair, and made me go with him to the welfare office. He stormed into the place, sat down right next to the supervisor, and said, "I'm not moving from this spot until you assign someone to look into the case of a woman who has been waiting for assistance for six months."

The bureaucrat asked for a copy of the form that the woman had filled out. They pulled it out of the files and the three of us read a note attached to it saying, "Rejected after investigation. Applicant has means."

Marcantonio fell into a rage. It was obvious that the family's case had not even been investigated. And the official, terrified at the sudden attention and afraid of a possible scandal, assigned a young woman to look into the matter.

But that wasn't enough for Marcantonio. From the office he went personally to the apartment and stayed there until the caseworker wrote out and signed her report and recommendation. Within a week the woman began to receive "relief" . . . And the most interesting part is that from then on the woman had a new lease on life, and in later years became an exemplary mother.

There were of course thousands of identical cases—people in desperate need of help—which were never attended to. Picket lines and demonstrations in front of welfare offices were practically an everyday occurrence. One of the measures aimed at repressing this sort of protest was a campaign initiated in the middle of 1935 calling for the "deportation" of all persons with less than two years' residence in New York who were on relief. Such a measure was implicitly directed against Puerto Ricans.

Marcantonio took charge of the protest movement. He appealed to Mayor La Guardia, who ordered an investigation. The scandal was exposed: hundreds of public employees were found to have been pocketing money earmarked for the poor, or using those funds for the exclusive benefit of certain privileged groups, to the detriment of blacks and Puerto Ricans. For his role in such protests, and his steadfast defense of Puerto Ricans and the most impoverished people in the city, Marcantonio earned the bitter hatred of all the forces of reaction.

For years to come, not an electoral campaign went by which failed to raise the ridiculous charge that thousands of our countrymen were being shipped in from Puerto Rico to cast their votes for Marcantonio. That's how stupid propaganda against the working people can be. But, actually, it's not that the organizers of those chauvinistic and discriminatory campaigns are really that stupid. They know all too well what they're doing and who pays for such prostituted writing!

At around that time the governorship of Puerto Rico was taken over by General Blanton Winship, another of President Roosevelt's unfortunate appointments. The legislative majority on the Island was dominated by the Republicano-Socialista coalition. The Partido Liberal—heir to the tradition established by Muñoz Rivera and his Partido Unionista—had the most electoral support but was, as a party, in the minority. Luis Muñoz Marín, who had become editor-in-chief of *La Democracia* in San Juan, was named senator by the Partido Liberal in the 1936 elections.

To complete the picture, the Partido Nacionalista had come under the leadership of Pedro Albizu Campos who set forth a policy of open combat against the colonial regime. The confrontation was not long in coming, and culminated in the trial of the Partido Nacionalista leadership in the Federal Court in San Juan.* On July 31, 1936, Pedro Albizu Campos, Juan Antonio Corretjer, Erasmo Velázquez, Clemente Soto Vélez, Juan Gallardo Santiago, Julio H. Velázquez, and Luis F. Velázquez were sentenced to between six and ten years in prison.

When the Puerto Rican community in New York heard about the conviction, it was up in arms. Protest rallies sprang up in every neighborhood. Almost every group joined the struggle in support of the political prisoners. Of those, mention should be made of the Mutualista Obrera Puertorriqueña, the Harlem Sections of the Communist Party, the Centro Obrero Español, the International Cigarmakers' Union, and the Committee Against War and Fascism. The

---

*The Nacionalistas were charged with conspiracy to overthrow the U.S. government in Puerto Rico by violent means.

Junta Nacionalista in New York received a flood of solidarity statements.

A major rally was held on 113th Street between Madison and Fifth with Vito Marcantonio the featured speaker. To the delirious applause of the crowd, a telegram to President Roosevelt was read, demanding freedom for the Nacionalista prisoners and an end to "the despotic measures of Governor Winship." Marcantonio took the occasion to announce that he would propose a bill granting Puerto Rico its independence, which he did soon thereafter.

Shortly before all of these events, on May 27, 1936, a Congreso Por Convención Constituyente de la República de Puerto Rico was held in New York. It was composed of fifty-one delegates representing twenty-three Puerto Rican organizations based in the city.

In early August an angry crowd, numbering in the thousands, gathered at the Park Palace. They were there in response to the sentences handed down against the Nacionalista leaders. Messages addressed to President Roosevelt, to Congressional leaders, and to Governor Winship proclaimed: "We demand the immediate release of the political prisoners . . . If Puerto Rico is not given its independence, we will take it." The statements were approved by wild acclamation from the audience.

A few days later there was another huge rally, this time out of doors on 113th Street between Madison and Fifth. The main speakers were Gilberto Concepción de Gracia and Vito Marcantonio. "The trial of Albizu and those who share his ideals," Marcantonio stated, "was nothing but an inquisition. Never in the history of this country has there been such a travesty of justice. That trial represents a dark page in our history, one that will fill future generations with shame. The crimes committed by the governing powers of our nation against that Island far exceed those of the Roman Empire against the colonial world in its time. Those of us who love justice and genuinely believe in democratic principles of government cannot and shall not close our eyes to acts of such blatant cruelty. We must protest, loudly and clearly, against this blood-stained act, which stands as an outrage and insult to the American people. It is the duty of all Americans who love justice to speak out fervently against the kind of gangsterism that would smother the inalienable rights of the Puerto Rican people."

In spite of his advocacy on behalf of the poor and disinherited,

Vito Marcantonio was defeated in his second electoral campaign. His Congressional seat was taken by J. J. Lanzetta. And the reasons were clear—Marcantonio was running on the slate of the Republican Party, which in New York had been the bulwark of the struggle against the corruption of Tammany Hall and the Democratic Party machine. The 1936 elections meant the deification of Franklin D. Roosevelt and the New Deal, and his landslide victory carried nearly all of the candidates in his party with him, including Lanzetta in New York.

But his defeat by no means weakened Vito Marcantonio's commitment to the struggle. On the contrary, it only heightened his dedication. He went on to affiliate with the newly constituted American Labor Party, while at the same time running as a candidate in the next Republican primary. Once again, despite opposition from the party's leadership, he gained the nomination, and appeared on the ballot as the candidate of both parties. In that way he won back his seat in the 1938 Congressional elections.

In the 1940 elections Marcantonio ran as the candidate of the American Labor Party with Republican Party backing, and again emerged victorious. Then, in 1942, the Republican Party refused to support him, forcing him to fight for the nomination of both the Republican and Democratic parties—and he won in both primaries. In Washington, though, he always identified himself as representing the American Labor Party.

When it came to the elections of 1944, the conservatives and reactionaries in the two major parties banded together in a smear campaign to oust Vito Marcantonio. One of their devious tricks was to alter the boundaries of his Congressional district, extending it to include the area from 59th Street to 99th Street. Their hope was that voters in that new territory—largely Germans and Irish—would be hostile toward Marcantonio's strong base of support among the Italians, blacks, and Puerto Ricans. But that's not what happened.

The dynamic "champion of the poor," as he had been named by those good pastors from Harlem at the beginning of his political career, redoubled his efforts. Sticking to methods that had been proven to work well, he opened a new campaign headquarters at 1484 First Avenue, off 77th Street, and it wasn't long before he had just as many people working for him there as he had in his main headquarters up in Harlem. So that in spite of all maneuvers to unseat him, the people sent Vito Marcantonio back to Congress in the 1944 elections.

In subsequent election years, Marcantonio's battle to hold on to his seat in the House drew nationwide attention. The active and outspoken Congressman had won the admiration of progressives throughout the United States. But his advocacy of the most far-reaching reforms promised by the New Deal, his staunch battle against racial discrimination and in favor of educational opportunities for blacks and national minorities, and his constant call for world peace also won him the hatred of the reactionaries. Even so, he won again in 1946.

There were many who thought it was a miracle that Vito Marcantonio managed to keep on winning so convincingly in the face of such formidable enemies. But it was no mystery. It was the result of strong popular support earned through consistent hard work and an untiring defense of the poor. To illustrate what I mean by work, let me recount an incident told me by Juan Emmanuelli.

Juan came to New York from Coamo, his hometown in Puerto Rico. After some time he became a member of the Communist Party of the United States. As an officer in the party, he organized the Communist section in El Barrio. At that time the Communist Party had a great deal of influence up in Harlem, and some of the local black and Puerto Rican leaders were outstanding figures in the community. They were also active participants in the Marcantonio campaigns.

It is worth pointing out that, in spite of continual charges to that effect, Vito Marcantonio was never, as far as I know, formally a member of the Communist Party. He was exactly what he said he was—the leader of the American Labor Party, a much broader political organization. Nevertheless, even in times of the most rabid anti-Communism, he never identified with anti-Communist positions, even if his office in the United States Congress was at stake. In fact, his point of view coincided on every issue with the general line put forth by the Communists, so that for all intents and purposes, as the reaction never failed to point out, he was one. And now the anecdote!

In one of his electoral campaigns Marcantonio needed a statement, signed by him, to reach the voters in his district. Time was short and there was Marcantonio himself, in his campaign offices, inspiring some volunteers involved in the tedious job of addressing and sealing envelopes. Juan Emmanuelli was supervising the operation, and in the early morning hours Marcantonio said to him, "Look, I've got to get some sleep. But these statements have to be in the mail before sun-up."

Juan assured him that it would be done.

They went on working for another hour or so, after which Juan Emmanuelli gathered all the envelopes together and headed for the nearest mailbox. As he stepped up to deposit the letters, he noticed a man sitting on the sidewalk, leaning against the mailbox, half asleep. It was Vito Marcantonio. He sat up quickly and exclaimed, "I just wanted to be sure that those statements would be mailed right away!"

The reactionaries would not give up their attempt to get Vito Marcantonio out of Congress. They resorted to a new trick. This time the New York State Legislature passed a law which required that all candidates who wanted to run in a party primary have the approval of that party's leading body. The aim was clear: what they wanted was to prevent Marcantonio from winning nominations in the Republican and Democratic primaries.

But even so, finding himself up against a virulent campaign within both parties and in nearly all the papers, Vito Marcantonio managed to score yet another triumph, this time as the candidate of the American Labor Party alone. It took an even more unscrupulous reactionary coalition to bring about the downfall of the "champion of the poor.". . . But I've gotten ahead of myself. Let's get back to 1936.

24. The end of the 1930s: Spain and other events that preceded World War II

If the grave situation in Puerto Rico in the middle of the 1930s stirred up the Puerto Rican community in New York, so did the events in Spain around the same time. I'm referring, of course, to the rebellion of the generals. The cause of Republican Spain became our own.

The democratic people of the United States stood alongside the Spanish people as they rose up in arms. Hundreds of young men of all nationalities wanted nothing more than to join the popular forces, and did so. Such was the origin of the Abraham Lincoln Brigade that fought so valiantly in Spain, and whose ranks included a fair number of Puerto Ricans. Among the many heroes of the antifascist cause who fell in combat in the Spanish trenches were our compatriots Jorge and Pablo Carbonell. And in New York, of course, there were many demonstrations of solidarity with the Republic and against the intervention of Hitler and Mussolini.

But however heroic the struggle of the Spanish people, things looked worse and worse for the Madrid government. The fatal blow was dealt by the United States Congress on January 6, 1937, when it decreed an arms embargo, which froze all shipments to the war zone. While the traitorous generals kept receiving weapons and troops from Italy and Germany, the democratic governments—first with their hypocritical declaration of nonintervention, then with the arms embargo—disarmed a people who faced the coordinated aggression of the Spanish Falangists, Italian fascists, and German Nazis.

At the beginning of that year a printed leaflet circulated around New York. It was signed by Pablo Casals, and said: "The Spanish people are in no way responsible for a war that was begun by the military . . . I cannot remain neutral in this conflict. I was born of the people; I am and always shall be with the people . . . Aside from being an artist, I am also a profound lover of democracy, and neither money nor success will ever change me. I shall never forget my humble birth, which binds me to my people. I pity those who bring shame to their past, to their race, and to their fatherland. Such a shameful example should not be followed. I shall never betray my people or their cause, which is sacred and just . . ."

Like the illustrious Catalonian musician, artists and intellectuals from all over the world showed their solidarity with the cause of the Spanish people. In New York there were many protest rallies against the arms embargo. One of the most memorable was held at the Palm Garden with Juan Marinello, the brilliant Cuban writer, delivering the keynote address. That was the first time we had the opportunity to hear him. Soon thereafter, up at the Club Juan Antonio Mella in Harlem, Marinello gave a lecture about Maceo, the great military leader of the Cuban independence struggle.

Meanwhile, union organizing among Puerto Rican workers continued. One event that drew a lot of attention in those days was a strike at an electrical appliance factory in the Bronx. Violence broke out between the strikers and the scabs, who were of course protected by the police. Many of the strikers were arrested, including Olimpia Méndez, a leader of the CIO. She was accused of throwing ground pepper in the eyes of a guard who had tried to rough her up.

The Committee for Political Prisoners also continued its campaign to free Pedro Albizu Campos and the other Nacionalista leaders. That was the atmosphere in New York when on March 21, 1937, news arrived of the Ponce massacre.* Immediately an indignant statement of protest circulated throughout the Puerto Rican community, signed by Vito Marcantonio, Gilberto Concepción de Gracia, and J. M. García Casanova. On the following night a crowd of angry Puerto Ricans filled the Park Palace. Erasmo Vando chaired the event, and the speakers, aside from Marcantonio and Concepción de Gracia, were A. R. Newhoff, R. Boneta, Filiberto Vázquez, and

---

*The Ponce massacre occurred in Ponce on March 21, 1937, on the occasion of a march and rally called by the Nacionalistas. The authorities denied a permit at the last minute, and when the organizers attempted to hold the march anyway, the police opened fire, killing twenty people and wounding over 150 others. An investigative commission, presided over by Arthur Garfield Hayes of the American Civil Liberties Union, agreed with the people of Ponce in referring to the event as a "massacre."

José Santiago, the latter an outstanding Puerto Rican Communist leader from Harlem.

From La Fortaleza, the governor's mansion, Governor Winship tried to portray the victims as criminals. Rafael Pérez Marchand, the district attorney assigned to the case, resigned because, in his own words, he "was not allowed a free hand to investigate the causes of the riot . . ."—that's what the police called the massacre. Pérez Marchand's letter of resignation went on to state: "The attorney general ordered me to turn my attention to new arrests of more young people and other persons who in my legal judgment had participated in the riot, and not to arrest any more police without prior orders, until such time as those further arrests had been made. I could not agree with the attorney general that this was a proper way to handle the case. The differences between us being so great, I cannot continue to work in this department . . . which is why I hereby resign."

This arbitrary action by the prosecution was conclusively exposed as the result of an investigation conducted by the Civil Liberties Union, which was directed by Arthur Garfield Hayes. The report, which was also signed by the editors of the Puerto Rican daily newspapers, rejected the term "riot" to describe what happened on the corner of Aurora and Unión streets in Ponce. Rather, it called the event "a mass murder committed in a premeditated and treacherous way by the guardians of public order." And it went on to charge Governor Winship with denying Puerto Ricans their civil rights and "arbitrarily overstepping the proper functions of the governorship."

That report, which constituted a thoroughgoing indictment of General Winship and his regime in Puerto Rico, was read at a public rally at the Park Palace on June 30, 1937. Presiding was none other than the president of the American Civil Liberties Union, Roger Baldwin. After Arthur Garfield Hayes read the report, Baldwin declared that the "police were the only ones responsible for the so-called riot. Governor Winship is to be held accountable for the twenty-one dead and one hundred wounded on Palm Sunday in Ponce."

For the first time a Puerto Rican, Oscar Rivera García, was elected to the State legislature. He had been nominated by the Republican Party, but he got his backing from the American Labor Party and Fiorello La Guardia's Fusionists. He also had the support of Puerto Ricans affiliated with the Democratic Party, who set up a committee that included José Cabán Soler, Ramiro Medina, Bienvenido Durán, and Gaspar Delgado.

Around that time the news spread in New York that Luis Muñoz Marín had split from the Partido Liberal and was starting a new movement called Acción Social Independentista, or ASI. Out of that group was to grow the Partido Popular Democrático.

In January 1938 Puerto Rican dockworkers—first in San Juan, and soon in every port on the Island—went out on strike. This strike action was of particular historical importance for two reasons: first of all, because the seamen working the ships, organized by the National Maritime Union of the CIO, totally supported the strike; and secondly because new elements, clearly identified with the Partido Comunista Puertorriqueño, played a leading role in the labor movement for the first time. In New York a strike solidarity committee was formed, made up of Manuel Ortega, Harry de la Cruz, Joaquín Rosado, Aracelio Pagán, Juan N. Maissonet, Consuelo Marcial, José Martínez, Homero Rosado, Juan Emmanuelli, J. Enamorado Cuesta, A. Pacheco Padró, and G. Concepción de Gracia.

On the initiative of José Camprubí, the editor of the Spanish daily *La Prensa,* another effort was made to bring the Puerto Rican organizations together in an alliance that would represent the entire community. Some of those who carried through on the idea were the legislator Oscar García Rivera, J. M. Vivaldi, Cabán Soler, César G. Torres, and Laura Santiago. After a series of meetings the Confederación de Sociedades Puertorriqueñas was founded with J. M. Vivaldi as president and Tomás Gares, José Santiago, García Angulo, Laura Santiago, and Angel Vidal as vice-presidents. Named to the board of directors were Isabel O'Neill, Vicente Medina, and Gregorio Domenech, among others.

The campaign in support of the Spanish Republic and against the arms embargo culminated in a huge rally at Madison Square Garden. The featured speakers were the Spanish leaders Juan Negrín, José Bergamín, and Carmen Meana. The gathering approved messages to the President and the Congress of the United States demanding that the embargo be lifted. Aside from what it paid at the door, the audience wound up contributing over $20,000 to the cause. And it is worth pointing out that the Puerto Rican workers did not scrimp in their economic support for the heroic struggle of the Spanish people.

At one point there was a delegation from Spain in New York, which was the occasion for organizing a march in El Barrio. More people took part in that demonstration through the streets of Harlem than had taken part in any other demonstration up to that time. It ended with a rally in front of the Park Palace; the main speakers were Frank Quintana, Juan Emmanuelli, and Gilberto Concepción de Gracia.

Even though most of our countrymen had no inkling of it, June 10, 1938, should have been a day of mourning for Puerto Ricans everywhere. On that day a man to whom Puerto Rico—and the Puerto Rican community in New York—owes recognition passed away. I am referring to Arturo Alfonso Schomburg, born in San Juan on January 24, 1874. His parents were Carlos and María Josefa Schomburg, long-term residents of Cangrejos, as the populous city of Santurce was known.

The only school Arturo Alfonso attended as a child was the Instituto de Párvulos, run by the Jesuit Fathers in San Juan. He didn't stay there for long. As far as is known, he educated himself on his own. But from his early boyhood he spent time among *tabaqueros,* and it is from them that he learned his ABCs.

When he was seventeen he left Puerto Rico and settled in New York. He worked as a messenger in a law office and gave Spanish classes in his free time. He also worked as a messenger in a bank, this time making his way up to head the lower ranking personnel. In 1896 he got a job as a Spanish teacher in the public school system.

Until the time of the Spanish-American War he lived in the Puerto Rican community. He later moved up to the neighborhood where North American Blacks lived, and there he stayed. This led quite a few Puerto Ricans who knew him to think that he was trying to deny his distant homeland, but nothing could be further from the truth. He always had a deep love for Puerto Rico. But his interest in the history of the Negro, their African origins and contributions to American society, led him to identify closely with black people in the United States.

That Schomburg maintained a constant interest in Puerto Rico was proved by the countless times he defended and upheld Puerto Rico in the newspapers. The polemics in *The Globe* in 1904, which I referred to earlier in these memoirs, are an example. By that time Schomburg had already moved away from the Puerto Rican community and was living in a black neighborhood over in New Jersey. He enjoyed great prestige in the cultural and progressive movement. He concentrated on the study of history, and for his contributions to this field he was awarded the presidency of the American Negro Academy in 1922.

In 1924 he left for Spain where, in the Archivo de Indias in Seville, he discovered a wealth of important information about the participation of blacks in the conquest and colonization of America. Among his many findings, he tells of how the first Bishop of Panama was a black man; how one of the batallions led by General San Martín in the Battle of Maipú was made up entirely of blacks; how the famous Latin scholar at the University of Granada, Juan Latino, was black; and so forth . . . Many other important facts about Haiti and the role played by black people in the history of our hemisphere were publicized by Schomburg in the United States.

Patiently, over the course of his life, Schomburg gathered a valuable collection of documents and a sizable library. In recognition of his accomplishments, Fisk University named him director of their libraries and archives in 1930. Part of his library is intact at the New York Public Library, at the branch on 136th Street off Lenox Avenue. It is known as the Schomburg Collection.

Schomburg was a prolific writer. He dedicated brilliant essays to Máximo Gómez, Antonio Maceo, and to Plácido, the ill-starred Cuban poet Gabriel de la Concepción Valdés. Even the style of his English attests to the Hispanic, Latin quality of his spirit and culture. And he retained the ability to write impeccable Spanish. He contributed to many periodicals in the United States and abroad, such as *The Crisis, American Review, African Times,* and *Orient Review.*

May this reminder of his work serve as a humble tribute to Arturo Alfonso Schomburg, the beardless boy who in April 1891 was recommended by a San Juan *tabaquero* to Flor Baerga, who extended his hand to him, as a Puerto Rican, in New York City. He came here as an emigrant and bequeathed a wealth of accomplishments to our countrymen and to North American blacks. What a magnificent example of solidarity among all oppressed peoples!

If 1938 was hard in more than one respect, 1939 was even more so for the whole progressive world. For those were the years when the Nazi and fascist powers in Europe and Japanese militarism in Asia were on the offensive. On January 26 of the latter year Franco's troops took over Barcelona and the Republican army was forced to withdraw to France. Madrid still held out for two more months, but on March 29 the forces there surrendered too, putting an end to the last vestiges of the Spanish Republic. With the downfall of that heroic bulwark of antifascism, the hopes of democratic and progressive people throughout the world seemed to fade. The fall of the Spanish Republic paved the way for World War II.

The withdrawal of the International Brigade, which was supposed to have been a condition for the withdrawal of German military aid and armed Italian troops, did nothing to improve the international situation of the Republican government. Around three thousand Latin Americans were fighting in Spain as volunteers, among them some three hundred Puerto Ricans, both from New York and from Puerto Rico itself—the latter figure would be well worth substantiating in greater detail.

In Puerto Rico, the movement headed by Luis Muñoz Marín awakened the hopes of the people. Acción Social Independentista soon became the Partido Popular Democrático, with the profile of a *jíbaro* and his well-known wide-brimmed hat as its insignia, surrounded by the slogan "Pan, Tierra, y Libertad." Muñoz Marín had by then begun to go out into the countryside, reaching the most remote rural towns, talking with the people, taking the pulse of the masses, explaining the problems ahead, and stressing the importance of voting. But no one at that time had the faintest idea that we were entering into a new stage in the history of our country.

Meanwhile, Pedro Albizu Campos remained in prison in Atlanta. Responding to reports he had received, he communicated to New York his differences with the activities of some of the leaders of the Junta Nacionalista. Soon thereafter, Don Pedro officially withdrew his backing of attorneys José Toro Nazario and Gilberto Concepción de Gracia, as well as Lorenzo Piñeiro. They all resigned their leading positions, despite the vote of confidence they received from the Junta itself in New York. The upshot was the founding of the Asociación Pro Independencia not long afterward.

In September Hitler's hordes invaded Poland. France and England found themselves drawn into the war. President Roosevelt asked Congress to lift the arms embargo. The United States was to remain on the sidelines for some time, but it was already clear what lay ahead.

I should mention that in December of that same year, 1939, Santiago Iglesias died in Washington. His body was brought to New York on the way to San Juan. Distinguished figures paid homage to him there, but the only one of his old-time comrades I saw at the event was J. M. Vivaldi.

I myself had spent those years living at my little place out on Long Island. There were some Puerto Rican families out there, in towns like Elmont, Babylon, Floral Park, and Smithtown. Without fail, on weekends we were plagued by unwelcome visitors—friends and relatives, and even some total strangers. They would be out for a ride in the country in their jalopies, and would invariably drop in, with or without invitation. I had to put up with my share of such nuisances, especially from people I had met at a meeting or demonstration. Just because we all come from the same country is no reason for concealing the sad truth that people often upset the peace and tranquility of those little towns with their childish noisiness and the disrespectful way they litter the streets with their empty beer cans. All of which only earns us more ill will from our neighbors. After all, we do have to learn to live with others!

But apart from that avalanche of freeloaders, many were the pleasant days I spent there, out in the fresh air on hot days, with some real friends and comrades. At Christmas and on the Feast of the Epiphany there would be roast pig and all of our other delicacies. My home was like a little corner of Puerto Rico, in spite of the snow.

Otherwise, life was peaceful. I tended my garden, where I planted tropical fruit trees—although hardly any of them ever yielded anything—as well as the kind of vegetables that grow in that climate. And I raised my chickens and hens. But one day I got tired of all the peace and quiet; my blood was stirring again inside me . . . Life (and the struggle) in the city were calling me!

Part 6
MID-CENTURY

25. I am on the move, determined once again to strike out against injustice

At Christmas time 1939 I went back to New York. I held onto the house in the country, but I intended to base myself in the city. I would go back to helping undo wrongs and to fighting for what more sensible people consider utopian fantasies. I made a New Year's resolution to leave my paradise of chickens and vegetables behind and to stick my nose back into the problems of my fellow countrymen. I was starving for some lively discussion, tough challenges, and noisy crowds. New York was awaiting me.

That the city was awaiting me, of course, is just a manner of speaking. But I had quite a few invitations to El Chico's, the Havana-Madrid, and the Casino Cubano . . . I decided instead to turn to our people, and to spend my nights with my fellow cigar-workers eating *pasteles* and *cuchifritos,* washed down with good old "bathtub wine."

One party I decided to attend was held at 1 East Third Street. Back around then Quisqueya, Pachín Marín's daughter, was living at that address. Some of the people I remember were there were Sandalio Marcial, Concepción Gómez García, José María Dieppa, Eduvigis Cabán, Valentín Flores, Lupercio Arroyo, Juan Rovira, and Arcadio García, all Puerto Ricans. The Cubans Generoso Reyes and Julio Velázquez were there too. And there were many more, nearly all of them *tabaqueros*—those still alive from the group that had come to New York in the first years of the century.

Although there are those who won't believe it—since *tabaqueros* are supposed to be such big drinkers—only a few of us really hit the liquor hard that night. Most of us were dead set against all drinking. But one thing is for sure: everyone ate to their heart's content. No matter how long we've been in New York, no one seems to be able to pass up a plateful of fried plaintains and *cuchifritos.* Not to mention blood sausage, *pasteles,* and roast pig. Conversation covered the same issues that had been discussed for half a century.

We talked about union struggles, housing problems, racial prejudice, socialism, anarchism, the colonial regime in Puerto Rico . . . I noticed ideological changes: those who had belonged to radical groups had become staunch advocates of national independence.

I hardly said a word. I just listened. I felt a touch of remorse for having been away from the struggle for the last few years. The party that night was like bathing in the Jordan again.

Not long afterward I had the pleasure of meeting our poet Julia de Burgos. She was already quite well known. When I heard her read her poems I decided she was one of the greatest people in America. My opinion has since been confirmed by the critics.

For some time Santiago Iglesias's old Partido Socialista, whose founding convention in Cayey in 1915 I had attended as a delegate, had been split into factions. Prudencio Rivera Martínez led one wing of the party against Bolívar Pagán, and attempted to set up a committee of their new Partido Laborista in New York. As those most involved were personal friends of mine, I attended the meeting. Some of those present were J. M. Vivaldi, José Barros, William D. López, Jesús Ugarte, and Felipe Rivera. I didn't agree with the idea and refused to take part in what turned out to be just another political "mishmash": the Partido Tripartita of Laboristas, Liberales, and Republicanos (Rivera Martínez, Ramírez Santibáñez, and García Méndez), which only served to break up the old coalition between the Partido Republicano and Partido Socialista and pave the way for the electoral victory of the Partido Popular Democrático in 1940.

By the beginning of March I was immersed in the crazy hustle and bustle. The French government, under the treacherous rule of Daladier, decided to get in the good graces of the fascist powers by ordering the deportation of all exiled republicans back to Spain. To allow them to be handed over to the vindictive rage of Franco was like condemning them out of hand to the scaffold. In every democratic city in the world, rallies were held in an attempt to hold back the hand of the executioner. I threw myself into this struggle in New York. Hundreds of us Puerto Ricans, and Hispanics in general, picketed the French consulate, and we went to Washington to picket the embassy.

We were the "antifascist upstarts," and they unleashed on us a whole squad of mounted police, swinging their clubs right and left. But we did help to stop the deportation order. The most important thing was time. Then came the struggle to get the refugees out of France. One of the first boats was the *Sinaia,* which made a stopover in San Juan en route to the Dominican Republic and Mexico. Thousands of Spanish Republicans—men, women, and children—were forced to start up a new life in the Americas.

On March 22, 1940, we commemorated the first anniversary of the Ponce massacre in New York. Two events were held: one was sponsored by the Junta Nacionalista, and was attended by Vito Marcantonio, Julia de Burgos, Octavio E. Moscoso, and Gonzalo O'Neill; at the other the most active roles were played by Gilberto Concepción de Gracia, Lorenzo Piñeiro, Erasmo Vando, and María Luisa Lecompte . . . Those separate events were already a sign of the two directions that the struggle for the independence of Puerto Rico was to take from that time on.*

That same March, toward the end of the month, the magazine *Scribner's Commentator* ran an article entitled "Welcome Paupers and Crime: Puerto Rico's Shocking Gift to the U.S." Among other lies, the writer asserted that for every 18 Puerto Ricans arriving in New York, not a single one turned out to be any good. The breakdown he gave was that 10 live off public charity, 1 is tubercular, 2 suffer from malaria, 3 have syphilis, and the other 2 shack up with women . . . And as for Puerto Rican women, all of them turned to prostitution to earn money to send to their husbands back in Puerto Rico.

Black Puerto Ricans were even worse. All they were good for was to add to the corruption and vice already rampant among blacks in the United States. In short, all Puerto Ricans were totally lacking in moral values, which is why none of them seemed to mind wallowing in the most abject moral degradation.

---

*These two tendencies, which had begun to emerge much earlier, are generally referred to as the "Independentistas" and the "Nacionalistas." The former advocated electoral participation as the main form of political struggle, while the latter—led by Pedro Albizu Campos—called for a boycott of established electoral processes in favor of direct action and armed struggle. This division in the movement assumed organizational form with the founding of the Partido Independentista Puertorriqueño in 1946. Despite their tactical and ideological differences, however, both the Partido Nacionalista and the Partido Independentista Puertorriqueño consider national independence to be the only strategy for addressing Puerto Rico's political and social problems.

That article stirred up real indignation in the Puerto Rican community. Several protests were organized, two of which stood out in sharp relief: one was at the Longwood Casino in the Bronx and the other was at the Park Palace in Harlem. The first was attended by representatives from forty community groups. It ended with a variety of resolutions, one being that Dr. Bailey Diffie—the author of the book *Puerto Rico: A Broken Pledge* and a good friend of Puerto Ricans—would answer the article in the pages of the same magazine. The second protest, called by the Asociación de Escritores y Periodistas Puertorriqueños, assigned Arturo J. Colorado to write a sharp rebuttal to the article. At both events the Puerto Rican community showed great public conscience and dignity.

I should not forget an event of importance to the history of the Puerto Rican workers' movement. On March 31, 1940, the Confederación General de Trabajadores (CGT) was formally constituted in San Juan. On June 29, the occasion of a visit to New York by their newly elected president, Francisco Colón Gordiany, a rally in solidarity with the CGT was held at the Park Palace. Aside from Colón Gordiany, himself, the speakers were Congressman Vito Marcantonio; the leader of the International Workers' Order, Jesús Colón; and Alberto E. Sánchez, general secretary of the Asociación de Choferes de Puerto Rico (an affiliate of the new federation) and general secretary of the Puerto Rican Communist Party.

The international situation was getting increasingly complicated. The famous Maginot Line, which the French swore was impenetrable, was easily crossed by Hitler's forces, which entered Holland and Belgium as though through the front door. Pessimism set in all over the United States. There were some Yankees who even began to learn German, assuming that it was only a matter of time before the new Attila would conquer the world.

In May 1940 President Roosevelt delivered a message to Congress, saying, "We shall not fight in Europe, but we shall defend the Americas against any and all acts of aggression . . . I am asking for the resources necessary to build the strongest navy in the world and to organize a reserve army of 800,000 men . . . Our system of government and the very independence of the country are in danger."

At the end of June, the leading statesmen in the hemisphere met in Havana. The Asociación de Escritores y Periodistas Puertorriqueños addressed a message to the conference, calling for an end to colonial rule in Puerto Rico. The group had been active for some time by then, and included in its ranks Rafael Torres Mazzorana, Angel M. Arroyo, Gonzalo O'Neill, Antonio J. Colorado, Erasmo Vando, José Enamorado Cuesta, Emilio Delgado, Manuel Ríos Ocaña, José Dávila Semprit, Antonio Coll Vidal, Max Vázquez, Lorenzo Piñeiro, Max Ríos, María Más Pozo, and Clotilde Betances . . . As might be gathered from such a list, the association had a brilliant membership.

Commenting on their message in a newspaper article, Torres Mazzorana had the following to say: "It is evident that my colleagues only wish to address two highly significant issues raised at the Havana conference. The first of these is that there was talk of the independence of Jamaica, Curaçao, and Trinidad, and other colonies in the hemisphere as a possible way of resolving the problems of those islands in the event of a German victory . . . It would be making a joke of justice and human dignity for the United States to foster the independence of those European colonies while denying Puerto Rico even the right to enjoy a greater measure of autonomy.

"The second issue is that the United States has set a precedent by declaring it necessary to guarantee the collective security of those peoples still subject to European colonialism. If the American nation believes that to be the case, then it is obliged to show equal concern for the fate of Puerto Rico. All that we have been told to date is that we are going to be the Gibraltar of the Atlantic . . ."

Around thirty thousand Puerto Ricans registered to vote in New York in the 1940 elections. Eighty percent voted for Roosevelt for president and Wallace for vice-president, and, of course, Vito Marcantonio for Congress. But the Republican Party candidate, Wendell Wilkie, also gained some favor among our countrymen, and a Puerto Rican committee was formed to support his candidacy. It was made up of Rafael Bosch, Eduardo González, José Matienzo, Aparicio Henna, Pedro Gotay, and others.

President Roosevelt began his new term in an atmosphere of growing tension. There was a strong smell of gunpowder in the air. In the streets of London people were dying like flies as a result of incessant bombings by the German airforce. Hitler was at the height of his infernal glory. The entire European continent was kneeling helplessly at his feet, and his ambition to conquer the world knew no bounds.

On January 6, 1941, Harry Hopkins, President Roosevelt's special ambassador, arrived in London. He was there to pledge unlimited United States aid to the defense of England. The entire machinery of U.S. industry was geared to war production.

On June 22 Hitler engaged his full military strength against the Soviet Union. The British and the Yankees immediately offered aid to the Moscow government. Within a week Special Ambassador Harry Hopkins was meeting with Stalin in the Kremlin. On his return to Washington, he assured President Roosevelt that the Soviet peoples were prepared to defend every inch of their native land, and would fight down to the last man or woman.

Meanwhile, a ferocious submarine campaign was launched from Berlin against the convoys carrying aid from the United States and England to the Soviet Union. But the Nazi powers were not allowed to gain supremacy on the high seas. Congress agreed to revise the Neutrality Law, making it permissible to arm merchant ships and allowing the navy to protect commercial sea routes. In addition, naval construction was stepped up significantly so that replacements for ships sunk by German submarines could be built. Many of those met their doom while crossing the Caribbean off Puerto Rico. Nearly every day there were reports of crew members rescued and reassigned to new ships after having been transported to San Juan.

Such was the state of open warfare when the Japanese navy executed its surprise attack on Pearl Harbor, Hawaii, on December 7. From that point on, the war raging on land, air, and sea truly took on a worldwide dimension.

When 1942 began we were in a full-scale war. There was an urgent demand for workers in the United States. The flow of migrants from Puerto Rico increased considerably. Thousands of our countrymen signed up for the armed forces. Hundreds of Puerto Rican sailors perished in the merchant ships sunk by German submarines. Puerto Rico itself fell victim to a submarine blockade, and in the first years of the war commercial vessels were unable to enter San Juan harbor for months at a time.

The top leaders of the democratic powers signed one declaration after another—the Atlantic Charter being one of them—solemnly reaffirming the right to self-determination of all peoples, and so forth and so on. But Puerto Rico, it seems, had to rest content as the "Gibraltar of America." Thank you very much!

The war absorbed the attention of everyone, and the Puerto Rican community in New York concentrated most of its energies on the war effort. For my part, I too was disposed to do all that was in my power to contribute—pardon the hackneyed expression—however little, to the defeat of fascism. Now I gave up my country retreat once and for all, closed up the little cigar factory I kept there, along with my garden and chickens, and offered my services to the government. After some time the Agency of Human Resources contacted me. They wrote, "Given your knowledge of foreign languages and experience in journalism, you are to present yourself at the postal censorship office . . ."

On March 12, 1942, having gone through the formality of an exam, I was accepted as a low-level clerk, which really didn't bother me in the least. As a Puerto Rican I knew very well that I was destined to be at the bottom . . . Such was our fate under Spain, and it has remained the same under the Yankees, with no sign of change.

There were over a thousand Puerto Ricans working in postal censorship in New York. For the duration of the war not one was promoted to an executive position of any standing—even though there were quite a few university graduates with professional titles, outstanding artists, and writers among them. What was most ironic is that hardly a single department head or supervisor knew more than one language, and they were generally uneducated and didn't understand what their sensitive assignments were about.

Judging from my own experience, I dare say that if the various agencies and departments under President Roosevelt had been left to function with anything like the crass inefficiency of the postal censorship office, the war would certainly have been lost, or at least greatly prolonged, at the cost of many more human lives. The majority of the upper level functionaries got their jobs not by virtue of any competence, but because of political patronage . . . In addition to which—let it be noted in passing—there was among the bosses a bevy of homosexuals, with all the attendant gossip and petty intrigue.

As happens so often in such situations, if you don't belong to the in-group, all doors seem to be closed. The way up is paved for those in better grace, and no attention is paid to talent or ability. The favoritism became so widespread that it led to several investigations. I might point out that as far as I know there were no Puerto Ricans among the homosexuals.

As I mentioned, some of our countrymen working in the postal censorship office were people of notable ability. Among them I remember Luis Quero Chiesa, José Pastrana, Bert Malavé, Esq., Francisco Carballo, Luis Torres Colón, J. Ramos, Esq., Elisa Belpré, Martha Lomar, Munita Muñoz Lee, and the attorney Bello. Of all of them, only Chiesa and Pastrana reached positions of any rank—something like foremen over menial laborers.

I must point out another relevant fact, which is that over 80 percent of the Puerto Ricans who applied for employment at the censor's office and took the Federal Civil Service examination demonstrated a command of at least two languages, as well as other qualifications. No other nationality had such a high average. On top of that, I can attest to the magnificent work performed by our countrymen. And yet we Puerto Ricans are still regarded as an incompetent people who never reached maturity . . . The truth is that those of us who get anywhere in this country must be superior to our equals.

In the pages that follow I will recount some of my experiences in those years. I am writing at a time when they have already become a thing of the past, although I am still filled with indignation and anger over the ridiculous hardships to which we were subjected. It is not some musty old sense of patriotism that so moves me, much less the wish to paper over the faults of my own kind. I am a man who feels that if my wine has gone bad, let's hold on to it and use it as vinegar . . . I write what follows because it pained me deeply to see so many good, cultured people subjected to shameful treatment and forced to accept injustice in order to stay alive.

And now, to the heart of the matter.

26. Where an account is given of how I joined the censorship office, and other wartime experiences

In 1942 Nazi Germany stepped up its submarine war in the Caribbean. So audacious did the Germans become that one day in March they bombarded Mona Island off the coast of Mayagüez. Early in the year the old steamer *Coamo,* which made regular crossings to New York, arrived in San Juan after a sudden and perilous change of course carrying seventy-one survivors from a Canadian ship that had been sunk off our shores. The *San Jacinto,* which made the same route filled with Puerto Rican passengers, also ended at the bottom of the sea . . . Because of the submarine siege, by mid-year food shortages in Puerto Rico became a matter of serious concern.

Many, in fact, were the vessels lost at sea. How much tonnage was destroyed, of course, was kept a dark secret, so that very few people in Puerto Rico were aware of the real situation. Only occasionally was news of a disaster allowed to reach the press. The people had no accurate knowledge of how effective the submarine blockade really was. The following dispatches may help give a better idea:

On February 25 a ship carrying cargo headed for Puerto Rico was torpedoed a mere twenty miles from Guánica. Twenty-two survivors, carrying four of their dead, managed to reach land in the lifeboats . . . On April 27 a ship that had been pursued by three German submarines reached port in Norfolk, Virginia, carrying fifty survivors from another sunken craft . . . On June 10, René Matos, a Puerto Rican merchant, told interested listeners in New York how German submarines had taken his ship by surprise in the waters off Trinidad.

"It was around four in the morning," he said. "Our ship was sailing with all its lights off. There was a strong wind. All of a sudden, before we even had a chance to get to the movable cannon we had on board, two torpedoes came crashing one after the other into the ship . . . Within minutes we began to sink. Four crewmen, all fellow Puerto Ricans, were blown to pieces in the explosion. The rest of us were able to make it to the lifeboats . . . The submarine left a bright torchlike light hovering over the waters, which made it possible for us to get away from the scene of disaster. For twelve hours we were adrift. We had already given up hope that we'd be rescued when we caught sight of an airplane and tried desperately to signal it down. It spotted us and contacted the Coast Guard . . . We were picked up by a boat headed for Ponce. We docked, and the wounded were taken to the hospital. The rest of us didn't wish to stay in Puerto Rico and asked to be taken to New York. And here we are, ready to get back to 'sea.' "

All of the islands of the Caribbean, including Puerto Rico, were on the brink of starvation. There was a dire need for staple foods. How painful and tragic are the symptoms of dependency! And our dependency remained unchanged, even after that crushing experience, and despite all the high-sounding words spoken in New York toward the end of that year by Luis Muñoz Marín in his capacity as president of the Senate. "Our political status," he declared, "shall be resolved no later than the establishment of peace, when victory has been achieved over the totalitarian forces. And it shall be resolved in accordance with the democratic sentiments of the Puerto Rican people and in harmony with the lofty ideals of the Atlantic Charter . . ."

Vito Marcantonio, speaking before Congress, delivered a lengthy report on the situation of Puerto Rico. Here are some of the points he made: "On the Island there are 325,000 unemployed . . . Food is scarce. There is no rice, beans, or codfish, all staples in the native diet. The cost of living has risen over 175 percent above normal. A pound of lard, for instance costs over $1.00. Black marketeering is rampant . . . I suggest that Puerto Rican workers be brought to the United States to work under decent conditions; that foreign ships (from Cuba, Santo Domingo, Argentina, and other countries) be allowed to enter all the country's ports so as to bring food; that seeds be sent to increase grain cultivation; and that regardless of the shipping costs, a given tonnage be allotted for products essential to the country's economy."

That was the kind of pressure Puerto Ricans in New York were living under, as we anxiously followed whatever news we could get about Puerto Rico from the papers, the radio, or by word of mouth. You can imagine what my state of mind must have been like the day I was interviewed by the postal censor's office. There I was, face to face with a rather corpulent man with a dull complexion, spruced-up clothes, and affected mannerisms. He asked me about my academic background and then went on to inquire about my style of living. Finally he started to test me on the specifics and rules of the Spanish language, his questions becoming cruder and more cutting as he went along. "Puerto Ricans can't speak or write proper Spanish," he concluded.

"I think I know my language quite well," I answered.

I immediately composed myself and became calm, accustomed as I am to that kind of foolish harassment. But the fellow, refusing to change his impudent tone, stood up and continued with the interrogation. He paced up and down in his office, swinging his big belly boastfully. It seems he had done some memorizing, and started spouting one term after another, the kind used in Spanish grammar books in the last century. This is what he fired at me point-blank: "Tell me, what I am speaking of when I use the words *prothesis, epenthesis, paragoge, sincope, aferesis, metathesis, antithesis,* and *sinalefa?*"

I felt the blood rushing to my head, but I kept my composure. Without saying a word I stood up, took my hat and coat, and turned to leave. My hand was already on the doorknob when he burst out triumphantly, "You see what I mean when I say that Puerto Ricans don't know Spanish?"

I turned around. For a time grammar had been one of my favorite subjects, and while rolling cigars, as a kind of mental exercise, I had memorized terms used in grammar and rhetoric. One thing for sure: that stuffy pedant wasn't ready for it. And without raising my voice, but in a cutting tone, I said to him:

"Look, sir, you have crammed your head like a bottle full of empty facts, but you don't know our language. But I did not come here to teach you. Nor did I come here to apply for a job at the Royal Academy of the Spanish Language. Nor do I see a scholar's cap on you, for that matter . . . However I would like to do you a favor. So that you aren't embarrassed when your bubble bursts, I'll teach you a simple trick to help you remember those terms from our grammar books. Take a pencil and write *pepsamas,* a rather curious sounding word that contains, in order, the initial letters of each of those grammatical terms. You see, *p* for *prothesis, e* for *epenthesis, p* for *paragoge* . . . and so on down the line!"

My blood boiling and without further ado, I turned on my heels and walked out. I left thinking that I'd be better off if I gave up my idea of contributing anything at all to the war effort . . . I would simply return to my cigar factory, that refuge of my dignity and fortress of my independence.

I'd already forgotten about the incident when, one day, I was called down to take the written exam. I later found out that the man who had interviewed me belonged to that clique of homosexuals. It is clear that he didn't want an ugly man like myself around.

Once I was accepted for work at the censor's office, they assigned me to the department that was in charge of reading through the soldiers' private mail. All but three of us were Puerto Ricans. I soon realized that we were carrying out a totally useless task. We spent all day reading nothing but family gossip, stories about the dog, the chickens and geese, what was happening on the little farm the soldier came from . . . And meanwhile there were thousands of Italian, German, and Japanese spies active all over the hemisphere.

The enemy agents were most intent on tracking down the movement of ships. As I pointed out, German submarines pursued naval convoys, especially when they were passing through the Caribbean. The convoys had no choice but to go between the islands of Cuba and Santo Domingo, or through the Mona Canal between Santo Domingo and Puerto Rico, or else pass north of the Antilles. It was certain that there were spies posted at various points in the Caribbean finding out about convoys and the departures of ships from different ports. Then they would send their reports in code through the international mail, disguising their communications as business letters or as private family correspondence. What they preferred, of course, was air mail, which had the advantage of reaching its destination before the ships left. And then, with little or no difficulty, they would cable secret messages to the submarines.

There were more than ample grounds to suspect that some part of that communications network was going through the censor's office in New York. But none of the higher level supervisors seemed to be able to figure out how to stem the flow of information. Their whole operation was confined to using the classical methods of censorship: chemical testing, darkrooms, labs, deciphering codes, and such.

We'd spend the days running back and forth, taking suspicious correspondence to the experts, peeling off postage stamps in search of microfilmed messages, smoothing out creased envelopes—and never discovering anything. And needless to say the maritime disasters continued.

One day, at a meeting of delegates from the different departments, a woman from our home country stood up to speak (she was a clever *jíbara* whose name I can't remember). "Look here," she said. "If the suspicion is that there are spies using air mail to send reports on when the ships are leaving port, why don't we just hold up that mail for a few days, the way they do with telegrams? That way, by the time the letters reach their destination the ships will be out of danger."

Her suggestion was pure common sense. Which may be why it had never occurred to those thick-headed supervisors, who so obviously lacked common sense and every other kind of sense as well . . . One of them, though (the most competent of the lot), looked on the suggestion favorably and sent it on to the central censorship office in Washington. It was adopted immediately, and it seemed to have worked very effectively. In fact, for three months afterward German submarine missions in the Caribbean became 50 percent less effective than they had been . . . And to think that if anything was responsible for the measure it was the suggestion made by our little *jíbara,* that unsung heroine!

Tired of reading so many letters from soldiers to their families, I asked to be transferred to another department. The people I was assigned to work with were a bunch of crotchety old aristocrats—a former count from one of the Balkan countries; an old Russian woman, at one time a lady in waiting in the court of a Russian prince; three retired diplomats; an elderly French woman, all dolled up, who believed in "free love"; four or five others hardly worth remembering; and four talented Puerto Ricans . . . The head of the department was our compatriot Luis Quero Chiesa.

It may seem far-fetched and you may think me a fanatic, but facts are facts: all the important work fell to the Puerto Ricans. We were the ones to examine all material of a diplomatic nature. But I didn't care for that job either, so that once again I asked to be transferred. And I was lucky enough to get assigned to the international unit, which was in charge of political matters, labor relations, conspiracies, and similar issues.

I wasn't in that department long before I became aware of some basic flaws in the whole censorship operation. I will say more about those later on.

In 1943 Washington stepped up its diplomatic campaign to win the support and good will of the countries of the world. That was the purpose of the various missions undertaken by Harry Hopkins and Wendell Wilkie. It was also the reason for Vice-President Henry A. Wallace's trip to Latin America. No North American had ever been so warmly received, which is because there wasn't the slightest trace of Yankee arrogance about him. "I speak to you as a farmer and as a friend," he would say in that tone so typical of his public speeches, "and not as an American diplomat . . . Nothing can do more to help wipe out misery among men than the scientific progress of agriculture in all nations . . . Agricultural development in Latin America should go hand in hand with industrial growth."

That same year the colonial "problem" of Puerto Rico was back on the agenda. On April 2 Senator Tydings introduced his independence bill.* Muñoz Marín responded two days later, saying, "My party has no mandate from the people concerning the question of status." With those words he succeeded in avoiding the big issue; and since he was the head of the majority party, what he really did was to kill the bill altogether.

For their part, the leaders of the Partido Republicano and Partido Socialista were outraged by the bill. They claimed that Tydings, who at that time was chairman of the Senate Committee on Insular Affairs, had failed to take into account the goals of those seeking statehood. On April 7, the Legislature hurriedly agreed to send a commission to Washington in order to present "recommendations concerning status and measures for self-government."

The reaction to the Tydings bill and the ambivalent attitude of the leadership of Muñoz Marín's Partido Popular Democrático led to

---

*The Tydings bill of 1943 called for immediate independence for Puerto Rico. It provided for a three-year period for the constitutional transfer of power, and twenty years for regulating the tariff schedule on exports to the United States. The bill, however, did not change matters concerning the U.S. military presence on the Island; nor did it seek to alter U.S. control of Puerto Rico's foreign affairs. Muñoz Marín and the Partido Popular Democrático opposed the bill because they did not wish to be diverted from their concern with economic issues into a debate on political status. The expulsion of Independentistas from the Partido Popular Democrático in 1944 marked the beginning of the party's public opposition to national independence.

heated controversy in the Puerto Rican community in New York. In an article in *El Diario*, Luisa A. Quintero voiced the feelings of many of us when she wrote: "The unfavorable reaction to this bill was to me both shocking and bitterly disappointing . . . Every day we hear nothing but screams of North American injustice and Yankee imperialism, and how they're sucking the blood from our veins. And yet when there is a decent and principled offer from the United States, the same people act like cowards. The Puerto Ricans get intimidated, fearful of all the work it will take to put the country back on its feet. They whine and whimper, saying that they do not want to be separate from North America . . . For the first time in my life I feel shame because of the inertia and lethargy that has hold of my people."

Even Senator Tydings himself had some sharp words, which he addressed in a letter to Luis Muñoz Marín: "It pains me to see that you have so little interest in a bill that bears so directly on the condition of your homeland."

On the initiative of the Asociación Pro Independencia, led by Gilberto Concepción de Gracia and Lorenzo Piñeiro, a meeting of Puerto Rican organizations was held on June 13, 1943, at the Oddfellows Hall on the corner of 106th Street and Park Avenue. The aim was to unify all forces supporting independence. It was on that occasion that Congressman Vito Marcantonio announced his own independence bill, in which he tried to take into account the objections and criticisms that had been raised against the Tydings Bill. His resolution guaranteed extended credit from Washington to the newborn republic and allowed for other economic concessions favorable to Puerto Rico. Delegates from the seventeen groups present pledged to continue working for the cause of independence, and formed a joint committee made up of Modesto Muñoz, Arturo Jiménez, Pedro Biaggi, Vicente Rolón, Luis Rivera, Erasmo Vando, Juanita Arocho, Carlos Cancél, Alfonso Pasarell, Juan Emmanuelli, José Santiago, and María Teresa Babín.

The weekly paper *Pueblos Hispanos,* edited by Juan Antonio Corretjer and backed by the Communist Party/USA, supported that movement. And it was the struggle to win backing for the independence bills introduced by Tydings and Marcantonio that gave rise to the first sign of a split within the Partido Popular Democrático. The first Congreso Pro Independencia was convened in San Juan, and had the endorsement of the majority of the legislators in the party as well as the majority of the party's mayors. Muñoz Marín did not come out against the initiative, and even went so far as to seek membership in the congress, which represented a unified spirit in favor of independence. But within a few years he found that membership in that group was becoming incompatible with his party affiliation, and the independence and "popular democratic" movements parted ways once and for all.

What happened in Puerto Rico, of course, was bound to repeat itself in the Puerto Rican community in New York. The sad truth is that the experience of World War II did nothing whatsoever to help resolve the problem of our colonial situation . . . Our fortunes, or misfortunes, were the same as ever, as will become clear in the following chapter.

27. Some anonymous achievements with no hope of compensation, and the crucial year 1945

In his early days, my immediate supervisor at the censor's office had been on the left, and may even have been a Communist. And as there's no one more reactionary than a repentant Communist, he was an archenemy of socialism, and especially of the Soviet Union.

The man was not without talent, but his phobia blinded him. It didn't even matter to him that the Soviet Union, and the forces of socialism and communism throughout the world, were fighting on the front lines against fascism; nor that at that moment the United States happened to be fighting on the same side of the barricades. And at work he was surrounded by nothing but the most rabid anti-Soviets.

That department, I might add, was the most important one in the whole censorship operation. That was where all the correspondence and documents having to do with international intrigue were examined. The group was like a Tower of Babel, made up as it was of citizens of Polish, Finnish, Hungarian, Russian, German, Italian, Arabic, and French descent, to name a few. After studying the staff carefully, I decided to find out more about the ones who were trying to sabotage the joint Soviet–United States war effort. The first thing I did was to get on the good side of the supervisor. Knowing from experience that vanity is the weakness of all men, I waited for an opportune moment during lunch hour and went over to him. "Do forgive me, Mr. So-and-so, for breaking in on you. I've been reading one of your books and am developing a keen interest in the Balkans. You are an authority on that part of the world, and I recognize my own ignorance . . . May I ask you a few questions?"

With an approach like that I of course won the man over, and from that day on he spent at least a half hour every day educating me. I followed his explanations humbly. Not that they were foolish;

it's just that everything he said was distorted by his emotional hatred. But his opinions really didn't interest me much, and did nothing to undermine my socialist convictions. The important thing is that by virtue of that relationship with him I was able to get involved in several major investigations.

I kept a file on Nazi agents in Latin America, and made it a point to follow their publications and learn all I could about how they operated. I have no idea whether my reports were of any value, but I will say by way of example that I prepared and submitted a lengthy memorandum on the activities of Karl Lunning . . . That agent was shot down in Havana on November 10, 1942.

I also remember compiling reports on Jacob Napp, Von Helmuth, and Dietrich Niebuhr, who were active in a German espionage ring in Argentina. There were others, and if I've mentioned these, believe me, it's not because I am looking to get any personal credit for my work.

Again, I do not know the concrete outcome of my reports. But it should not be forgotten that around that time the Berlin government was cooking up the most unbelievable plans for Latin America. The countries of the Southern Cone, with their large populations of German and Italian descent, were the most coveted targets. One of Hitler's fondest dreams was to form a German South American republic.

Today such an idea seems no more than sheer fantasy, but that is no reason to minimize the importance of those agents from Berlin and Rome back then. They were very able individuals, with far-reaching contacts in all the Latin American countries. Many of them enjoyed the highest respect among members of the oligarchies of those countries, and were on intimate terms with the ruling circles. It was not until around the middle of 1943 that protests and demonstrations by labor groups and democratic organizations began to counteract the spread of fascist propaganda and espionage operations in the hemisphere.

One day a diplomatic pouch with hundreds of Spanish and Portuguese birth certificates landed in our department. When those documents reached my desk, the first thing I thought of was the racket in birth certificates from Puerto Rico. I became even more suspicious when I found out that they were going to lawyers in Mexico, Buenos Aires, and Río de Janeiro.

I detained that correspondence and did some detective work at the New York consulates of those countries. The names of the professionals in question did not appear in the bar association registries for the various countries. I was convinced that those birth certificates were destined to be put to illegal use, possibly as covers for new spies . . . As a result of my report, the documents were confiscated!

Among those papers I found one that seemed to be of particular importance. It contained a set of instructions from the top brass in the Spanish navy to all ships, including merchant vessels, sailing under the Spanish flag. They asked to be notified, from that moment on, of the exact position of any United States convoys within two hours of the time they were spotted. And, of course, it was well known that the German submarines paid close attention to any signals or code coming from the Spanish navy.

I like to remember all of these things, and do so without meaning any pretentiousness, because I am proud to have contributed in some way to the world's victory over the fascist powers. Nothing, however, makes me prouder than the truly humanitarian things I was able to do at the postal censor's office on behalf of the Spanish Republicans, socialists, and Communists. I don't know how many lives I saved, but I am sure that it was no small number.

All correspondence from Spain passed through our department. Unfortunately, the man who was in charge made me very suspicious. You could tell from his ideas and opinions that he was a Falangist through and through. On more than one occasion I heard him say, "There's not a Spanish Republican who isn't an agent of world Communism."

It should be recalled that in those years there was a large number of fanatics from the Spanish Falange active in every capital city in Latin America, including San Juan, Puerto Rico. And it was in the Americas (especially in Mexico) that thousands of Spanish exiles found refuge after the fall of the Republic.

There were still open wounds from the bloody Civil War. Mail from Latin American cities was full of accusations against people living in Spain. There were a lot of anonymous letters denouncing alleged conspiracies against the Franco regime being planned by Republican, socialist, or Communist leaders living in exile. Some of the letters were even signed by well-known figures, men who had served honorably during the civil war and were now talking about new conspiracies, handing over names and all that. It didn't take much imagination to know what would happen to those named in the letters when they reached the censor's office in Madrid!

As soon as I figured it all out I made sure a stop was put on all such correspondence. There were letters signed by people of no less stature than Negrín, the last head of the Republican government; Aguirre, the Basque leader; Prieto, the head of the Partido Socialista; and Comorera, the Catalonian leader. I suspected that they were all forged, and that the entire thing was part of a huge diabolical plan that would allow Franco to keep on murdering old militants from the Republican and workers' parties in Spain.

I resorted to every bit of *jíbaro* shrewdness I had in me. What I did was to get hold of the authentic signatures of the Spanish leaders; then I forced the head supervisor to call in an expert in calligraphy. It was proven that the letters were forged. And that's how I prevented those criminal letters from reaching their destination.

To carry out my work I had to develop close friendships with all the other employees. Most of them were women. I'd bring them gifts, like vegetables and fruit from my garden. Whenever I went out to eat I would invite one of them to come with me, and I treated all of them—young and old, good-looking and homely—with equal respect . . . I got a terrible reputation for being a Don Juan. But I don't regret it—I am confident that the work I did exonerated me from such an unjust image.

But that wasn't all my efforts earned me: they also won me the ill will of many of the bosses. I knew that the consequences wouldn't be long in coming. I decided to move fast. At one of the meetings that were held now and then to discuss how the work was progressing, I asked to say a word and burst out with everything that was bothering me. I railed against the incompetence of the supervisors and the inefficiency of the whole operation . . . Nearly all of my fellow workers applauded me, and supported every point I made.

It was because of that support that I wasn't written up on charges. But I knew that my days were numbered. A week later I handed in my resignation. Once again I went back to the country, to my garden and my little cigar factory. And my exciting days undoing wrongs at the censor's office in New York during those years of World War II came to an end.

I also returned to my books. I might mention that ever since I had come to New York I had been buying books, so that by then I had assembled quite a library. In my first years here I would go to all the second-hand bookstores down on the Bowery and along Fourth Avenue between Astor Place and 14th Street. I enjoyed going through those bookstores, looking through hundreds of old books and collections of periodicals. Back then you'd find a lot of books in Spanish. There wasn't much demand for them, either, so that you could pick them up for a few cents. Which is why by 1920 the living room of my house was already lined with a collection of no fewer than six hundred volumes. Which, to be sure, was the cause of a good deal of discord in my house. Given how often we moved, it was always a formidable task to pack and transport all the books. Sometimes it was even more of a burden than moving our few pieces of furniture.

Around the mid-1920s interest in studying Spanish culture began to grow, as did the demand for books in our language. That put an end to the bargain prices, and my acquisition of books slowed considerably. My library also dwindled during the economic crisis— many were the times that I had to sell off some books to pay for my lunch.

But even so my library went on growing, to the point that when I went to live on Long Island I decided to donate over a hundred volumes to the Liga Puertorriqueña. I held on to the most valuable ones. At the back of the house, in the backyard, I built a wooden structure, which is where I put the two things most dear to me: my books and my little factory.

One day, tired of having been away for so long, a homesick feeling crept into my bones and I longed to return to Puerto Rico. I had recently attended an event at the Club Obrero Español in Harlem celebrating the victory of the Partido Popular Democrático in the 1944 elections. It was a landslide; Muñoz Marín swept all the electoral districts. Present on that occasion were Consuelo Marcial, a Puerto Rican labor leader in New York who had been on the Island during the electoral campaign; Alberto E. Sánchez, then general secretary of the Puerto Rican Communist Party and one of the leaders of the CGT; Jesús Colón, president of the Hispanic Section of the International Workers' Order; and many other leading members of the various radical groups. I was thinking of that celebration, where despite some reservations all of us harbored high hopes for the new government.

I dreamed of the trip to San Juan and back to Cayey, and pictured myself climbing *la Piquiña,* the mountain road that winds its way up to the little town I had left behind in 1916. I thought of traveling around the Island . . . But my longed-for trip never came to pass.

Filled with pain and sorrow, I returned to the iron Tower of Babel, and for some time it looked as though I'd be forced to live through the hardships of the new emigrant all over again. To add to my woes, I got back to my house in the country only to find that my "library"—which was also my factory—had been flooded. It was an irretrievable loss, and included some of my most treasured books and papers. I saved what I could, and in the process I came across some pages from a diary I had been keeping for some time. In what follows I quote from notes written in the course of 1945.

January 4: To this day I haven't had a chance to read the article published in the *New York Times.* I never would have thought that such a serious paper would print such biased information. The article was titled: "Puerto Rico: A Case to Be Heard," and included outrageous statements like, "The economic problem of that Island stems from the inability of its inhabitants, after forty years of generous aid from the Mother Country, to work out an adequate life for themselves . . ."

Since when is the United States our mother country?

January 5: Luisa A. Quintero answered the *Times* article by saying: "First of all, the United States is not the Puerto Ricans' Mother Country . . . The problem is that all our industry and trade are controlled by foreign interests . . ." And so on.

That helps!

January 14: Today is my birthday. I have lived sixty stormy years. I just had a phone call from Gloria Canejo, one of my co-workers from my days at the censor's office. She just wanted to wish me well, and to ask about my health. She got back last night from Buffalo, where she went to spend her honeymoon. While there she had been to Graciela Rivera's debut, and spoke of her performance in glowing terms.

February 4: We are all very happy. General MacArthur landed triumphantly at Manila. The Soviet army is thirty-eight miles from Berlin . . . The war will soon be over!

March 5: Today hearings began in Washington on the Tydings Bill for the independence of Puerto Rico. Juan Antonio Perea spoke on behalf of the pro-independence forces. He attacked Muñoz Marín

. . . What a role my old friend Muñoz Marín is playing! With every passing day he seems more and more like his father at the time of the Treaty of Sagasta.

March 7: Senator Tydings stated to newsmen that "Puerto Rico will never be a state of the Union." He said he had polled other members of Congress and found that "all of them are of the same opinion." He concluded by saying, "It would be wrong to deceive the Puerto Rican people with false hopes and expectations."

March 9: In a message to the Congressional Committee on Insular Affairs in Washington, 11 of the 19 members of the Puerto Rican Senate and 22 of the 28 members of the Assembly, called for passage of the Tydings Bill. The position of these legislators, all from the Partido Popular Democrático, is a direct challenge to Muñoz Marín . . .

March 11: The rationing of fuel continues. My house is without heat. For nearly three years we have stoicly sacrificed in order to win the war. There can be no question but that the North American people have responded bravely . . . The question is, what does the future have in store for us?

April 12: I am making cigars in my little factory. I am listening to Tchaikovsky on the radio. A sudden interruption, and in a deep, emotional voice it is announced that President Roosevelt has just died at Warm Springs, Georgia. His successor will be Harry S. Truman . . . What a shame that it isn't Henry Wallace!

April 24: We're having a party at my house. It has just been announced that the victorious Soviet and Yankee troops are embracing in the streets of Berlin. What I wouldn't give to feel confident that the fraternal spirit they are feeling today won't turn to ice come tomorrow!

April 27: Muñoz Marín has declared that his party is committed to holding a plebiscite. The United States Congress, in his opinion, should be called upon to propose alternatives. In the same breath, however, he states that the Island would not be able to remain independent without economic aid . . .

April 28: News of the death of Adolf Hitler. Unconditional surrender of Germany.

June 4: The Puerto Rican Legislature sends Senator Tydings an alternative proposal to his independence bill. The very senators and representatives who had so recently been demanding outright independence are now vacillating on the issue.

June 20: Attended a meeting in Harlem aimed at consolidating the Puerto Rican community . . . A committee was named.

August 5: I read in the San Juan newspapers that wealthy Puerto Ricans are busy investing in Florida. Mention is made of Serrallés, Roig, Ramírez de Arellano, García Méndez, and Cabassa . . . Every day I am more convinced that the capitalist class in Puerto Rico is not established on native soil. Yesterday the people of real means there were Spaniards; today they are Americans. Every dog has his day!

August 6: The United States drops an atom bomb on the Japanese city of Hiroshima.

August 8: Another atom bomb, this time on Nagasaki.

August 17: Peace.

September 7: Senator Tydings, speaking to a commission of pro-independence figures who have come from Puerto Rico: "I am not in favor of the confusing measures proposed by the Legislature. The only thing to discuss is my plan for independence. Everything else is to be tabled."

November 4: Attended a party in honor of Francisco Colón Gordiany, the outstanding CGT leader. The impression I came away with is that the split in the CGT is final. No reconciliation is possible! I'm afraid that from here on in, the labor movement in Puerto Rico is going to turn into a can of worms.

Those notes should give you some idea of the situation we were living in. Peace had arrived, and we were entering a new epoch . . . It turned out not to be so new after all!

28. Confronting hate campaigns; further struggles in defense of Puerto Rico

With the war's end all Puerto Ricans, no matter what part of the world they found themselves in, assumed that the issue of the sovereignty would be speedily resolved. One of the most important matters under discussion in international circles was the abolition of colonialism itself. Who would think that it would begin to disappear so rapidly in Africa and the other continents, and even right in the Caribbean—in Jamaica, Trinidad, and Barbados—while Puerto Rico would continue to languish in the same colonial condition!

The "status" question, then, was a major issue in 1946. Another reason Washington had to address itself to the demands raised on behalf of Puerto Rico was the contribution we had made to the war effort. The Puerto Rico office in Washington, in fact, had the following to say in its September 16 information bulletin: "Recent estimates, based on the official figures, of Puerto Ricans fallen in the world war place Puerto Rico second only to Hawaii as to the number of soldiers killed and wounded. Calculations were made proportionate to the population for each state."

On January 5, 1946, in New York the Essex House conference on the political problem of Puerto Rico opened. Up until that time there had never been such a well-attended event in the United States having to do specifically with our country. It was sponsored by a whole range of progressive North American organizations, including the Council of the Sciences, Arts, and Professions, the National Lawyers' Guild, the Workers' Council on African Affairs, the National Negro Congress, and the Council for Pan-American Democracy. There were some celebrated figures at the conference, such as Joseph M. Coffee, Elmer Benson, Paul Robeson, Vito Marcantonio, Howard Fast, and Canada Lee . . . The notable Puerto Ricans in attendance were the representative from Puerto Rico in Washington, Jesús T. Piñero, and legislators Baltasar Quiñones Elías and Vicente Géigel Polanco.

The position emphasized throughout was that "there can be no free world without a free Puerto Rico." At the conclusion of the meeting, a statement was unanimously adopted stating, "We demand that the United States immediately recognize Puerto Rico's right to self-determination, including independence, with an assurance of just economic guarantees . . ."

On April 24 the bill prepared by the commission of the Puerto Rican Legislature was presented to Congress. It consisted of a long-winded series of status alternatives: an independent republic, federated statehood, and an associated state. If the bill was approved, a plebiscite was to be held, allowing voters to choose among the three options. The proposed bill was so ridiculous that nobody—whether in San Juan, New York, or Washington—took it seriously. The *New York Times,* in fact, encapsulated its response with the following remark: "They want divorce, but with alimony."

The main concern of the United States, meanwhile, was how to move from a wartime to a peacetime economy. There were massive lay-offs and attempts to lower wages. The labor movement threatened to resist. But in the long run there was a convergence of interests which allowed the nation to come out of its dilemma with flying colors. It was clear that the economic prostration of Europe was of no benefit to the United States. It was necessary to help in the reconstruction process, and to do this it was necessary to keep the powerful machinery of U.S. industry running full steam ahead. Such was the origin of the so-called Marshall Plan.

The goal was to strengthen the capitalist system, nationally and internationally. In the national arena, new measures to hold down the democratic rise of the working masses were not long in coming. One such measure was the amendment of the progressive Wagner Labor Relations Act. Coming right on the heels of World War II the first signs of the "cold war" were already evident.

As has happened so often in the history of the United States, the non-Anglo Saxon sectors of the population became the scapegoats. The chain always gives at the weakest link. Puerto Ricans were once again subject to the cruelest mistreatment. And the reactionaries and chauvinists had no trouble justifying the abuse, since in those years it seemed as though all of Puerto Rico was being dumped into New York.

On July 2, 1946, the *Marine Tiger* set sail for our great city carrying a thousand Puerto Ricans. From then on that boat—which was hardly fit to carry passengers—carried one load of emigrants after another. The ship itself became part of a new Puerto Rican folklore, to such an extent, in fact, that the new arrivals to New York were referred to as "marine tigers." That month Pan American also inaugurated its first regular flights between San Juan and New York.

The census reflects clearly this huge increase in Puerto Rican emigration to the United States. The figures show 1,904 persons arriving from Puerto Rico in 1940, 988 in the following year, and 1,837 in 1942. From that point on, the number skyrocketed: 2,599 in 1943; 7,548 in 1944; 14,704 in 1945; 21,531 in 1946; and by April 1947, in those first four months alone, 26,000 Puerto Ricans landed in New York . . . Added to that, 60,000 Puerto Rican children were born in New York in the seven years between 1940 and 1947.

The ongoing smear campaign against Puerto Ricans led our compatriot Pilar Pacheco to write, in an article published by *La Prensa,* "The *New York Journal* and the *World-Telegram* are now laying off the Japanese, the Germans, and the Russians, and have opened up their attack on the Puerto Ricans . . . Now we are once again open game for the cheapest, most sensationalist, and filthiest kind of journalism."

Vito Marcantonio was back on the warpath, calling a rally to repudiate the defamatory press campaign. The Park Palace was packed with people from El Barrio. The main speakers were Manuel Medina, Jesús Colón, Pedro Hernández, and Vito Marcantonio himself. I also took my turn at the podium. All of the speakers agreed that something had to be done about the vicious slander. A committee was named, headed by Dr. Leonard Covello, and charged with the task of composing a manifesto and developing a plan of action that would give continuity to the defense of the Puerto Rican community.

At the next meeting, held in the same place, the manifesto was read and approved. It was also resolved that the meeting should become permanent, and be called the Convención Pro Puerto Rico. The manifesto was distributed widely in the universities, churches, and labor unions, and was sent to the press. The board of directors chosen to lead the new group consisted of José Ramos López, Maisonave Ríos, Carmen Cintrón, Juanita Arocho, and myself.

Little did we suspect that the smear campaign was to become even more odious. But that's what we realized was happening on October 20, 1947, when the *World-Telegram* began running a series of articles about Puerto Ricans. Unfortunately, we simply had no press organ capable of fighting it out with that paper on its own ground.

But we did have *Liberación*. That newspaper had started out as the official organ of the Comité Coordinador de la República Española, its main interest being the struggle against Franco. This exclusive focus on Spain inevitably limited its audience and success. A movement arose which recognized this and called for a broadening of the paper's coverage, which meant, first and foremost, broadening the extent to which it addressed the needs of the Puerto Rican community. Carmen Meana, the steadfast Spanish Republican leader and guiding spirit of the newspaper, endorsed the idea enthusiastically. Thus, early in 1946, while still upholding the cause of Republican Spain, *Liberación* became a mouthpiece more fully in tune with the city in which it was published.

The weekly *Pueblos Hispanos* had folded. There were other Hispanic papers published in New York, but none had the kind of vigor and outspokenness that was needed. We pinned all our hopes on *Liberación,* and many groups pledged their support. Several Puerto Ricans began to contribute, and Rafael López Rosas and later José Luis González joined the editorial staff. I myself was responsible for selling advertising space, a job to which I devoted most of my time that year. I did manage to assure the paper's economic solvency for the time being.

Liberación was a front line in the defense of the Puerto Rican community, and of all Hispanics living in the city. But the truth is that we needed more than one. Even the meetings we held at the Park Palace, spearheaded by militant Congressman Vito Marcantonio, never had an impact beyond the boundaries of Harlem. To have a greater impact on public opinion in the United States, we had to broaden our struggle even further. That was how I saw it, and when I voiced my concerns at a meeting, everyone present agreed with me. So that after discussing the problem at some length, we concluded that the only way to break out of our isolation and widen the range of our campaign on behalf of the Puerto Rican community was to win the backing of one of the large labor unions based in New York.

There were several unions with a growing Puerto Rican membership, one of them being the International Ladies' Garment Workers'

Union . . . The problem was that the upper level officers in the union bureaucracy were deaf to the needs of the Puerto Rican workers. We decided that we'd be better off trying to awaken interest and win support for our cause by approaching the National Maritime Union, which in those days was one of the most militant unions in the CIO and also had a rapidly increasing Puerto Rican rank and file.

And we were on target. On October 22, at the request of a large number of Puerto Rican merchant marines, a massive meeting was held at the NMA's main hall to organize a demonstration protesting the articles that had appeared in the *World-Telegram*. Our countrymen Juan Alejandro, Benito Hernández, and Luis Díaz, union members in good standing, chaired the meeting. It ended with the appointment of a delegation of twenty seamen who were to go to the editor of the paper and inform him of our protest.

I accompanied the delegation when it carried out its mission. The editor-in-chief, Lee B. Woods, agreed to receive us. As soon as we entered his office we stated that the purpose of our visit was to voice our protest against the campaign of falsehoods and lies perpetrated by his paper against the sons of Puerto Rico. We demanded that it be officially retracted and publicly rectified.

He let us speak without interruption, like someone listening to the falling rain. Then he sat up stiffly in his armchair and said condescendingly, "I believe that everything in those articles is true."

We disagreed, and repeated our protest. But all he did was make a gesture with one hand, swinging it around in a half-circle, saying, "Men and women from the tropics are incompetent people who lack maturity."

At which point one of the merchant marines exclaimed angrily, "It's because of those very ideas of racial superiority that we had to fight a war against the Nazis!"

The editor-in-chief only smiled with the same condescending air and, obviously trying to provoke us, cracked a disgusting joke about Puerto Rican women. What he wanted to do was drive us to the point where we resorted to violence, probably so as to be able to add a new incident to his newspaper's campaign.

We realized that we were in a snake pit, and that an incident of that nature would not help our cause. We managed to restrain ourselves and withdraw with dignity.

We withdrew, but with the derogatory notions that kept appearing in the *World-Telegram* ringing in our ears. Here is a sampling:

"The Puerto Ricans are destroying the economy and suffocating the culture of their adopted community . . ." (meaning, of course, New York!).

"[Puerto Ricans] are the cause of the incredibly bad housing situation . . ."

"The most serious thing about the poor health of those [Puerto Ricans] who have just arrived is that the large majority of them work in the city's restaurants, hotels, and clubs, where they handle food, plates, and other kitchen utensils, and in commercial laundries where they handle clothing."

"The problem is that they [again, Puerto Ricans] have a high frequency of tuberculosis."

"And as if that weren't enough, there is the growing amount of venereal disease among them, plus typhoid and other ailments, all of which are transmitted through the food and utensils they handle all day."

"Puerto Ricans have a stranglehold on jobs in hotel kitchens, restaurants, hospitals, and laundries."

"Being so uncivilized, a trait common to people from the tropics, many of them buy furniture on credit and don't even have the decency to keep up with their payments."

And on top of such broadsides, there was an even lower blow: "The police have followed groups of them arriving at the airport in Teterboro, New Jersey, and heading straight for the welfare offices in East Harlem."

"The city has no need for these workers . . . The government should throw them out." Short of that, the suggestion was to "announce that there exists a serious health problem in Puerto Rico, reaching epidemic proportions, and to set up health stations to subject them to a physical examination on arrival at all airports and ports of entry."

And then, as a final blow, "They are finding a way of easing their hunger in Marcantonio's political club . . . There are rumors, at least, to the effect that Marcantonio sends money down to the Island in order to increase his votes and political base in the district he represents."

Our answer to that barrage of gratuitous insults came on November 1, 1947, in the form of a boisterous, huge picket line in front of the *World-Telegram* offices. Three days before, delegates from thirty-three groups had met at the National Maritime Union headquarters to plan the event.

The day of the picket threatened to be cold and rainy. But nothing could dampen the militant spirit of our people. Hundreds of placards and posters expressed that traditional Puerto Rican dignity, and blasted the editors of the paper for abusing the freedom of the press in order to slander an honest hard-working people. At our side marched Congressman Vito Marcantonio and City Councilman and black leader of the United States Communist Party Ben Davis.

That picket line, which was several blocks long, had a great impact. It is worth pointing out that several well-known Puerto Rican personalities observed from the sidewalk across the street. Among them were the millionaire Pedro Juan Serrallés and performing artists Rosita Ríos and Bobby Capó. I repeat, they were there as observers . . . Once again, the task of standing up in defense of Puerto Rico fell to the workers.

The campaign against Puerto Ricans and the protest activities held in New York were the cause of some concern in Puerto Rico. As a result, a movement grew up in solidarity with our struggles. And for the purpose of coordinating action on both fronts, I took a trip to San Juan, paying my travel costs out of my own pocket.

In Puerto Rico I met with many, many people. Various delegates agreed to participate in our next convention of Puerto Rican organizations. One idea that was gaining favor was that of founding the Casa de Puerto Rico in New York. But these new activities only ended in the usual internecine squabbling and bickering . . .

On my return, it was clear that a new situation was in the making. At a meeting of the board of directors of the Convención Pro Puerto Rico, a question was raised about my recent trip to Puerto Rico. Right away I suspected the motive behind the query. In San Juan I had become aware of how suspiciously the politicians, especially those of the Partido Popular Democrático, viewed our efforts. They resented the influence of Vito Marcantonio, and his role in Puerto Rican struggles. They themselves were obviously hoping to impose their own leadership on Puerto Ricans in New York through the newly established offices of the Puerto Rican government in New York. They dreaded our political radicalism and pro-independence stance.

The subject of my trip was thus no more than a pretext, although it did give rise to a heated debate. It was alleged that I identified with the Communist Party and other groups on the left, and therefore should not have presumed to represent the Convención Pro Puerto Rico in San Juan. Those who made the accusations were forgetting—in bad faith, of course—that it is these very left groupings that always march in the vanguard when it comes to defending the rights of our people. But when people are blinded by their passions and prejudices, there can be no reasonings with them . . . I chose to resign.

I had done my job, which was the important thing. And, as so often before, I went back to my small factory to roll cigars!

29. An unfinished chapter with an unwritten moral: it is always more interesting to live than to write

On August 5, 1947, the United States Congress granted Puerto Rico the right to elect its own governor. After all that effort, and after having gone through a world war where the right of peoples to their independence was the very issue at hand—a war in which we took an active part—that was all we were conceded by way of recognition. An elephant gave birth to a mouse!

A few days later the Soviet delegates to the United Nations, speaking on the subject before the General Assembly, accused the United States of maintaining a "colonial system in Puerto Rico." And a few months later, on November 12, a delegation made up of Rafael Pérez Marchand and Antonio Ayuso Valdivieso—the managing editor of *El Imparcial*—arrived in New York to submit a petition on behalf of Puerto Rico to the secretary general of that respected body.

Explaining the reasons for their trip at a rally held in New York, Ayuso Valdivieso stated: "Our mission before the United Nations is nothing more than to ask that there be an investigation into the political situation in Puerto Rico and that the population be allowed to express its will. The document we have submitted has been signed by 105 prominent citizens who repudiate the colonial status of our country."

Reading such a statement, I am gripped once again by a longing to return to Puerto Rico. But at the same time a new perspective that is opening up here tugs me in the other direction. A movement is just getting off the ground, calling for a "third party" headed by presidential candidate Henry A. Wallace—a man who enjoys the sympathies of Puerto Ricans, Chicanos, and of all the Hispanic and Latin American sectors of the population. It would be a real contribution to start organizing their support. It would be a great opportunity to help our people . . .

[*Here ends the manuscript of the* Memoirs of Bernardo Vega.]

Index of names